W9-ABX-654

A Treasure Hunting Text

Ram Publications

Hal Dawson, Editor

The New Successful Coin Hunting
The world's most authoritative guide to finding valuable coins, totally rewritten to include instructions for 21st Century detectors.

Modern Treasure Hunting
The practical guidebook to today's metal detectors; a "how-to" manual that carefully explains the "why" of modern detector performance.

Treasure Recovery from Sand and Sea
Precise step-by-step instructions for reaching the "blanket of wealth" beneath sands nearby and under the world's waters, totally rewritten for the 90's.

Modern Electronic Prospecting
Explains in layman's terms how to use a modern detector to find gold nuggets and veins of precious metal.; includes instructions for panning and dredging.

Modern Metal Detectors
Advanced handbook for field, home and classroom study to increase expertise and understanding of any kind of metal detector.

Buried Treasure of the United States
Complete field guide for finding treasure; includes state-by-state listing of thousands of sites where treasure is believed to exist.

Treasure Hunter's Manual #6
Quickly guides the inexperienced beginner through the mysteries of full-time treasure hunting with easy explanations of equipment and techniques..

Treasure Hunter's Manual #7
The Classic book on professional methods of research, recovery and disposition of treasure; designed to supplement THer's Manual #6.

Weekend Prospecting
Offers simple "how-to" instructions for enjoying holidays and vacations profitably by prospecting with metal detectors and gold pans.

Gold Panning is Easy
This excellent field guide shows the beginner exactly how to find and pan gold; follow these instructions and perform as well as any professional.

Treasure Hunting Pays Off
A basic introduction to all facets of treasure hunting...the equipment, the targets and the terminology; totally revised for the 21st Century detectors.

True Treasure Tales -- Gar Starrett Adventures
The Secret of John Murrell's Vault
The Missing Nez Perce Gold

Garrett Guide Series -- Pocket-size Field Guides
Find More Treasure With the RIGHT Metal Detector

Metal Detectors Can Help You Find Wealth	Use the Super Sniper
You CanFind an Ounce of Gold a Day	Find Wealth on the Beach
Metal Detectors Can Help You Find Coins	Find Wealth in the Surf
Money Caches Are Waiting to be Found	Avoid Detector Problems

~the new~
TREASURE
RECOVERY
FROM
SAND & SEA

by
CHARLES GARRETT

ISBN 0-915920-70-0
Library of Congress Catalog Card No. 89-63316
Treasure Recovery from Sand and Sea
Second Edition.
© Copyright 1990
Charles L. Garrett

All rights reserved. No part of this book may be reproduced or transmitted in any form or by any means, electronic or mechanical, including photocopying, recording or by any information storage and retrieval system, except in the case of brief quotations embodied in critical articles and reviews. For information, address all inquiries to Editor, Ram Publishing Company. Printed in Korea for worldwide distribution.

Second Edition Printing, March 1990.

For FREE listing of related treasure hunting books write
Ram Publishing Co. ● P.O. Box 38649 ● Dallas, TX 75238

DEDICATION

To all of those over the world who seek treasure with Garrett equipment... may the close of every day in the field and surf find you returning home with a pouch overflowing with newfound treasure. It is my fondest hope that techniques and ideas presented in this book will add to that overflowing pouch.

By CHARLES GARRETT

Treasure Hunting Texts
Treasure Recovery from Sand and Sea
The New Successful Coin Hunting
Modern Metal Detectors
Treasure Hunting Pays Off
Treasure Hunting Secrets

With Roy Lagal
Modern Treasure Hunting
Modern Electronic Prospecting

True Treasure Tales
The Secret of John Murrell's Vault
The Missing Nez Perce Gold

Garrett Guides
Metal Detectors Can Help You Find Wealth
You Can Find Wealth on the Beach
You Can Find Wealth in the Surf
Metal Detectors Can Help You Find Coins
Find More Treasure with the Right Metal Detector
Money Caches Are Waiting to be Found
You Can Avoid Detector Problems
Use the Super Sniper to Find More Treasure

Contents

The Author
Author's Note
Introduction

About the Author

The name of Charles Garrett ranks high on the list of those men and women who have pioneered the use of metal detectors for discovery of treasure under and near the waters of the world. His XL 500 Sea Hunter detector is the workhorse for most professionals who search oceans and lakes, and his Beach Hunter expanded the horizons of all who search at the water's edge and in its surf.

Charles Garrett did not set out to become a leading manufacturer of metal detection equipment. He prepared himself well, however, to become one of the world's foremost treasure hunters. Since boyhood he has been enthralled with stories of hidden wealth...tales which brought excitement to his semi-rural youth in the Piney Woods of Deep East Texas. Throughout his life he continually sought to learn all that he could about available techniques and equipment.

A quarter century ago, Mr. Garrett was a young electrical engineer deeply engrossed in development of systems and equipment required by America's space effort. In devoting himself to his lifetime hobby of treasure hunting, however, he also designed and built metal detectors in his spare time. Because his detectors were obviously more effective than any available commercially, they became popular with fellow treasure hunters for whom he was soon making them. This avocation became a career when he founded Garrett Electronics to produce his inventions.

Today, the name Garrett stands as a synonym for the treasure hunting metal detector. Mr. Garrett himself is known as the *Grand Master Hunter,* which is also the name of his company's new computerized instrument, described as "the finest metal detector ever manufactured."

Along the way, Mr. Garrett has also become recognized as an unofficial spokesman for the hobby of treasure hunting and the metal detecting industry through a long list of honors, personal appearances and books. He is the author of several major works which have been accepted as veritable "texts" for treasure hunting. In addition, he recently began publication of the popular line of *Garrett Guides,* modestly priced, pocket-sized books designed to be used by treasure hunters in the field.

Another significant contribution is his introduction of Gar Starrett, a metal detecting hero who has already been featured in two novels, *The Secret of John Murrell's Vault* and *The Missing Nez Perce Gold.* The author reports that we can expect to hear more about Gar's exploits as he looks for Jim Bowie's mine in West Texas and encounters pirates in the Caribbean!

Charles Garrett was born and reared in Lufkin, TX. After service in the U.S. Navy during the Korean Conflict, he earned an engineering degree from Lamar State University. He is married to the former Eleanor Smith of Pennington, TX, who has played a key role in the growth of Garrett Electronics. They have two sons and a daughter.

As a graduate engineer and a businessman, Mr. Garrett introduced discipline to the manufacture of metal detectors. He has generally raised the standards of metal detecting everywhere, while the hobby has grown from a haphazard pastime to almost a science. He has used a metal detector of his own design to search for and find treasure on every continent except Antarctica. He has also scanned under the lakes, seas and oceans of the world.

Hal Dawson
Editor, Ram Publishing

Dallas, Texas
Winter 1989-90

From the Author

A Personal Note

When this book was first published, I expressed my thanks to a number of people and admitted numerous debts of gratitude. In the period since, additional names have been added to this list...

A very special *thank you* to my wife, Eleanor, and my children, Charles Lewis Jr., Deirdre Lynne and Vaughan Lamar.

Virgil Hutton reviewed my chapter on Cleaning and suggested several changes. Monty Moncrief with his experience contributed to the section on Aerial Photography; plus, he supplied many fine photographs taken at Galveston. Walter E. "Rip" Parker, Dallas attorney, reviewed the chapter on Laws and made excellent suggestions and additions. George Sullivan freely provided excerpts from his engrossing book *Treasure Hunt,* which tells the story of Mel's Fisher's search for and discovery of the *Atocha*, for use in my chapter on the Archaeologist and the Treasure Hunter. Robert Marx graciously offered research reference data from several of his superb books on underwater salvage and archaeology.

I especially thank Hal Dawson for his many days spent improving my manuscript and making sure "every last thing" was correct prior to printing. Marie England spent countless and uncomplaining hours typing and retyping the manuscript. Special thanks also to Ken Durham, Georgia Montgomery and Mary Penson for their endeavors.

Thanks to Tom Edds, Jack Lowery, Ed Morris and others who read portions or all of the manuscript and suggested improvements in treasure locating and recovery techniques.

Concerning illustrations and photography, the First Edition of *Treasure Recovery from Sand and Sea* contained credit lines for many of the pictures. My Editor convinced me to change the caption style for this Second Edition in the interests of brevity and readability. I regret that the names of numerous friends and associates were thereby omitted. Yet, I am grateful to so many that it would be impossible to list them all. Mel Climer's professional contributions are to be found throughout the book. His wife Lisa also assisted during several photography expeditions to the Texas Coast. Other photos were taken by my *delayed shutter* camera.

To all who helped me with this book, I expressed my profound thanks two years ago. I emphasize it even more strongly today.

Charles Garrett

Dallas, Texas
Winter, 1989-90

Introduction

Shortly before the First Edition of *Treasure Recovery from Sand and Sea* went to press, I presented a slide talk to some 500 treasure hunters. It covered this book's basic outline, and I explained a few of the techniques that beach and surf hunters use in locating lost treasure. Following that talk, a crowd gathered around the Garrett Metal Detector exhibit, eagerly seeking to purchase copies of this still-unpublished book and to learn more about treasure recovery in, around and under the water.

This was no surprise to me. I had already experienced the keen interest in water hunting with the eager and immediate acceptance of my company's AT3 Beach Hunter detector, designed specifically for use on the beach and in the surf.

It was because of this desire by treasure hunters to enter the new frontier of the water that I began writing *Treasure Recovery from Sand and Sea* several years ago. It was obvious that a good percentage of the tens of thousands of land hunters also wanted to pursue and find treasures in the water. I set about applying knowledge and experience gained over a lifetime of treasure hunting on land to every aspect of successful searching for all types of treasure that could be found in and around water. I had to learn for myself before I could instruct others!

As thousands of you have already discovered from reading this book, I left very few stones unturned in my quest for knowledge and experience. And, let me emphasize that I enjoyed every minute of every field trip I made to learn--first hand--what water hunting was all·

about. I learned also that there are many professional water hunters who have filled bank vaults with their discovered treasure. I learned something else though...something very important to *you.*

While many fortunes in treasure have been taken from beaches and surf as well as under the water, only the *surface* has been scratched, so to speak. The amount of treasure left to be discovered cannot be comprehended. Believe me!

To those of you who own or have read the first edition of *Treasure Recovery from Sand and Sea,* this may look like an entirely new book. And, it does have considerable new material...plus more than 50 beautiful color photographs. Major significant change between this book and the First Edition, however, is the inclusion of considerably more material concerning the use of computerized detectors. This material is important! Each time I hunt with the new Grand Master Hunter CX II, I fall even more in love with it and with how this detector's greater depth and increased sensitivity provide real *shortcuts* to treasure recovery. You must experience its Ground Track™ and Fast Track™ features for yourself to appreciate how they can make it so much easier for anyone to find more treasure.

Let me leave you now to the reading and study of this book with what I consider the wisest course of action...my belief in an eight-letter word that must begin all treasure hunts. That word is *research!* Do your homework, find the best places to search and you'll find more treasure than you ever dreamed or imagined was possible.

You can also count on something else. I practice what I preach, and...

I'll see you in the water!

Charles Garrett

Garland, Texas
Winter, 1989-90

Lure of Instant Riches

The lure of instant riches...that's what treasure hunting is all about. The discovery of a single coin, a gold ring, or a chest of doubloons...each in itself is thrilling. And, when treasure is found, the search for more begins immediately. The lure of lost, buried or sunken riches beckons people from all walks of life. Treasure hunters range from the armchair adventurer to the seasoned professional. Some only dream of finding treasure while others set out with determination born from the belief that the next turn of the shovel is certain to unearth *instant riches*.

Yet, no one ever has enough wealth. The desire for more is always present...even in the most serene individual. Thus, no one ever loses the desire or the dream of discovering treasure. Sales of treasure hunting equipment reflect this yearning. When the price of gold reached $800 an ounce in 1980, sales of metal detectors jumped nearly 400% in a single year. Production at Garrett Electronics lagged nearly two months behind sales orders during that period of high gold value. The company simply could not keep up with the demand.

After a network television program presented a story about treasure hunters finding coins and jewelry in a California surf, metal detector dealers were swamped the next day with purchasers. When Mel Fisher announced discovery of a $500-million-plus treasure from a sunken Spanish galleon and reported hauling up silver and gold by the bucketsful, adventurers beat a path to shops where they could buy metal detectors and other treasure hunting equipment. When local news media report stories--or,

1

even rumors--of treasure being discovered, sales of detector equipment in that area take a noticeable leap.

It is obvious, therefore, that the desire for instant riches is always present. It may be depressed into the subconscious, but only a small spark fans this desire into full flame. *The fever hits!* When it does, there can be no cooling down that fevered person until some effort is made at treasure recovery. Perhaps this effort never gets beyond the pages of old newspapers or other reference material. More than likely, however, the would-be treasure hunter will not be satisfied until both time and money have been spent on some form of recovery effort.

Whether doctor, lawyer, movie star, teacher, plumber, electrician, librarian or whatever, everyone is a prime candidate to respond to the lure of treasure hunting. People of all ages find the prospect of discovering riches irresistible. Whether you have a grade school education,

The network TV program *PM Magazine* has presented programs on both land and water treasure hunting. George Mroczkowski, at center, hosted one documentary on THing in Southern California.

a high school diploma or a doctor's degree, the reward of instant riches probably appeals to you...even if you hesitate to admit it!

As a manufacturer of metal detectors, I try to meet as many of our customers as possible. So, you can be certain that I have witnessed first hand the onset of *treasure fever.* Let me assure you that there is nothing wrong with finding lost wealth. The *Bible* speaks of a man who found a treasure hidden in a field and sold all he had to get money to buy that field. Treasure hunting is recognized by many as an activity with merit beyond greed alone. Countless men and women of all ages welcome it as a lifetime hobby.

Of course, many of those who crave instant riches do not understand treasure hunting or have any idea about metal detectors. Still others have heard the fabulous stories, yet refuse to believe that such lost treasure even exists...much less that a man-made device can find it. We manufacturers continually devise programs to instruct in the use of metal detectors and show how they find treasure.

Lest I lead you astray, let me emphasize at the outset that treasure hunting *is not easy.* In fact, more often than not, it is downright hard work. The actual truth is that success is measured in direct proportion to the time and effort spent...not only in selecting the right equipment and learning how to use it, but basing all efforts on methodical research that leads to successful recovery.

When I was young I repeated the maxim, "Practice makes perfect," but was corrected by my Mother who pointed out that "*correct* practice makes perfect." How right she was! When you learn the *correct* way to use your detector...when you learn the right way to research and locate potentially rich treasure sites...when you properly and persistently apply this acquired knowledge, you will be successful. You'll never be satisfied, however, because you'll always know of a place to search for treasure that's just a little more promising. And, you'll always to ready to improve your skills...with new techniques or more effective equipment.

The waters of the earth constitute a tremendous treasure bank. There is wealth to be found, and treasure hunters will always seek their share. Thrills await you when you join the ranks of these beach, surf and underwater hunters. The sheer joy of the chase itself will come first...just scanning your detector over a sandy beach or in splashing surf. Then, what a delight awaits when you find your first coin! When mere nickels and quarters become so commonplace that they cease to excite, you'll begin searching for rare and more valuable coins and rings, jewelry, relics and sunken treasure.

Your determination will stimulate more research and literally force you to discover history and to experience its fascination. Whether young or old, male or female, you'll not turn back after you find your first treasure. This book is designed to guide you along the path you'll want to take. Start right, and you'll follow it successfully!

One final admonition before we begin...*always enjoy yourself and try to have fun*!

Gar Starrett is a fictional character I created to tell about some of the exciting treasure hunts in which my friends and I have participated. In each of the novels featuring him, Gar makes the same statement about treasure hunting. His observation is so pertinent that every treasure hunter should heed it:

"If nobody gets hurt or spends money he or she can't afford, every treasure hunt is a genuine pleasure!"

I couldn't have said it better myself!

Treasure is Waiting

The surest antidote to failure in treasure hunting is correct knowledge.

Karl von Mueller

If all lost treasure and items of value could be recovered from Davy Jones' locker--which includes all beaches, lakes, streams and rivers--and if these riches could be evenly distributed, I am confident that every man, woman and child on earth could be supported comfortably for the rest of their lives.

Seventy percent or nearly 200 million square miles of the earth's surface is water. Since the dawn of mankind, man has lived on or near water. Warfare, commerce, recreation, exploration and the search for food have made water, in one form or another, essential to the very continuation of human activity on this planet. Man has continually returned to it. And when man makes contact with water, he generally brings wealth with him.

Such wealth takes many forms. It may be a single coin or a diamond ring, but it may also be a ship laden with millions of dollars in cargo. Countless possessions of man have been lost and will continue to be lost in the world's waters--if not today, then tomorrow.

What is mankind doing to retrieve this wealth? Comparatively speaking, practically nothing! This statement is accurate even though men each day execute elaborate plans to search for sunken wealth. As they say, talk is cheap. It also requires at least a little effort. Some, however, are making the necessary effort. Recovery teams attempt to find and recover ships and lost cargo. Archaeologists and historians meticulously locate and retrieve artifacts from buried or sunken historical sites and shipwrecks.

Treasure hunters scan beaches and surfs. They dive under water looking for coins and items of jewelry. Lost treasure worth literally millions of dollars is recovered yearly. In reality, however, the amount of wealth currently being *lost* each day exceeds the amount being recovered.

All lost wealth can never be recovered. Man's best efforts can locate but a small percentage of the lost treasure and recover only a part of this. The purpose of this book is to help you learn how to search for, and find, *your share* of this lost wealth. Much of the "how-to" material explains the use of the modern metal detector. Since most wealth that can be recovered is metal, a detector is the perfect tool for finding it. We all dream of discovering a rich Spanish treasure ship laden with thousands of silver pieces of eight and gold escudo coins. But, on a more practical note the realistic treasure hunter would gladly settle for just those coins and rings lost daily by those who use the water for recreation and commerce.

Your Guidebook

This book gives basic instructions for locating sunken ships and underwater treasure of all kinds. Its main purpose, however, is to teach you how to find and recover coins and jewelry from the earth's recreational beaches, surf areas and accessible waterways. Only a minimal, but diligent, effort will leave you extremely pleased with new-found wealth. Beachcombing, surf searching and shallow water recovery techniques are quick to master, yet long on rewards. Surf searching begins where beachcombing ends. Shallow underwater searching begins where surfing ends.

Found treasure delights the mind and puts a sparkle in the eyes. There's nothing like the thrill of instant wealth in your hand. You'll experience it for yourself very soon...when you master simple research methods, metal detector skills and recovery techniques. The amount of

6

wealth recovered daily by men and women like yourself is staggering to contemplate. And, it's not necessary for you--or anyone else--to be a soldier of fortune trekking off on a distant country or sailing to a Caribbean island in search of a lost pirate chest. The wealth that can probably be recovered just within the city limits of your home town--most likely, that which can be found within your county--is substantial, no matter what the size of your community. I can assure you that the lost treasure within your state totals thousands upon thousands of dollars.

In the next chapter I'll introduce several people just like you who ventured forth, followed the rules of the game and won. Countless volumes would be required to present all those who have been successful in treasure hunting. You may know some of them. I wish this book could be large enough to list them all. But, that's not our purpose. We want to help you get on a beach or in the water and we want you to be equipped to wrest from Davy Jones some of the wealth stored in his treasure vaults.

The First Step

This book is for everyone who dreams of discovering lost and sunken treasure. Whether you seek treasure from the beach, the surf or the depths of the sea, you'll need an earnest desire, a lively imagination and a keen interest in finding riches.

Besides offering wealth, treasure recovery is a delightful activity. You'll enjoy the smell of springtime and the warmth of summer...even the crisp winds of autumn and the chill of winter can bring pleasure. Treasure hunting is one of the safest and most enjoyable hobbies in the world. Depending upon an individual's skill, it can be one of the most rewarding.

For the beginner, this book is the first step toward successful treasure recovery. "How-to" knowledge presented here results from more than 40 years of study and experience. Metal detector and treasure hunting instruction might not, at first, seem important. Take this opportunity for a *proper beginning* to your knowledge, however, and you'll become more successful in finding treasure later.

For the seasoned treasure hunter, this book has assembled the most current information about metal detectors and detecting techniques to help you sharpen your skills. The latest revision has added equipment developments that have occurred since the first publication of this manual some two years ago. The *book knowledge* you gain here can certainly add to your knowledge of modern water hunting techniques.

Yet, even a lifetime of treasure hunting is not sufficient to learn all there is to know about this fascinating hobby and its primary tool, the metal detector. I know because I learn more each time I use one. A metal detector is perfectly obedient and will do exactly what it is told to do--either find a ton of trash or locate the treasure you are seeking. Your detector will never lie to you. Its performance, however, will always depend upon the knowledge and skill of its operator.

Very little educational material is available on the use of metal detectors for recovery in beach, surf and water locations. This fact was made doubly clear to me upon publication of this book. Messages of appreciation poured into my office literally from all over the world. They generally told me just what I had suspected...that the advice available on beach and surf hunting usually consisted only of first-person accounts that included a rambling and completely unorganized assortment of suggestions. Unfortunately, some of the information and advice has proven to be inaccurate and can limit your opportunities to find treasure.

You can search the right way, or the wrong way. If you are fully prepared, if you understand your equipment and know how to use it properly, treasure hunting will be thrilling and profitable. You'll finish with more wealth to show for your efforts than you ever imagined.

8

Find Lost Treasure

Recently, I passed the forty-year "anniversary" of the day I found my first treasure. By eyesight I found a walking liberty half-dollar and a watch lying partly concealed in grass near the front entrance of the Lufkin, TX, High School building. Since that time I have found more than my share of lost wealth, but the amount of treasure that I have seen others discover exceeds mine many thousands of times.

It would be easy to fill this chapter with nothing but names of people who have shown me their discoveries or who sent photographs of the wealth they have found. Occasionally, I encounter so much treasure that I am left speechless when I realize the vast amount that is just waiting for all of us!

Long-Time Treasure Hunters

In a sense, I am a full-time professional treasure hunter. Much of my time, however, must be spent directing Garrett Electronics, a company that my wife and I founded in the early 1960s. Often I work alone in my quest for treasure, but I also join forces with other treasure hunters. During all my treasure hunting activities I put many "miles" on my metal detection equipment.

Often, I help others search for valuables they have lost or for treasure they expect to find. I spend a good percentage of my time testing new Garrett equipment and accessories. Whenever possible, I test equipment at actual treasure sites, thus seeking "double-barrel" success. I test and prove Garrett equipment while finding lost, buried and sunken treasure.

9

The majority of my hunting has been done on land, which includes beaches. More recently, I have begun to search for treasure in the surf. And, since I have been a scuba diver since the early 60s, my searches often lead me into and under water. Consequently, the amount of treasure I have found, or have witnessed, bestows upon me real authority to state that if you sincerely want to "strike it rich," you should become a beachcomber, surfer or a shallow water treasure hunter.

If you are not yet convinced that beachcombing or water hunting is for you, read on.

James "Monty" Moncrief

Monty resides near one of the world's greatest treasure vaults, the Texas coast. It was this coast that "converted" him from land hunting to beach and surf hunting. Monty served several years in United States Naval Intelligence before accepting a position with the National Aeronautics and Space Administration. He and his wife, Becky, now reside in Nassau Bay near Galveston. Monty and I often talked about the need for a combination land/underwater metal detector. As a result of these discussions, he became instrumental in the mechanical design and development of the Garrett Sea Hunter detector. While testing it on Galveston beaches, he began to find lost coins and jewelry. These early successes whetted his appetite for further discoveries. Consequently, he now spends much of his free time searching productive coastal sites. His finds are measured not in items but rather in pounds of coins and jewelry. At a recent South Texas treasure hunter's gathering he showed me a beautiful 18-karat ladies bracelet he had recently added to his collection of found jewelry. While his beach and surf finds are spectacular, he continues in other phases of treasure hunting, especially electronic prospecting.

Jack Lowry

Jack began his treasure hunting career as a coin hunter searching local recreation areas and homesites. He amassed buckets filled with coins of all descriptions. While he found an occasional piece of lost jewelry, he was not satisfied. He decided to try his luck on a Texas recreational beach. Since that first day, he has become an avowed beach/surf hunter. Even though he lives in the Dallas area, about 300 miles from Galveston, he makes the trek to the beach every chance he gets. He still finds coins, but his ring and jewelry collection has sharply increased in size and value. To improve his beach and surf hunting efficiency, he keeps track of storms and tides. Whenever there is an exceptionally low Texas tide, you can expect to see Jack in the surf, regardless of weather conditions. He occasionally travels to Arizona or New Mexico to electronic prospect and cache hunt, but he will quickly tell you that his first love is water hunting. While I was writing the first edition of this book, Jack showed me a 14-karat man's ring he had recently found. The ring with a large ruby and two diamonds mounted in the crown is worth more than $800.

T.R. (Tom) Edds & Walter Stark

Tom Edds and Walter Stark are ordinary folks like me

Jack Lowry, a Garrett Electronics executive who has found this vast horde of treasure searching local parks and the surf along the Texas coastline, will quickly admit that his first love is water hunting.

11

and perhaps like you. If you happen to meet them, they probably will have beach sand in their cuffs and a deep tan--instant clues that they like the great outdoors. Beyond that, you might never know they are two of the world's most successful treasure hunting beachcombers.

Their Florida residence gives them instant access to countless miles of recreational beaches that might better be described as storehouses of lost treasure. Should you be lucky enough to see them display some of their finds at a treasure meet, you won't believe your eyes. The gold, silver and platinum rings, diamond rings, high school rings, gold and silver bracelets, religious medals and other jewelry they have found would put a well-equipped jewelry store to shame. You'll listen spellbound as they describe these various treasures and as they tell you exactly when and where each object was found. You may be equally surprised at the tremendous quantity of lesser-valued items they have recovered from the sand: toys, locks, keys, sunglasses and an endless list of ordinary metal items.

Listening to these men and watching them search is an

Eleanor Hube of Connecticut, quite possibly the world's most successful lady surf hunter, hasn't gone back to dry land hunting since she first ventured into the water at a local swimming beach.

education. They're never in a hurry. They methodically pursue their hobby with precision and deliberate slowness and they know what they're doing. They have developed beach treasure recovery into a fine art, perhaps, even a science. Should you meet them on the beach, they may take a few minutes from their scanning to give you tips on how you can find your share of beach treasure. "There's plenty to go 'round, join us and let's find some treasure," they'll tell you.

Eleanor Hube

Eleanor's eyes are always sparkling and she never loses her smile. Perhaps she's thinking of what tomorrow may bring when she'll again seek lost treasure. Eleanor is a surf hunter. She used to search the land and has spent many thousands of hours in local parks, playgrounds and ghost towns. But since the day she ventured forth at a local swimming beach and found her first gold ring, she's never gone back to dry land hunting.

She has spent so much time enjoying the rewards of surf searching that she's as much at home in the water as out. Because she rarely removes it from the bank vault, you'll never see much of Eleanor's found treasure. Occasionally, however, she'll bring out a few choice pieces for a talk before some local treasure hunting club. She has, on occasion, let me photograph a few of her valuable finds. I assure you, if you could see the rewards that have come from this dedicated surfer's persistence, you would quickly follow in her footsteps.

Of course, those footsteps don't end at the local beach. She, her husband and friends travel throughout the United States, the Caribbean and to England. The first thing she packs is her underwater Sea Hunter metal detector. Usually the results of her first day of surf hunting on the Caribbean beaches more than pays for the entire trip.

"It's not work," she once told me. "It's pure vacation. I love every minute of it. I'm hooked--but who wouldn't be if they could spend the rest of their life enjoying a rewarding hobby like the one I pursue."

Ed Morris

Ed is a retired Air Force officer who lives in Santa Maria, CA. Upon retirement he began spending his leisure time treasure hunting. Over the years he developed a knack for beach hunting because he lives immediately adjacent to miles of prime swimming and recreational beaches. He gained mastery over his first detector and as new instruments came along he quickly became proficient in their operation. Over the years he amassed a large quantity of rings, coins, jewelry and other valuable items discovered by his metal detector in the sands of the beach. Since he was heavily involved in journalism in the Air Force, he began writing articles about his hobby and published them in the various treasure hunting magazines. You may have read some of Ed's helpful articles. "There has never been any need for me to search for another hobby," says Ed. "The activity of metal detecting on local beaches is all I need. It's solid fun. I enjoy it, and it's very rewarding. It's one of the most healthful activities I can think of. I'm hooked on the great outdoors and the sunshine and, of course, the rewards of treasure hunting."

Don Cyr

A resident of Burlington, Ontario, Canada, Don has been a water hunter for many years. In spite of the cold weather and frozen lakes during a good portion of the year, he and many other Canadians continue their quest wearing hip waders or wet suits. He reports that he likes water hunting because many of his best treasure finds came from the water.

Don's activities often take him throughout Canada, as well as into the United States. Because of his dedication to the hobby, he was elected President of CMDA, Canadian Metal Detecting Association. He worked diligently to help form a coalition between CMDA and FMDA (United States Federation of Metal Detectors and

14

Archaeological Clubs. In other chapters in this book you will see photographs of many of Cyr's finds.

Sherrill Williams & Bob Darnell

These two lake hunters found themselves featured in the *Lake Country Banner* of Tiptonville, TN. During the "good old days," thousands of sun lovers frolicked on the beaches and swam in the warm water at several nearby recreational areas. Until Sherrill and Bob began their underwater recovery work, no one thought much about or believed that those early day fun seekers lost their wealth. There were a few remembered instances of missing rings, but that was about it. The newspaper article tells their true story, and readers are awed by the treasure they have discovered.

Many of the class rings they found have been returned to their owners who lost the jewelry as far back as 1931. Much of the treasure, however, is on display at Sherill Williams' True Value Hardware in Hornbeak, TN. At last count the treasure included more than 3300 coins, 334 of which are silver. There are 28 buffalo nickels, 118 mercury dimes, 108 Roosevelt dimes, 84 silver quarters and 24 silver half dollars. The oldest coin dates back to 1894. Other items included 5 gold rings with stones, 30 silver rings, 14 class rings, 8 gold bands and 2 diamond rings. There are 19 religious items, a 5-gram gold piece and a large assortment of knives, lighters, buckles, keys, bathing suit pins, chains, bracelets, watches, lifeguard whistles, pendants and sunglasses.

Harry & Lucille Bowen

This man and wife from Spokane, WA, have been active metal detector enthusiasts for three decades. Harry is a retired Spokane police officer. Years ago they began to think about life after Harry's retirement and they decided to open a treasure hunting specialty shop. They believed many people in Spokane would be interested in treasure hunting. With the experience they had gained in the past, plus the experience they would gain in the next few years, they could teach their customers about this great hobby.

As the years progressed, Harry continued to concentrate mostly on land hunting. However, Lucille began to occasionally search local beaches. It soon became obvious that her rewards were great. Whenever the opportunity presents itself, Lucille and some of her friends head for swimming areas. Though she hasn't given up her love for searching ghost towns and other promising sites, the lure of treasure in the sands and shallow water is very strong. She has found thousands of coins, rings, religious medallions, bracelets, necklaces and other forms of jewelry. Lucille has never claimed to be a professional treasure hunter. Her success simply proves it!

Ken Schaffer

You could never tell by looking at Ken Schaffer, the owner of H & S Detector Center at 184 Boggs Avenue, Virginia Beach, VA, that he often spends eight hours a day treasure hunting in the local Chesapeake Bay area surf. One look at his showcases, however, would convince you immediately. After a few minutes of conversation with Ken, you'll be satisfied that he knows his business and that he has learned how the hobby of shallow water metal detecting can pay off.

He won't tell you how many gold, silver and platinum rings he's found in the past two decades nor will he tell you how many diamond rings he's added to his collection since January 1 of the present year. But, he often searches eight hours a day. "Because it pays off!" he'll quickly answer. No one spends that much time searching the cold water of Chesapeake Bay unless it pays dividends. Ken admits that most of his hunting is done in the winter. The tides run in two directions along these beaches, he says. During the warm, summer months the tides cause the sand to pile up. During the colder months, however, a reverse tide removes the accumulation of sand. That's when he goes to work, when the gold rings and other valuables are at their

16

shallowest depth. If you are lucky enough to meet Ken, ask him about surf hunting and he'll give you quick, straight answers.

Bob Trevillian & Frank Carter

This pair of water hunters really need no introduction. They discussed their success in *Diamonds in the Surf* and *First and Second Adventure*. Bob and Frank's early finds were so spectacular that the men retired and now devote their energies in searching recreational beaches and surfs for treasures lost by sun lovers. They have discovered an amazing quantity of wealth others left behind. The treasure hunters began their activities mainly in the water, but research kept turning up promising land sites such as abandoned beaches and ghost towns. Curious, they searched these places and their results were so spectacular, they wrote a third book, *The Poor Man's Treasure Hunter*. Bob and Frank's success story is remarkable but, as they point out, it is within the reach of anyone with the time, desire and determination to succeed.

Wallace Chandler

I first met Wallace Chandler in 1972 at a prospector's meeting in Southern California while he was on vacation. Though his home base is in Michigan, he travels around the United States searching beaches. Not a water man, he's content to make his living--a quite acceptable one-- searching for treasure that sun worshipers leave behind. He's been a full-time beachcomber going on two decades and he says he wouldn't give it up for anything. He's come by the Garrett Metal Detector factory several times to show me his latest treasures. Photographs in the first edition of this book included many of these finds that establish him as a man who knows what he is doing.

It's easy to understand why he searches the beaches full-time. It would be difficult to make that kind of money working at a regular job. He drives a Volkswagen Rabbit equipped with a diesel engine and at this writing he has driven the car one-quarter million miles. Wallace told me one day he could afford to drive a larger, more expensive car, but why should he? Wallace gets 50 miles to the gallon out of that Rabbit and it's never yet failed to take him to a place he wanted to search.

Wallace plans well into the future. Each spring he knows where he's going to be the next springtime. Research is one of the key reasons for his success and it seems obvious that Wallace has built a pretty good life for himself. He goes where he wants to go and stays as long as he likes when he gets there. Since he finds more treasure than he needs, most of his most valuable rings are transferred to a bank safe deposit box. Should he need a little extra cash for gas or other expenses, he sells a few rings and keeps going to his next job--or rather his next vacation spot.

World of the Divers

You've probably heard or read about men known the world over for the vast amounts of sunken treasure, relics and artifacts they've found. Robert Marx, Mel Fisher, Burt Webber, the famed Jacques Cousteau, and others have become household words. They have found so many kings' treasures consisting of mountains of silver, Spanish pieces of eight and gold escudo coins and other treasures, they probably have lost count. Of course, these men are notable exceptions to the rule. They have gone well beyond finding their share and have found hundreds and probably thousands of other people's shares as well! The wealth they recovered didn't fall into their laps. They worked long, hard hours and spent countless months researching the locations of treasures they knew existed. And, do you know what? They probably enjoyed every minute of it!

Facing: Mel Fisher, left, and author

Over: Monty Moncrief

18

Successes like theirs don't come very often, but when they come, the rewards make the effort worthwhile.

Robert Marx

This adventurer, historian, marine archaeologist and treasure hunter has written more than 30 books and has published hundreds of scientific articles and reports. He has been an editor for *Argosy* and *The Saturday Evening Post.* Since the age of 10, Marx has been an active deep sea diver.

During his early days he was a treasure hunter, but he has abandoned most of these adventures to become a serious archaeologist. Marx now focuses his attention on educating governments on the importance of not only protecting archaeological areas, but also actively supporting qualified projects. His numerous books are astonishing in their descriptions of various projects in which he has participated.

Marx is known as one of the most successful and well-known specialists in the field of marine archaeology and he has an equally strong reputation for his work in naval and maritime history. He studied at UCLA and the University of Maryland and served in the U.S. Marine Corps where he was a diver and worked on salvage operations. Among his more popular writings are *Shipwrecks of the Western Hemisphere, Into the Deep, The Underwater Dig, Treasure Fleets of the Spanish Main, Following Columbus, Voyage of the Nina II, Quest for Treasure* and *Buried Treasure of The United States.*

In *Quest for Treasure,* Marx discovers the remains of the Spanish treasure ship, *Nuestra Senora de la Maravilla* which sank in 1656 off the Bahamas. Marx vividly describes the find and recovery of a vast fortune in gold and silver

Facing: Robert Marx

Over: Don Cyr

coins and ingots, jewelry, ship's cannon and relics. He and his crew battled the sea, sharks, corrupt government officials and modern-day pirates who wanted to take the treasure for themselves. To read this book is to learn the true life of a modern-day adventurer who searches for and recovers fabled wealth that most of us can only dream of finding.

Though he has spent a lifetime in an exciting field, his discoveries and recoveries represent only a minuscule fraction of the lost wealth awaiting the underwater explorer. Marx's books contain a wealth of information. Anyone interested in this fascinating and rewarding hobby is encouraged to read his material and learn from a true professional. Marx's wife, Jennifer, is a professional as well. She is a diver, historian, author and lecturer. One of her best known books, *The Magic of Gold,* is a fascinating story about gold that you'll be unable to put down. Robert and Jennifer Marx are a perfect example of the accomplishments that a husband-and-wife team can make in the exciting field of underwater discovery.

Mel Fisher

Mel Fisher

"Today is the day!"

Mel Fisher has lived by this positive statement for more than two decades. It became Treasure Salvors' marching cry as the group searched the Florida Keys for the Spanish treasure galleon *Nuestra Senora de Atocha* which went down in 1622 with a cargo of valuables. When the *Atocha* sank in a hurricane it nearly caused a depression in Europe and almost threw the Spanish Court into bankruptcy. The ship's manifest listed more than 600 pounds of gold, 1200 silver bars weighing upwards of 70 pounds each and 250,000 silver coins and rare art objects of extreme value. Precious cargo totaled nearly 40 tons of treasure, valued at more than $400 million! What's more, it often has been said that most Spanish treasure ships carried from three to four times the amount of treasure listed on the manifest.

Smuggling apparently was rampant in those days and tremendous quantities of unregistered treasure has been found on most Spanish shipwreck sites.

Fisher's first big treasure find came in the mid-1960s when he and his partners discovered part of the 1715 Spanish Plate Fleet of 10 treasure galleons between Vero Beach and Fort Pierce, Florida. After discovering more than two million dollars worth of gold and silver, he decided to go after the *Atocha.*

Even though he has witnessed tragedy and has found himself in many legal battles, most of which were decided in his favor, Mel's faith remained firm. One July morning in 1985 he came into his office and once more said, "Today is the day!" Little could he know that 41 miles west of Key West, in what has been described as an underwater desert, his team members had already dived 55 feet to check out a strong electronic reading. While scanning over ballast stones, their underwater metal detectors screamed an alert. With a mass of solid silver bars stacked all over the sea floor, they had found the Mother Lode.

In the first week the crew recovered nearly five hundred silver bars, each one weighing seventy pounds. Treasure chests, similar to those you would visualize, some complete with hinges, were located. Seven contained up to two thousand pieces of silver. Each treasure chest was worth about two million dollars. The eighth chest was filled with gold bars.

This remarkable find and recovery placed him at the pinnacle of success. Through many trials and discoveries, Mel Fisher and his wife, Dolores, have carved for themselves a niche in the annals of treasure hunting history.

Burt Webber, Jr.

Burt Webber made a name for himself when he searched for and discovered the famous ship, *Nuestra Senora de la Concepcion.* His quest for treasure, described in John Grissim's, *The Lost Treasure of the Concepcion,* is an exciting adventure to read. He brought up millions of dollars in treasure, proving once again that earth's oceans contain treasures beyond imagination.

Barry Clifford

While diving off the Massachusetts town of Wellfleet, a modern- day adventurer named Barry Clifford located the remains of the ship--with its remains still containing cargo--sailed by the notorious 18th century buccaneer, Samuel "Black Sam" Bellamy. When it sank in 1717 in sight of the beach, the *Whidah* was carrying a treasure valued today at hundreds of millions of dollars. Among the recovered treasure were gold and silver coins, ingots, jewelry, weapons and artifacts. Shipboard booty, captured from 22 ships, includes 180 canvas bags that each held 50 pounds of jewels.

The ship is also of great historical value in that it is the first pirate ship discovered. "Black Sam" Bellamy roamed the Caribbean and left a legacy of misadventures as spectacular as those of the fabled Blackbeard and Captain Kidd. Clifford's plans are to keep all of the recovered treasure intact and establish a museum to exhibit his findings.

Jack Kelley

Tulsa architect and oilman Jack Kelley is basking in the glow of a crowning achievement--the discovery of a cargo ship that sank off Turkey about 1400 B.C. This discovery and excavation has been called the most exciting event in the decades-long search for ancient artifacts in the Mediterranean Sea. Cargo from the merchant ship totals an estimated 20 tons. Kelley believes the shipwreck to be the next most significant archaeological find since the discovery by Howard Carter of King Tut's tomb.

Kevin McCormick

Kevin McCormick, project manager for Sub-Sal, Inc., reported the salvaging of the sunken sailing vessel, *HMS deBraak*, from Delaware Bay. The 18th century British brig sank nearly two centuries ago and carried a cargo valued at several million dollars.

Mike Hatcher

Explorer and treasure hunter Mike Hatcher achieved fame when he discovered a sunken Chinese junk containing millions of dollars worth of Ming porcelain. More recently, he located the remarkably rich sunken cargo of the Dutch East Indian merchantman *Geldermalsen,* which went down in the South China Sea in 1752 with 270 men on board. The gold and porcelain recovered brought over 10 million pounds at a Christie's auction in Amsterdam. Should you have the opportunity to view the documentary, *The Nanking Cargo,* don't miss it.

And, You've Heard About

In various books, magazines and trade publications, treasure hunters regularly reveal their successes, some of which are phenomenal. I wish space in this book would let me include all their stories. Among the successful beach, surf and water hunters (and this acknowledgment is by no means complete) are Richard and Heather Ambrose, Keith Hetherington, Australian author of *Beachcombing with a Metal Detector,* Bill and Sherie Kasselman, Rene LeNeve, Don Littlejohn, Joe Maenner, Kay Modulling, George Mroczkowski, Ettore and Diana Nannetti, Mike Numann, Roy Volker, Betty Weeks and Ken Wherry.

Other Success Stories

Louisiana state officials released information that an 18th century shipwreck found off its coast yielded nearly a half million dollars in gold and silver. The Spanish vessel, *El Constante,* was lost in a hurricane in 1766. This ship was one of six in a fleet bound from Veracruz, Mexico, to Spain. A hurricane drove it into shallow water and smashed it to bits. This find could lead to a total recovery of several hundred million dollars as records indicate that the entire fleet carried over 50 million pesos worth of gold, silver, copper and pottery.

The *U.S.S. Hatteras*, a 210-foot iron ship, was a Union vessel used during the Civil War. It was sunk by a Con-

27

federate ship in 1863. Using sophisticated equipment, Jeff Burke and Charles Rose found the ship near Galveston in 20 feet of water. The men have plans to raise the *Hatteras* and convert her into a floating museum.

A World War II Wellington bomber was found resting on the bottom 230 feet deep in Scotland's Loch Ness.

A few miles off the coast of Egypt, French and Egyptian divers discovered the wreck of the *Orient*, flagship of the ill-fated fleet that convoyed Napoleon Bonaparte and his army to Egypt. The fleet was destroyed and sunk in 1798 by the British.

After 73 years of solitude, the mighty ship, *Titanic*, was found at a depth of two and one-half miles. Using sophisticated underwater photography equipment, a group of professional marine explorers located the ship. It was mostly intact and covered by only a light silt sediment.

You have already read my belief that more treasure is being lost than is being recovered. People continue to lose valuable items on the beach and in the surf. Ships continue taking their precious cargo to the bottom. And, old treasure continues to be redistributed as storms arise and literally churn up the beaches and shallow waters. Treasure from ships that have gone down recently as well as riches that disappeared centuries ago is picked up by storms and hurled into the shallow surfs and even onto land. Pounding surf, changing tides and relentless winds deposit untold amounts of treasure in troughs, washes and other sites along the beaches.

Travel to any popular beach and watch people at play. They engage in horse-play or, perhaps, play ball. Without knowing it, they lose coins, rings and other valuables. Gold and silver chains break and fall to the ground to be lost. Sunbathing on towels is a popular activity. All too often, sunbathers remove jewelry which they promptly forget about. When they leave, they grab their towel and swing it to shake off the sand. I have discovered "pockets" of coins and jewelry on the beach, and others have told me of similar recoveries. I believe hurrying sunbathers are the reason for these abandoned collections of valuables.

Swimming draws people into the surf. All too often swimmers forget about their gold and silver rings, even diamond rings. They just don't realize how easy it is to lose rings off fingers made slippery by suntan lotions and oils. Plus, hot summer sun expands metal in the rings, making them slightly larger than normal. Swimmers dash into the surf, not realizing that they are about to add more treasure to Davy Jones' locker as rings slide off their fingers and into the water. By the time they discover their jewelry is missing, they have no idea where to look. Many scratch through the sand, but more often than not, the search is futile.

Only the modern day treasure hunter, equipped with sophisticated, high-tech metal detection equipment, can locate these lost treasures. When found, it is no longer "lost wealth." It is, more properly, *sudden wealth!*

Use Proper Research

We inherited these lost fortunes, but we must seek them out.

Roy Lagal

Treasure is where you find it. You may diligently seek it or you may stumble upon it. The choice is yours. You can increase your chances of finding treasure one thousand fold if you will learn how to research projects through to successful conclusion. Without research, treasure discovery comes only by chance and luck...and the booty is often of little value.

Treasure found by accident represents but a small percentage of that found by persons using good, acceptable research practices. Research can consume up to 99% of a successful search and recovery undertaking. Without proper research you'll be as lost as a driver without a map in a strange city. You need a waybill...directions to guide you to the best locations. These waybills, these directions, come from many sources, both public and private.

I *never* advise either buying a treasure map or taking the word of anyone else as gospel. You must always find the primary source for yourself. To begin at the beginning involves a study of basic research material and sources. You must know *what* you are looking for and that it exists. Certain forms of treasure hunting require a knowledge about where specific types of treasure, can be found. You don't search for pieces of eight in a city park or seek lost gold rings in a child's sand box. (Even though tiny children's rings and mother's rings are occasionally found there!)

Since failure to prepare groundwork generally results in wasted time, effort and money, I have included this chapter to give you a headstart. Also, other chapters contain specific research information.

Unfortunately, there is no one-two-three step procedure I can outline. One hundred people reading this book may begin looking for one hundred different treasures. The main thing is to get started by defining these goals, which you can call...

A Treasure Check List

What are you looking for?
Does it exist?
Where is it?
Will you have clear title to it if you find it?
Have others looked for it?
How do you know they didn't find it?
What will it cost you to find it?
Is it worth what it will cost you to find it?

Certainly, these questions are rudimentary, but yet very important. Don't go searching for the will-o-the-wisp. Spend your time wisely and efficiently. Don't waste time looking for treasure unless you are sure, based upon your research, it exists. Use the sources listed here and others to discover how to track down the information about the treasure you seek.

Establish your goal. Then believe in this work and your ability to achieve it. Finally, work like the dickens to make it come true.

To repeat a truth, successful treasure hunting can often be 99% research and 1% recovery. Do not think of research as though it were an uninteresting stint in the back room of some dusty, ill-lighted library where you must pore over volumes of scarcely legible books, articles and newspapers. Research can be fun. It can become something you enjoy and look forward to.

When you become obsessed with beach and surf hunt-

32

ing, you'll continually think about it. You'll scan newspapers and magazines for stories and data about local sites. When you talk with people, especially oldtimers, you'll ask them about such-and-such a place. You'll ask them if they remember whether the present swimming beach is in the same location as it was decades ago. You'll ask them if they remember incidents when sunbathers lost jewelry and other valuables.

The other day I was walking around the lake where I have spent time writing portions of this book. I came upon three elderly men resting on a bench. After a brief discussion about the weather, I asked them if swimming ever took place anywhere other than at the presently designated location. They told me the present swimming area is the only one ever used. I then asked if they recall anyone ever losing rings or other valuable jewelry.

They first said they didn't remember any such incidents but then one of them quickly added that, yes, there was a person who lost a watch...back in the 1960's. The reason the oldtimer remembered the story and when it happened

These finds by a West Coast THer, especially the turquoise Indian jewelry, illustrate the author's contention that certain categories of jewelry and other items can be found at certain beach locations.

was that his father was caretaker at the time. He said that this swimmer reported to his father that she had dropped a watch down through the floorboards of the bathhouse. She asked the caretaker if he would keep his eyes open for the watch. Sure enough, sometime later, the man spotted the watch gleaming in the sun as it lay a few inches deep in the water slightly back under the edge of the bathhouse. Then one of the oldtimers looked at me and said, "You do know that there used to be clothes-changing booths built on the present pier?" I told him I didn't know that. "Yes, there was," the oldtimer replied, "and I'll bet that they lost a lot of coins and valuables as they changed clothes."

In that brief conversation, I fairly well had the history of the beach and swimming area. Plus, I now had even more reason to don my dive suit and work beneath the pier.

When you read the newspapers, be alert for leads. I remember an issue of the *Dallas Morning News* that featured a large, front page, color photo of a mass of young people playing on an ocean beach. The photo was captioned, "Where the Joys are!" The article described thousands of teenagers taking spring break frolicking on a South Padre Island beach. When school spring break comes for a week, students from far and wide flock to the beaches where they release pent-up frustrations; these treks to the beaches have been going on for decades.

I talked with my son, Vaughan, who spent two of his high school spring breaks on Padre Island. He said that spring break is the time when students like to show off. "They do their best to impress everyone else; they give it everything they've got." He continued, "They wear their best clothes and swim suits and certainly their best jewelry. Many of the girls are husband-hunting and they really put on the dog. Things often get so wild, I don't see how they can keep from losing lots of money, jewelry and other valuables."

The moral to that story is for the beachcomber and surf hunter to work those beaches immediately after the parties have ended, if not during.

Be alert to news reports of modern day heists and robberies. When a safe, for instance, is stolen, the thieves must do some thing with it. Usually, "hot" items are discarded in some convenient nearby pond or stream. A fellow repairing the roof on one of our Garrett buildings, told me an interesting story. He reported that a friend of his had stolen a private coin collection. Realizing that the property could be traced, the thief hastily threw the collection into a nearby creek. The roofer promised to show me the exact spot. Well, embarrassing as it is, "to tell the rest of the story," I delayed too long. A few months later when I tried to locate the roofer, I could not. The fellow had moved and no one knew his whereabouts. So, the moral to that story is, when you hear of a "good one," *Go Immediately.* Don't delay. Check the story to a *satisfactory conclusion!*

Robert Podhrasky, Garrett Electronics' Chief Engineer, and I taught an underwater metal detector seminar for the local Garland police. Following classroom instruction we drove to a North Texas rock quarry filled with water. During our training activities, we located a safe, two coin changers and, believe it or not, an automobile...proof positive that thieves discard stolen property.

There's an unlimited amount of research information available to you. The only limits will be those you impose upon yourself. Since you know that *everyone* has shortcomings, it is better never to rely entirely upon the work of others. After all, if someone is willing to write about a treasure...you can be sure the person abandoned searching for it for one reason or another. You must, therefore, analyze the data with a cautious eye. Failure of the writer to complete the research and recovery could be due to lack of funds, time, or simply interest. But, if a person took time to travel to a site and investigate it, that person must have believed in his story.

Do not become discouraged if in the early stages of your treasure hunting activities, you cannot achieve expected success. You'll notice I said, "expected" success. I could have used the word,"satisfactory," but I want to stress that you must set goals--realistic ones, to be sure. Only when you establish goals will you have a target at which to shoot. Set goals for your success and strive to achieve them. Do not become discouraged in the early stages. Success will come if you persist.

You must never doubt that you will be successful. Dogged patience, perseverance, continued study and research and field practice are necessary ingredients in the formula of success in this fascinating and rewarding hobby. If you are skeptical and do not continue unswervingly in your quest, you will achieve mediocre results. But, when you one day "round the corner" and begin filling your pouch with coins, jewelry and treasure, then you will know you have "made it" and can look forward to successes of which you may never have dreamed or envisioned.

Research Sources

Modern Day Photographs: The undisputed value in photography lies in the fact that photographs will reveal objects and features you normally might overlook or not even see when scanning hurriedly. You can do your own photography or obtain photographs from many public and private sources.

The U.S. Forestry Service maintains an extensive photo library through which you can obtain aerial photos of Forest Service and soil conservation sites. For information on this service contact your local U.S. Forestry Department or you can write the Engineering Staff Unit, Forest Service, U.S.D.A.,Washington, D.C. 20250 or the Cartographic Division, Soil Conservation Service, U.S.D.A., Federal Building, Hyattsville, MD 20748. From your local forester or the Engineering Staff Unit in Washington,

D.C. (address above) you can obtain the address of the various regional Forest Service field offices.

Two additional aerial mapping photo sources are the Tennessee Valley Authority, Map Files and Records Section, 200 Haney Building, Chattanooga, TN 374011 and the U.S. Geological Survey, EROS Data Center, Sioux Falls, SD 57198. Refer also to Eugene Avery's Book, *Interpretation of Aerial Photographs.*

Old Photographs: They capture forever the activities of man. Sooner or later a photographer is bound to show up at every recreation and swimming site. The photographers of yesterday seemed to enjoy photographing swimmers of the day in their funny-looking (to us) costumes. Old time photographs offer a world of information and in many cases the exact spot where swimming took place. Unfortunately, most old photographs are not identified. No one took the time to write, on the reverse side, the site location. But a little research can lead to the site being pointed out by an oldtimer.

Oldtimers: The oldtimer is one source of information that you must never pass up. In fact, these storage vaults of treasure locations should be actively sought out and quizzed for every last scrap of information that can guide you to a fruitful location. When talking with oldtimers about old locations, quiz them about jewelry items that they may know of being lost years ago. Oftentimes they'll tell you of valuable rings and other jewelry items that were lost by their companions. If they'll take you to these treasure sites, all the better.

Insurance Agents: Your insurance agent is likely to be a warehouse of information. If he has paid claims on lost jewelry, he'll have records specifying the value and the probable location of the loss.

Beach Managers or Proprietors: Oftentimes lost items are reported to managers or proprietors in the hopes the lost article will be found. One fellow I struck up a conversation with at an old abandoned swimming site described the probable location of a safe that was stolen by two men * approximately 15 years earlier. One of the men was this man's friend who told him that they stole the safe and hauled it part way across the dam. During their attempt to open the safe they were fearful of being caught by the police so they rolled the safe down the dam's slope into the water. I investigated the area and determined that the dam was soft earth and, in all probability, the safe quickly sank several feet into the earthen dam below water level. I earmarked that one for future investigation.

Libraries: Here's where you can spend lots of time that can pay off. Unless you're familiar with library cataloging, ask the librarian to give you a short course. Tell her you're looking for history books, periodicals, maps and other sources that will list early day swimming sites and beaches. Take your time and look through every reference you find. Either use the copier to gather the information you need or take along some 3x5 cards and list each site on a card. The more specific you can be with the librarian as to what you're looking for, the more help you will get.

Newspapers: When you have free time, go down to your local newspaper office and ask to browse through their old newspapers or microfilm of past editions. Scan the lost and found column for items lost by persons visiting local beaches and swimming areas. Study the travel sections for information about beach resort sites. Read articles that describe severe storms, especially hurricanes, in which beach homes were flooded or destroyed. These areas could be a true treasure vault of many types of lost valuables. Especially be on the lookout for photographs of people swimming and enjoying beaches of bygone eras.

Chambers of Commerce: Contact chambers for maps and literature they have regarding swimming and recrea-

Because proper research is certainly necessary before carrying out the expense of underwater diving, the author carefully checks finds here to validate his search site.

tion beaches. Often chambers of commerce promote special programs to encourage residents and tourists to participate.

Departments of Parks and Recreation: Write, call or go by and request lists of all recreational facil ities that include a swimming area. Ask them to send you all promotional literature describing the type of sites you're searching for. Don't forget aerial photographs, especially the old ones that show the locations of lakes, ponds and other swimming sites, many of which may be no longer in use. When you study these photographs, keep your eyes peeled for piers, landing docks, bath houses and other promising sites.

Old Atlases: Your library or historical society may have old community issues you can review. From these you can learn the location of long-gone communities, railway and stage stations, fords, Indian encampments and the like. Old city maps will show the location of the oldest recreational parks where you can find, perhaps, the oldest coins...where that gold coin might be waiting.

Department of Permits: If there is one in your area, they may have a list of swimming spots for which, in order to swim, a permit is required.

Yearbooks: School and college yearbooks often abound with photographs taken by young, enterprising photographers. These yearbooks can be a valuable source of swimming sites that could keep you busy for years to come.

Historical Books: More and more historical books seem to be appearing. They are written about practically every town, city and county in the United States, and the authors and editors all seem to try to outdo each other. Rare, even valuable, photographs are often included, along with data

Successful THers realize that even hunting for pieces of eight such as this requires research to determine the precise *where* and *when* for optimum searching times.

concerning activities. The early-day recreational sites are true bonanza locations where you'll want to scan for lost treasure of yesteryear. When you examine such historical books, be on the lookout for millponds and other water areas that could have been used for swimming.

Maps: Never pass up the opportunity to scan both new and old maps for location of swimming beaches. United States topographical maps show remarkable detail for all bodies of water in any given area. Deeds and surveyors' notes describe or include maps showing bodies of water.

Museums: Don't be content just to browse through your local museum. Tell the curators what you're looking for; they can dig back into dusty files and come up with some true treasure vault locations you might not find down any other avenues. Be sure to browse photograph and old book departments since valuable relics such as these are often donated to museums. Your local museum can be as good as the library in providing good research material. You are more likely to meet resistance when it comes to trying to work with museum curators and other personnel, so a good idea is to develop an *historical research thesis* of the local area. You may get lots more assistance.

Ghost Town Books: Be on the lookout for books written about ghost towns and old sites of your area. Many towns of bygone days have their own swimming tank, blue hole or whatever they might have called it. Certainly you'll want to locate these long-neglected treasure vaults and clean them out.

Hotel and Motel Lobbies: They'll almost always have a literature rack containing free brochures that describe various vacation and tourist spots.

Historical Societies: If the town or city is large enough, there'll be a "home" where the historical society has its headquarters. Not only will the persons on duty probably be well versed in local sites of interest, there may be a library of invaluable maps and books that contain the locations of more places than you can search in a year.

U.S. Forest Service: The U.S. Forest Service maintains an excellent photo and map library that may contain photos of areas that are of interest to you. Check with your local Forest Service office or write the Chief, Forest Service, U.S.D.A., South Building, 12th and Independence Avenue, S.W., Washington, DC 20013, for information.

Paper and Timber Companies: These companies have millions of acres accessible to vacationers. Contact them to obtain information on swimming and recreational sites.

National Forests: Write to them and request information and locations of swimming and recreational areas open to metal detectors.

National Park Service Recreation Areas: For specific information write to the Regional Office, National Park Service, Room 3043, Interior Building, Washington, DC 20240.

Bureau of Reclamation: The Federal Reclamation office assists all levels of government with the management of water and related land resources. Current reclamation maps and data available from older maps will loca tions of many interesting sites. Write to the Bureau of Reclamation, U.S. Department of the Interior, Washington, DC 20240.

National Cartographic Information Center: Available to you are 1.5 million maps and charts, 25 million aerial and space photographs and 1.5 million geodetic control points. Write to the National Cartographic Information Center, U.S. Geological Survey, 507 National Center, Reston, VA 22092.

U.S. Government Printing Office: The U.S. Government Printing Office offers more than 25,000 books and pamphlets through a centralized mail order office and 24 bookstores throughout our nation. To have your name added to this free descriptive booklet distribution list, write the Superintendent of Documents, U.S. Government Printing Office, Attention: Mail List, Washington, DC 20401.

National Weather Service: Climate data and flooding information will be of interest to every beach and surf hunter. For information about general information offered, write to the National Weather Service, National Oceanic and Atmospheric Administration, 8060 13th Street, Department of Commerce, Silver Spring, MD 20910.

Bureau of Outdoor Recreation: For information on outdoor recreation programs, write to the Bureau of Outdoor Recreation, Department of the Interior, Washington, DC 20240.

State Archives: During normal working hours, you can search through historical documents, maps, charts and prints relating to the history of just about any state. Since the archives are funded by tax dollars, you certainly shouldn't overlook this source.

State Tourist Bureau: Write to your bureau and request specific information related to your investigation.

Municipal Government Information Sources: Cities and towns change with time. Study available maps and look for defunct parks and other gathering places.

Maps: Various state and federal agencies make available to the public an almost unbelievable array of maps. They cover practically every subject under the sun. Here are a few suggestions for your consideration as you research a given locale. Treasure maps and charts (Superintendent of Documents) River Charts (Corps of Engineers), Historical/Military Maps (National Archives), Selected Civil War Maps (Supt. of Documents) and Township Plats (National Archives).

River Authorities: A good source of information for old boat landings, river ports, forts and long-past ghost towns.

Corps of Engineers: Contact the Corps of Engineers in your area to learn where salvage contract records are kept. These records may contain information about particular lakes and rivers that concern the shipwreck you are researching.

Life Guards: These lifesavers often know where valuables have been lost; for sure, they will know where activities take place. Strike up a conversation and tell them what you have in mind.

Local Treasure Hunting Clubs: If you are not a member, sign up now! Active members will know where the hot spots are. Don't miss out on the rewards that can come from being an active member of your local and/or state clubs. Join national clubs devoted to helping members find treasure.

More Books: This is one of the best sources for finding swimming and recreational beaches. Check with your local library and bookstores to learn what has been printed. For instance, the books, *Mid-Atlantic Treasure Coast, West Coast Beaches* and the *New England Beach Book,* all listed in the bibliography, contain the location of popular and once-popular beaches in their respective areas where you can search for coins, rings and jewelry to your heart's content.

And Magazines: Treasure and other magazines can be a source of good information, but be cautious. Articles contained in these publications make interesting reading and many contain factual information. But, use common sense when spending time and/or money seeking out the "hot spots" that authors boast about. If the hunting there is that good, would *you* write an article and tell the world about its location? You know that when you talk about your treasure finds, you probably paint a more glowing picture than actually exists. And, probably, the person listening to your story sees it as even more romantic and rewarding than you intended to describe it. Always, if possible, obtain two or three creditable references about a subject before striking out on the treasure trail.

Shipwreck Research

The United States National Archives: Located in Washington, DC, this is the largest source available concerning shipwrecks.

The United States Coast Guard: Reports of thousands of marine disasters since 1915 are available from the Public Information Division of the U.S.C.G.

The United States Life Saving Service: From 1872 until 1915 when it became the Coast United States Coast Guard, it maintained records of all United States Life Saving Service Districts.

The United States Lighthouse Service: You'll find reports of maritime disasters in the records of the Lighthouse Service. These records contain information on shipwrecks that took place within the jurisdiction of any given lighthouse.

United States Maritime Commission: Located in Washington, D.C., this is another valuable source of shipwrecks and other maritime disasters.

The United States Weather Bureau: Shipwreck charts and much other valuable information can be obtained from the Weather Bureau.

The U.S. Coast and Geodetic Survey: Since 1900 wreck charts have been published covering the area from Newfoundland to the Gulf of Mexico.

The United States Steamboat Inspection Service: Since the Steam boat Inspection Service was founded to insure that steamboats were sound and safely equipped, careful records for analysis were kept of steamboat disasters.

Library of Congress: The LC is the nation's library that serves researchers throughout the world. Its current holdings exceed 75 million items with more than seven thousand new items added each work day. When you need additional information or have exhausted all research sources, write to the Library of Congress, Information Office, Washington, DC 20540.

The Site Search

There are two areas of approach to site research, one is to explore probable area sites and then concentrate your research on a particular site that you have located. The second is to select one or more area sites as objectives, then conduct in-depth research before any attempt is made to locate and excavate. In every country in the world there are many research sources. As stated before, you must know what you are looking for and then doggedly go after the research information. A good filing or computer system will be necessary for you to keep track of the voluminous material that you will encounter. Several books, including *The Underwater Dig*, by Robert F. Marx, and *Treasure Diver's Guide* by John S. Potter, Jr. are recommended sources for those who are just entering the realm of shipwreck research. These men gained vast knowledge and experience and have presented it in fascinating form in the above publications. You would do well to learn from them.

Sources of information and other valuable research data include books, archives, newspaper reports, maps and charts, marine insurance companies of which Lloyd's of London is probably the largest, ships' manifests, ships' logs, official reports, letters, eyewitness reports, testimony, court martial records, interviews and many other sources.

This tremendous cache of 500 Spanish silver pieces of eight buried centuries ago was found by two Florida treasure hunters who worked a beach area based on research that led them there.

The Encyclopedia of American Shipwrecks by Bruce D. Berman includes information on ships wrecked in United States Waters. As a result of eight years of intensive re-search, the author collected data on more than 50,000 wrecks in American waters. He wrote about some 13,000, excluding all vessels of less than 50 gross tons. Some of these wrecks are pre-Revolutionary and his list includes ships lost prior to 1971. Included in the information about each wreck is the name and tonnage of each vessel, the year of construction, the date, loss and locations.

A Guide to Sunken Ships in American Waters by L. Lonsdale and H.R. Kaplan lists ll,000 wrecks off the coasts of the United States as well as many in rivers and the Great Lakes. Although most of the wrecks mentioned in this book are also listed in *Berman's Encyclopedia,* they are covered in somewhat greater detail. Dozens of other books deal with shipwrecks in particular areas or describe ships lost at specific times. For the Great Lakes you can read *Memories of the Lakes* and *Shipwrecks of the Lakes,* both by Dana Thomas Bowen.

New England wrecks are dealt with in *Wrecks Around Nantucket* by Arthur H. Gardner and another book, *Shipwrecks of Cape Cod* by Isaac M. Small. A good book on West Coast ships is *Shipwrecks of the Pacific Coast,* by James A. Gibbs, Jr. An excellent book about river wrecks is *Steamboat Disasters and Railroad Accidents,* by S.A. Howland. For information on almost every military and merchant ship lost during the Civil War there is the 42-volume work entitled *Records of the Navys of the Civil War,* published by the U.S. Government.

For Spanish ships there are two major works: *La Armada Espanola,* in nine volumes, and *Disquisiciones Nautical,* in six volumes, both by Fernandez Cesareo de Duro. For French ship losses you should consult the *Histoire des Naufrages,* by Gene L. Desperthes. The best work on British warships is *The Royal Navy,* in three volumes, by William L. Clowes.

Shipwreck source book information falls into two categories, descriptions written at the time of the disaster and data compiled at a later date...perhaps in modern times. Books written at the time of the disaster may be more reliable, as they often contain firsthand information and eyewitness reports. Books written at a later date contain the best information the author was able to obtain. Books published in recent years can be quite helpful in selecting and locating a site, but it is still wise to go back to the primary source whenever possible. Every state in the United States has many books about its history, and it is a good idea to acquire and read the ones of interest. Try to obtain the oldest and those written soon after the time of a particular ship loss.

Books written before 1800 are generally difficult to locate. Check with your local library and, perhaps, with large city libraries through inter-library loans. Your librarian can suggest book titles.

Newspapers: Journalistic accounts are a valuable source of information, and they may be the best source relating to the exact location of the vessel for which you are seeking. Newspapers were first printed in the American Colonies in 1690. In addition to listing the movements of all ships in and out of port, and their cargoes, the journals printed a great deal of information on shipwrecks, not only in America but throughout the world. To determine which newspapers were being published or were published nearest to the site of the wreck, it is helpful to consult the following excellent works, *History and Bibliography of American Newspapers 1690 to 1820*, 2 volumes, by Clarence S. Brigham, and *The Dictionary of Newspapers Periodicals,* Ein W. Ayer and Sons, which covers the period until 1880. *The New York Times* was founded in 1851 and is a comprehensive source of information on later shipwrecks.

You probably know that you should read newspaper accounts carefully in order to obtain and separate the factual information from the excitement of the times. You may find it difficult to gather sufficient factual information from newspaper reports alone.

Original research undertaken in archives may be by far the most rewarding as well as the most challenging and time consuming method of learning about underwater sites. The greatest collection of Spanish Colonial documents is stored in the handsome building near the Cathedral in Seville which contains the Archivo de las Indias. There are many other depositories of information in Spain as well.

Documents describing shipwreck locations can be vague. In the very early days (which would apply primarily to Spanish ship wrecks) there were few fixed place names on charts used by navigators. In Florida, for example, on most 16th century charts only two places are named: Martires (spelled a number of ways) in the Florida Keys and Cabo de Canveral or Cape Canaveral. By the mid-17th century a few more places names had been added to charts including Las Tortugas (the Dry Tortugas), Vivoras and Matacumbe (two island in the Florida Keys), Rio de Ais (Fort Pierce Inlet on the East Coast) and La Florida (St. Augustine). By the beginning of the 18th century many other names were on charts rendering them more accurate.

Another important factor to keep in mind when working with primary source material is that there was no standardized calendar system followed by all countries. In 1582 Pope Gregory XIII ordered that ten days of the year be omitted to bring the calendar and the sun once again into alignment, thus creating the Gregorian Calendar which we use today. All the Protestant countries stuck to the old calendar, however, for many years. Until England adopted the Gregorian Calendar in 1752, her new year began March 25; so a date of February 11, 1733, to the English was February 21, 1734, to the other European nations.

In England primary sources of shipwreck research are the British Museum, the Public Records Office, the Admiralty Library, the National Maritime Museum and the Archives of Lloyd's of London. Because of the great fire of London in 1666, there are virtually no available documents on British shipwrecks in the New World before the mid-17th Century.

In 1740 a newspaper called *Lloyd's List* was founded and is still published. It charts the movement of British shipping around the world and gives brief accounts of ship losses and the movement of important foreign shipping, such as the Spanish fleets or ships engaged in the East Indies trade. *Lloyd's List* has also published information regarding salvaging of ships. Until recently it was necessary to go to England to consult these lists. Now, however, all the lists dating from 1740 to 1900 have been republished in a multi-volume work which can be found in a number of large United States libraries, including the Library of Congress in Washington, D.C. and the New York Public Library.

Before attempting any research in United States depositories, either on American or foreign ship losses, one should consult the *Guide to Archives and Manuscripts in the United States* by Philip M. Hamer to determine which archives or library contain relevant materials. The National Archives in Washington, D.C., is the most important source of shipwreck data postdating the American Revolution, but there are many others with original documents also. Each state has archives which should be consulted for information about a wreck off the coast of, or in a river or lake of, a particular state. In some cases many of the most important documents in the state archives have been published, as have indexes of what the archives contain.

If you are interested in shipwrecks off Virginia, for instance, the first step in researching them would be to consult the *Calendar of Virginia State Papers and Other*

Manuscripts, preserved in the capitol in Richmond, an eleven-volume edition edited by Kraus Reprint Corporation of New York.

In addition to the state archives, many state and private universities have large manuscript collections. Some contain a wealth of information from foreign archives. At the University of Florida, for instance, there is a collection of documents on microfilm obtained from the Archivo de las Indies and other depositories abroad, dealing with early Florida history. Thus, when seeking primary source material about Spanish shipwrecks off the coast of Florida, one should first consult this source, which can make an expensive--though pleasant--trip to Seville unnecessary. The Bancroft Library of the University of California at Berkeley has a good collection of documents and microfilm gathered from many archives. These are relevant to ships lost not only off the California coast, but throughout the Pacific.

A number of maritime museums also have original documents and microfilm. All countries of the Western Hemisphere and many of the Caribbean Islands have national archives worth consulting. Archives of the countries bordering the Mediterranean have a great amount of original documentation on ship losses after the year 1400.

Museums

Museums are an excellent source for the dedicated researcher. The Peabody Museum in Salem, MA, has some of the finest information obtainable and will allow a researcher to use its facility. The Mystic Seaport in Mystic, CT, is another institution available to the researcher. They have photographic files and research libraries, along with lifesaving and service records and even records of early wrecking companies. Another museum claimed to be the finest source of information relating to government owned-vessels in the United States is the Mariner's Museum of Newport News, VA.

Maps and charts are often valuable sources for locating underwater sites. Some will reflect astonishing accuracy and others equally astonishing inaccuracy. A number of important facts should be considered in referring to old maps and charts. Over the century, shorelines have receded in some places and extended farther out to sea in others. Many small islands that existed years ago have disappeared. Others have built up; new ones have been made by man. The mouths of rivers and streams have in some cases meandered considerable distances. The present Fort Pierce Inlet is now two miles south of where it was about 1750.

Most depositories of primary source material have a good collection of maps and charts. The most extensive, covering the entire world, is the fabled map room of the British Museum. In the United States, the two best sources are the New York Library and the Library of Congress. Innumerable books containing fine reproductions of old maps are also available. An excellent guide to colonial maps and charts of Florida and several adjacent states is The Southeast in Early Maps by William Cummings which lists locations of hundreds of old maps and charts covering these areas.

A number of charts showing locations of ships lost during the last 20 years of the 19th century are available. In 1893 the U.S. Hydrographic Office produced a "Wreck Chart of the North Atlantic Coast of America," covering the area from Newfoundland to the mouth of the Orinoco River in South America. It shows the locations and gives pertinent information on 965 vessels lost between 1887 and 1891. The U.S. Weather Bureau published two charts about the same time, the "Wreck Chart of The Great Lakes," which lists 147 ship losses between 1886 and 1891.

Modern navigational charts are sometimes useful in locating the sites of long-ago shipwrecks. Many of them list geographical place names associated with wrecked ships. Throughout the world are many places named

"Wreck Point" or "Wreck Bay" or other names indicative of past shipwrecks. In the Caribbean there are dozens of places with such evocative names as "Money Cay" or "Treasure Cay," implying ships sank with treasure or that treasure was hidden ashore.

Research should not overlook historical societies from whom much general information can be obtained. The United States Army Corps of Engineers destroys obstructions to navigation and ships sunk in shallow harbors that pose a problem to other vessels entering the port. Data from the Corps of Engineers pinpoints these sites.

Another approach to gathering information is to start with anyone who might have accidentally found an underwater site. Fishermen, sponge divers and others may know where shipwrecks lie. Commercial salvage divers and operators of dredging barges are also good sources of information. Fishermen and shrimpers must know the surrounding sea bottom to avoid snagging their nets on shipwrecks and other obstructions. They also know that fish feed around wreck sites, and many have their own "wreck charts," to locate choice fishing grounds or avoid areas where they might lose valuable nets.

Each location chapter in this book contains its own research information. Review this material to obtain additional, specific information that will further guide you toward your specific treasure site.

How They Work

In trying to explain how a metal detector operates I've said many times that there's no "magic" to the way it can so easily locate a coin in the sand, buried deeply in coral or in murky surf waters. It's all a matter of electronics. That's what I say.

But, yet...there's a bit of *magic* there, too...at least, for every avid beach and surf hunter. In point of fact, a metal detector might simply be an electronic device that detects the presence of metal, primarily through the transmission and reception of radio wave signals. When you're scanning it across a spot of beach, and it makes a noise that alerts you to the presence of a ring several inches deep in the sand...don't say it isn't magic!

But, let's consider for a minute just what a metal detector is and how it works. If you've read any of my other books, some of the following will probably sound familiar. As I've said so often, however, the physical *laws* and the mythical *lore* of metal detecting never change...just the people involved and their experiences.

To start, let's consider what a metal detector is *not*. A metal detector is not an instrument (Geiger counter) that detects energy emissions from radioactive materials. It is not an instrument (magnetometer) that measures the intensity of magnetic fields. It does not *point* to jewelry or any other kind of metal; it does not measure the abundance of metal. A metal detector simply detects its presence and reports this fact.

When a piece of jewelry or a coin is made of metal--and, most of them usually are--a metal detector can signal the location of this item a reasonable distance beneath its searchcoil. How all this comes about is a somewhat more complicated story.

Knowing how a gasoline engine operates really doesn't make you a better driver. Similarly, it isn't necessary to understand the scientific principles of metal detection for you to be able to find coins with a detector. But, we all know that understanding an internal combustion engine and knowing a little about how it makes the wheels turn helps you become a better operator of a motor vehicle. In the same manner, understanding the how and why of metal detection results in a better beach hunter. Since better beach hunters find more treasure, it would be well if every hobbyist had some understanding of the basic scientific principles of metal detections. So, here we go, to explain in laymen's language just how a metal detector locates lost jewelry and coins as well as all other metal.

By Radio Waves

Like any other metal object, an earring in the sand or a coin in the surf is detected essentially by the transmission and reception of radio wave signals. This is the scientific "principle" that governs operation of *all* metal detectors. If all of them are the same, you may quickly ask, why do some models cost so much more? What distinguishes quality metal detectors such as those manufactured by Garrett from those that don't seem to find many coins or much of anything? Primarily, it's the methods by which the detectors transmit signals and the sophistication with which the signals are received and interpreted. In a word, it's the *circuitry*.

When a radio signal is produced in the searchcoil of any metal detector, an electromagnetic field is generated that

Metal detectors may be products of modern science and engineering, but they seem somehow "magical" when locating golden coins and jewelry in coral such as this.

56

flows out from the coil into the surrounding medium, whether it be earth, rock, water, wood, air or any other material. This electromagnetic field doesn't particularly seek coins or any other kind of metal; it just flows out into the air, earth, water or whatever medium is present. But, the "lines" of this electromagnetic field penetrate metal whenever it comes within the pattern of the detection path. The extent of this pattern depends to a large degree upon the power used to transmit the signal and the resistance of the medium into which the signal is transmitted.

The electromagnetic field generated by transmission from a detector's searchcoil causes something called "eddy currents"to flow on any metal object detected by this field. Generating these currents on the metal causes a loss of power in the electromagnetic field and this power loss is sensed by the detector's circuitry. Electromagnetic field lines passing through a metallic object and generating eddy currents on it distort the normal electromagnetic field. This distortion is another of the clues that alert a detector to the nearby presence of metal.

These eddy currents on the coin create a secondary electromagnetic field and send it into the surrounding medium, which gives the detector still another clue. A receiver in the searchcoil detects these signals at the same time the loss of generating power is being detected. The circuitry of a modern metal detector is designed to interpret all these sensations simultaneously and generate appropriate signals to the operator. The detector, therefore, instantly reports that some sort of metal is present.

If you think all this interpreting and generating requires complicated electronic circuitry, you're right…especially

Penetration depth of the electromagnetic field into the sand as a detector's searchcoil skims across the beach depends to a large extent on the circuitry of that detector.

for a detector that expects to detect deeply and to report accurately on the identity of the metal target it has discovered. That's just one of the reasons for the vast differences in the quality--and prices--of metal detectors. Those instruments with more sophisticated circuitry designed to do a better job of sending out signals and then receiving and interpreting them for you simply cost more to develop and manufacture.

But, they find more treasure!

Electromagnetic signals from the detector's searchcoil cause eddy currents to flow on the surface of any metal object (or mineral) having the ability to conduct electricity. Precious metals such as silver, copper and gold have higher conductivity and, appropriately, more flow of eddy current than iron, foil, tin or other less desirable metals. Since metal detectors can "measure" the amount of power that is used to generate eddy currents, the detector can "tell" which metals are the better conductors.

Quite simply, the quality of signals generated, received and interpreted by the metal detector and the ability of the beach hunter to act upon them determines the difference between"digging junk" and finding coins or other treasure.

Oh, that it could be so simple!

Penetration of the electromagnetic field into the "search matrix" (that area over which a metal detector scans) is described as "coupling." Such coupling can be "perfect" into air, fresh water, wood, glass and certain non-mineralized earth. Unfortunately, life is seldom perfect. The search matrix which a metal detector "illuminates" (through transmission and reception of signals) contains many elements and minerals...some detectable and some not, some desirable and some not.

A metal detector's response at any given instant is caused by all conductive metals and minerals and ferrous non-conductive minerals illuminated in the search matrix by the electromagnetic field. Detection of minerals is, in most cases, undesirable.

And, wouldn't you know it? Two of the most un-desirable are also two of the most common: natural iron (ferrous minerals) found in most of the earth's soil and wetted salt found in much of the earth's soil and water. Not only do these minerals produce detection signals, but they inhibit the ability of instruments to detect metal.

When iron minerals are present within the search matrix, the electromagnetic field is upset and signals are distorted. Iron mineral detection, therefore, presents a major problem to manufacturers and users of metal detectors. This has been true since the earliest days of the first crude metal detectors. Although detection of such minerals may be desirable when a prospector is seeking ferrous black sand or magnetites that could contain gold or silver, it is a nuisance to the hobbyist who is looking for coins.

A primary design criterion of any detector, therefore, must be to filter or eliminate responses from undesirable elements, informing the treasure hunter only of those from gold and silver or other desirable metals. This is

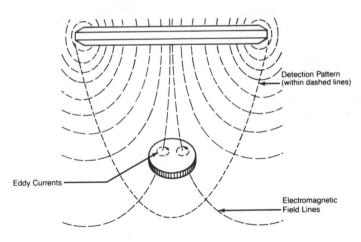

When any metal comes within the detection pattern of a searchcoil, "eddy currents" flow over its surface, resulting in a loss of power in the electromagnetic field, which the detector's circuits can sense.

accomplished in a variety of ways depending upon the type of metal detector.

Such words as ground balancing, ground canceling, discrimination and elimination are used moreorless interchangeably to describe the ability of a detector to seek out only desirable targets while ignoring ground minerals, trash and junk.

It is in this area that many of the significant advances have been--and continue to be--made in the design of metal detectors. Electronic engineers have long known that this task could be accomplished through various methods of circuitry which properly manage the normal electrical phase relationship among resistive, inductive and conductive voltage.

Don't let that preceding sentence confuse you. Simple phase shifting itself is a phenomenon basic to the understanding of electricity. Anyone who has studied physics or understands electricity knows that.

It's the *management* of phase shifting that makes detectors so different from each other. Management of this phase shifting to enable a specific metal detector to "dial out" iron mineralization or other undesirable targets, while still permitting the discovery of coins and jewelry, involves highly proprietary knowledge and circuitry protected by U.S. patents. The author and other Garrett engineers, incidentally, hold a number of these patents, including some that are primary in the manufacture of metal detectors.

Depth of Detection

The electromagnetic field transmitted by any detector flows into the search matrix, generating eddy currents on the surface of conductive substances. Detectable targets that sufficiently disturb the field are detected. But, why, you may ask, do some detectors detect deeper than others? And, for goodness sakes, why do some detectors even detect better targets than others?

Those are good questions, and the answers are simple. The better quality detectors detect deeper, and they can be relied on to reject unacceptable targets. Circuitry of these quality detectors is more intricate, enabling them to penetrate deeper into the soil while avoiding unwanted targets. Not only will this circuitry project a stronger electromagnetic field, it is designed to interpret disturbances in this field with more precision. Of course, the materials present in the search matrix further determine how deep the electromagnetic field will penetrate.

Of the factors that determine how deeply a target can be detected only the electromagnetic field and the circuitry to interpret its disturbances are a function of the detector. Two other important factors, size and surface area, are determined, of course, by the target itself.

Simply stated, the larger a metal target...the better and more deeply it can be detected. Larger detection signals

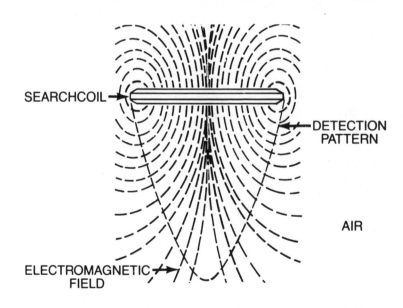

This diagram of "perfect coupling" illustrates the general shape of a detection pattern that occurs when the electromagnetic field from a searchcoil penetrates earth or any other nearby object.

come from targets that produce more eddy currents. An object with double the surface area of another will produce detection signals twice as strong as those of the smaller object, but it will not necessarily be detected twice as far. It is true, however, that a large target will produce the same detection signal as a small target positioned closer to the searchcoil.

Surface Area

Generally speaking, modern metal detectors are surface area detectors. They are not metallic volume (mass) detectors. How a detector "sees" a target will be determined to a large extent by the surface area of a metal target that is "looking at" the bottom of the searchcoil. You can easily prove for yourself that the actual volume or mass of a target has very little to do with most forms of detection.

With your detector operating, move a large coin across the bottom of the searchcoil with the face of the coin "looking at" the searchcoil. Note the distance away from the searchcoil at which the coin is detected. Now, move

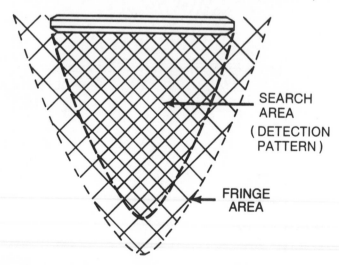

SEARCH AREA (DETECTION PATTERN)

FRINGE AREA

Targets can be located outside the normal detection pattern, but signals are too weak to be heard except in the immediate fringe area around the electromagnetic field's outer edges as shown here.

the coin back and rotate it so that the narrow edge "looks at" the searchcoil. Continue to hold the coin sideways, and move it across the bottom of your searchcoil. You will notice that it must come far closer to the searchcoil to be detected. The mass of metal itself did not change, only the surface area of the coin facing the searchcoil.

Another proof is to measure the distance a single coin can be detected. Then, stack several coins on the back side of the test coin and check to see how far this stack of coins can be detected. You'll find that the stack can be detected only a little farther away, illustrating that the greater volume of metal has minimal effect on detection distance.

Fringe-area detection is a characteristic whose understanding will enable you to detect metal targets to the maximum depth capability of any instrument. The normal detection pattern for a coin may extend, say, nine inches below the searchcoil; the detection pattern for a small jar of coins may extend, perhaps 18 inches below the searchcoil. Within these areas of detection an unmistakable detector signal is produced.

Does detection take place outside the detection pattern? *You bet!* Signals from this detection, however, are too weak to be heard by the operator except in the fringe area directly adjacent to the outer edges of the normal detection pattern.

If you want to hear fringe area signals, a good set of headphones is a must, along with training in the art of discerning those faint whispers of sound that can signal the presence of a coin in your fringe area. You can develop the ability to hear fringe area signals with practice, training, concentration and faith in your detector and its ability. Those of you who develop this fringe area detection capability will discover valuable items that other beach hunters miss. Combine your newfound capability with a modern instrument that can detect deeper and more precisely, and you have a metal detecting team that can't be beat!

The Equipment

This chapter contains discussions about metal detector configurations available for beach, surf and underwater hunting. These configurations include standard models, pistol-grip types, hip mounts, chest mounts, as well as models designed to be convertible or used only under water. The various types of searchcoils, headphones and other accessories are also discussed. This material should help you select a configuration to fit your requirements.

Detector Configurations

The traditional metal detector represents the *standard* configuration with control housing attached to the handle and stem. Several sizes of searchcoil are available. This style is restricted to land or very shallow water hunting. Our Garrett Master Hunter configuration is often called the *wrist action* model. Lightweight models such as the Grand Master Hunter whose balance lets the detector "float" in your hand can be used for long periods without causing much fatigue.

The *pistol-grip* configuration with built-in arm rest is identified in photographs accompanying this chapter. This style is also used for land and shallow water hunting. Lightweight, properly balanced models can be used for long periods without causing much fatigue. Some hip mount models with a pistol-grip stem, such as the Garrett AT4 (All Terrain), are designed for use in rain and in the surf.

When non-submersible models are used in shallow water, the control housing must be must be flotation or high body mounted. Either mounting keeps the detector housing above water and lessens the risk of the detector circuitry and other components being damaged by a sudden wave or other mishap. The *chest mount* configuration gives good protection when the control housing is mounted high up on the chest just under the chin.

The *hip-mount* configuration model is especially popular for hunting both on the beach and in splashing surf waters. The control housing, mounted on a belt, can be worn around the waist (hip-mounted) or slung over the shoulder. Most hip-mounted configurations are non-convertible because they cannot be assembled into the standard detector configuration. An adjustable-length stem and an armrest are supplied. Belt clips are attached to the control housing. Some hip-mount styles permit use of more than one searchcoil. Ideally, the meter is protected and all controls are easily accessible.

A special accessory kit permits you to convert your *standard* configuration into *hip-mount*. Generally, the control housing is mounted on a belt and slung around your waist or across one shoulder. Equipping your detector with hip-mount components may require minor fabrication such as drilling a hole and/or mounting one or more strap clips. If you are hesitant to put a tool to your detector, ask your dealer for instructions. Some dealers are factory-trained in this procedure.

The use of the *hip-mount* configuration requires searchcoil cable that is longer than normal. Ninety inches is the normal length. Using a standard-length cable on a hip-mount unit necessitates the use of an extension cable two or three feet long with mating conductors. If the unit is to be used under water, the connectors must be waterproof. Hardware kits are available that allow you to waterproof such connections, see Chapter 22. Also, you can cut off the closed end of a balloon, slip the balloon over the connector, use silicone grease under the ends before tightly binding them with rubber bands.

The *chest-mount* configuration while quite functional,

has never enjoyed popularity. Usually, the control housing is suspended with a cross-shoulder x-type strap that holds the housing flat against the upper part of the chest. The control housing should be as slim as possible to permit an unrestricted view of the ground. If a meter is provided it must be mounted either on top of the control housing or on the lower part protruding away from the body so that it can be readily viewed. The knobs should be readily accessible, but should not interfere with clothing.

Convertible configuration detectors are designed to permit the control housing to be attached to the stem (standard operation) or worn on the body. The *body-mount* configuration requires a cable length of about 90 inches. The extra weight of the cable is noticeable when the detector is used in the *standard* configuration.

Flotation mounting locates the control housing on a flotation device when the detector is used for surf searching. Almost any type of detector is suitable for flotation mounting if extra searchcoil cable is available. Flotation mounting is satisfactory for lakes and ponds with calm water but is risky when operating in ocean surf. Some floats are made from inflatable articles; others are made of styrofoam. Most surfers build their own flotation devices.

They can be built with a wire mesh sifter, preferably one that is hinged to facilitate quick dumping of accumulated rock and debris. Of course, metal trash should not be dumped but brought in for proper disposal. Compartments on the float are designed to hold treasure finds and trash. Hook arrangements can support digging equipment, and some THers carry food and drink to permit a snack without leaving the water. The float can also be used as a "life raft" when flotation support is needed. In Chapter 22, recovery tools and flotation devices are discussed in greater detail.

Operating Considerations: If you have never worked in water, the first time you get a detector signal and start to dig an object, you will immediately encounter a problem: "What do I do with the detector?" Holding it with one hand while operating the scoop with the other is usually best. If you find this awkward, there are several other methods. Secure the detector to your body with a short cord and, if necessary, attach a buoyancy device (styrofoam or a plastic bottle) to the housing. Try to keep it floating in the correct position with the searchcoil down to make it easier for you to start scanning again.

Underwater Detector Configuration: In this section, we will discuss submersible detector configurations that can be used to depths of 200 feet. The underwater detector shown in illustrations in this book is a Garrett Sea Hunter XL500 Pulse Induction detector. Designed for efficient land, surf and underwater hunting, it is built in the hip-mount configuration. Design of the detector also permits the control housing to be mounted on an arm, leg or the upper chest.

When searching under water (not surfing), I have found it awkward to have a long stem attached to the searchcoil because this arrangement makes it difficult for me to dig and retrieve discoveries. With the searchcoil several feet in front of you, it is inconvenient to swim to the point of detection. Also, it is difficult to search your hole thoroughly because the long stem keeps the searchcoil far in front of you. A short (12-inches) stem keeps the searchcoil at arm's length. When you detect a target, you simply extend your free hand to the point of detection, dig or fan the sand away. To check the hole, you scan the searchcoil back over the spot. The XL500 Sea Hunter is convertible into the stem mount. An accessory, the Scubamate, as pictured in the underwater color photo in this chapter, allows conversion from hip-mount to the "short arm" "standard" configuration. The searchcoil is attached to the lower stem; the cable is wound around the stem or crisscrossed below the control housing support. An arm rest and grip then keeps the detector firmly "locked" to your arm.

Detector Searchcoils

Think of the searchcoil on your detector as having the same functions as the wheels on your automobile. Wheels take power from the motor and interface between the automobile and the ground. They roll along, take the bumps, grinds and shocks to get you to your destination. Searchcoils take power from the oscillator via the searchcoil cable. They are the interface between the metal detector and the ground. They scan along and take the bumps, grinds and shocks. They get you to your destination...the target.

Most searchcoils have electromagnetic transmitter and receiver antennas. These antennas are embedded within the searchcoil. The searchcoil is mounted on the lower end of the metal detector stem to be scanned over bare ground or a specific object. An invisible electromagnetic field generated by the transmitter winding flows out into the surrounding medium...air, wood, rock or whatever.

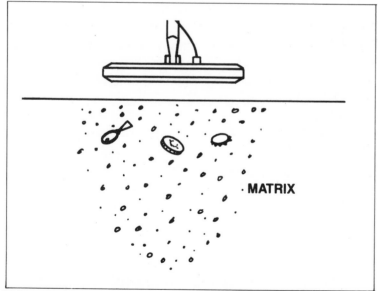

MATRIX

This typical matrix beneath a metal detector's searchcoil illustrates how the electromagnetic field generated by the antenna in that searchcoil "illuminates" every metal target in the area it reaches.

Because a metal detector without a searchcoil simply would not function, coils constitute a vital element in its operation. They come in many sizes and shapes, ranging from about four inches in diameter to the very large, deepseeking depth multiplier. Generally speaking, the smaller searchcoils detect smaller objects, and larger searchcoils find larger and deeper targets. Of course, this is not altogether true since I have found tiny coins with a large searchcoil and also detected quite deeply with the little 4 1/2-inch Super Sniper.

For hunting large objects at great depths, the most popular cache hunting searchcoils are those 12 to 14 inches in diameter. These are large enough to give excellent depth, yet small enough to be reasonably light in weight. Larger searchcoils obviously make it more difficult to maneuver around obstacles. Under water, however, the extra weight is no problem.

Waterproofing Designations

Searchcoils are built with varying degrees of waterproofing. *Splashproof* indicates that operation will not be affected if a small amount of water gets on the searchcoil, such as moisture from wet grass. *Waterproof* means the searchcoil can be operated in a heavy rain and operation will not be affected. *Submersible* means that the searchcoil can be submerged beneath the water as deep as the cable connector without affecting the detector's operation. Standard configuration metal detectors, generally, have searchcoils that can be submerged about 30 inches under water (to the connector on the detector housing). Hip-mount models have searchcoils that can be submerged about five to six feet. *Underwater* metal detectors have searchcoils designed to withstand great depths, even down to 200 feet.

Electronic Shielding

There are two types of electronic field potential, electromagnetic and electrostatic. Electromagnetic field potentials are the radiated power field that illuminate the matrix being scanned. When the electromagnetic field penetrates metal, eddy currents are generated on the metal's surface. Power is drawn from the electromagnetic field, thus alerting the operator to the presence of the metal.

An electrostatic field potential is of a constant voltage nature. This electrical phenomenon occurs whenever two objects come in close proximity to one another. When wet grass, for instance, comes close to the searchcoil, a "false" detector signal may occur. Fortunately, well engineered detectors have solved the electrostatic potential problem. Quality manufacturers construct what is called a Faraday Shield that literally shields the windings from nearby objects.

You are advised not to purchase a detector without an electrostatic shield on each of its searchcoils. To test a searchcoil pull a handful of weeds and wet them with water. Turn your detector on and adjust its threshold. When you drag the weeds across the bottom of your searchcoil, very little change should occur in the threshold sound. If there is a noticeable change, the searchcoil does not have effective shielding. Slight audio changes are not objectionable when grass is passed over the top of the searchcoil.

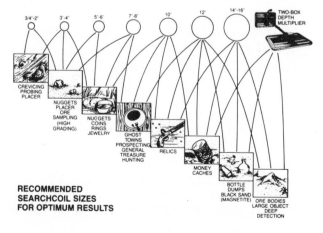

RECOMMENDED
SEARCHCOIL SIZES
FOR OPTIMUM RESULTS

Generally, the standard searchcoil accompanying most metal detectors is the on that gives the best general purpose results. The chart on Searchcoil Sizes on the preceding page will guide you in your understanding and selection of characteristics and capabilities of the various sizes of searchcoils. For more information on searchcoils and the operational characteristics of metal detectors, I refer you to my book, *Modern Metal Detectors*.

For most beach and water hunting you should select a searchcoil that ranges in diameter from about seven or eight inches to ten inches. Searchcoils that size will scan a wide swath and give good detection depth. As searchcoils increase in size, however, it becomes more difficult for them to pinpoint detected objects.

When working in high trash areas, you should consider using a smaller searchcoil, usually about four inches in diameter. These Super Sniper-class searchcoils offer an extra measure of success by "helping" the detector to read individual targets. This increased capability is especially valuable when the discrimination mode is being used. Larger searchcoils obviously can cover more objects at any given time. Consequently, the detector's circuitry has greater difficulty identifying these objects simply because there are so many of them. Small Super Sniper coils eliminate this problem for the most part. They usually won't detect as deeply as larger coils, but can often be far more efficient, especially in trashy areas. You can learn more about the smaller coils by reading my *Garrett Guide* entitled *Use the Super Sniper to Find More Treasure*.

Facing
Hip mount configuration is ideal for easy detector handling in rough surf or over uneven beach terrain.

Over
Configuration of Sea Hunter XL500 can be changed for hunting beneath the water or on land.
(Underwater photo by Rick Sammons, CEDAM)

Shipwreck Searching

When searching shipwrecks, there are several situations to consider. In loose sand an initial search should use a larger searchcoil for good detection depth. This is important because soft sand permits digging to such depths. When there are many small targets, however, you should consider a smaller searchcoil, especially if you are using discrimination. For such precise pinpointing as that required when you are digging coins from coral, the smaller searchcoil will be best. Since digging in clay or coral is generally difficult and time consuming, pinpointing and target identification are vital.

Determining Target Center

Any given searchcoil may or may not produce maximum audio when small coin-size targets are directly beneath its exact *physical* center. To determine *target* center of detection, set your detector's audio at its threshold level and place a small coin directly on the bottom of the searchcoil near its center. Slide this coin around and listen closely to the sound from your detector. The target center is the spot where you hear maximum audio sound. Mark an "X" with a felt tip pin at this point on the searchcoil both on top and bottom. Knowing this target center enables you to pinpoint targets precisely. Since, pulse induction searchcoils are generally constructed with an open center, it is not possible (nor necessary) to mark the center of these coils.

Dynamic Detection Range

As used by detector manufacturers this term indicates various target sizes a searchcoil can detect to a practical depth. Examples of dynamic detection range:

Smaller searchcoils are especially suitable for searching in tight places like this rocky stream. Before using a searchcoil anywhere under water, make certain it is submersible.

- A *12-inch searchcoil* can detect objects from BB shot size to very large targets and detect this wide range of objects to practical depths. It functions most effectively on larger targets at greater depths.

- A *4 1/2-inch searchcoil* can often surprise you with the depth it can achieve. For the most part, however, it works best on smaller targets at relatively shallow depths.

- An *8 1/2-inch searchcoil* is selected for most "general" searching because it offers a wide range of both target detection and depth. In addition, its size and weight insure good maneuverability

A few minutes study of the searchcoil charts in this chapter will reveal the relative dynamic detection ranges of the various types and sizes of searchcoils.

Specific Gravity

When manufacturers produce searchcoils for use both on land and under water, they must achieve a happy medium. The searchcoil must be light enough for practical land use yet have slightly negative buoyancy for use under water. An example is the special Crossfire searchcoil now used on Garrett's AT4 Beach Hunter. It is a few ounces heaver than the normal 8 1/2-inch coil and requires no extra weights for use in the surf or elsewhere under water. Hobbyists who formerly had to devise various means of weighting their searchcoils used sand bags on the coil or lead weights on the stem. Of course, there was a problem here since the lead could not be too close to the searchcoil.

While this truly is only a minor consideration, searchcoils with slightly negative buoyancy require considerably less effort to use under water than coils that try to rise to the surface. When in doubt about equipment for surf or underwater use, contact your dealer and/or factory for specific information.

Searchcoil Diameters

3 to 4 Inches: This size is referred to by Garrett as a Super Sniper. It projects an intense electromagnetic field which gives good detection of small objects. The narrow detection pattern permits excellent target isolation and precise pinpointing. This size scans a more narrow width that larger searchcoils, and it will not detect as deeply. The ability for close scanning of metal objects such as fences and concrete with reinforcing bars is an added plus.

Treasure hunters rate these searchcoils highly, but not all detectors are capable of using them, nor do all manufacturers provide them. The purchase and use of one is suggested, especially if you hunt in worked-out or high junk areas.

7 to 9 Inches: Most detector types and brands are sold with searchcoils about eight inches in diameter (Garrett offers 8 1/2-inch models) as standard equipment. These are the best general purpose sizes because they generally are lightweight, have good scanning width and are sensitive to a wide range of target sizes. Objects as small as BB shot can be detected. Good ground coverage can be obtained with scanning width at shallow levels equal to the approximate diameter of the searchcoil. Scanning width

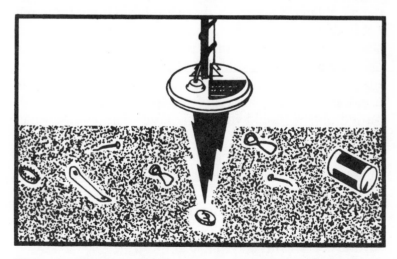

When a smaller searchcoil is used, fewer targets are beneath it at any given time, enabling the detector to locate valuable objects in a trashy area where signals might have been masked by junk metal.

becomes less toward the bottom of the detection pattern as shown in the previous chapter. Since the detection pattern of all searchcoils is somewhat cone-shaped, overlapping of each detector sweep is necessary to lessen the possibility of missing targets. Pinpointing is good but can be made even better by electronic pinpointing and proper use of target center.

10 to 12 Inches: Searchcoils of this size, while still able to detect small coin-size objects at great depths are classified as the smallest searchcoils to be used for cache and relic hunting. Precise pinpointing is more difficult with these larger sizes, and the extra weight usually necessitates use of an arm rest or hip-mounted control housing. This is especially true when the detector is used for long periods of time.

When do you use a larger searchcoil? Reason it out for yourself. Suppose you find a target in the fringe area of detection with your 8 1/2-inch searchcoil. Weak audio signals indicate you're reaching the outer detection limits of the searchcoil. By using the next larger size you will detect deeper. Of course, there are limitations. You may not find tiny targets as easily with a large searchcoil. You'll stand a much better chance using a Super Sniper. Practically speaking, when you're hunting on the beach or in the surf, a 10-inch coil is generally the largest size you should use. Only if you're looking for a specific large or deeply buried object should you use a larger coil. On the other hand, you'll find many uses for a Super Sniper on the beach. How about hunting among rocks...near metal...or, in areas with lots of metal trash?

The chart on Page 73 illustrates recommended searchcoil sizes for optimum results. Note the overlapping capability of all searchcoils. The wide dynamic range of several searchcoils is obvious.

Depth Multiplier Attachment: Just as its name implies this valuable attachment can multiply the depth that your detector can search effectively. A good depth multiplier can double or triple the depth to which your detector can find a large target, such as a large cannon or safe.

The depth multiplier is easy to use. It can be attached to your detector in a matter of minutes. No adjustments are required. Simply turn your detector on and select the All Metal mode. Adjust your threshold sound and begin searching. More information on this important accessory can be found in my *Garrett Guide* entitled *Money Caches Are Waiting to be Found.*

The depth multiplier is recommended when searching for money caches, large relics, safes, cannons, ore veins and mineral structures. It's not an accessory normally required in beach or surf hunting, but it's one with which every detector operator should be familiar.

Headphones

You should *always* use headphones whenever you search with a detector. They are especially useful in noisy areas, such as the beach and near traffic. Headphones enhance audio perception by bringing the sound directly into your ears while masking "outside" noise interference.

There is no question that most people can hear weaker sounds and detect deeper targets when quality headphones are used. As proof, bury a coin at a depth that produces a faint speaker signal. Then, use headphones and scan over the spot. You'll be amazed at how much better you can hear the detector signals with headphones than you can with the speaker alone.

Headphones come in many sizes, shapes and configurations, the most popular being stereo types that cover the ears. Many fine detectors do not have volume controls since they are not particularly necessary. Headphones equipped with volume controls allow a wide degree of loudness adjustment while not degrading detector sounds.

Manufacturers know that reducing sound volume of the detector's signals is accompanied by loss of detection depth and sensitivity. Reducing circuit "gain" reduces the sharp, quick audio turn-on necessary for good operation.

Even on detectors with volume control, the manufacturer usually recommends that volume be set to maximum. Most detectors are operated at full volume with the tuning (audio) control adjusted so that a faint sound (threshold) is coming from the speaker. When a target is detected, the sound volume increases quickly from threshold to maximum loudness. Headphones allow this threshold to be set even lower, giving improved performance. Modern detectors can be operated "silent" or with slight threshold sound.

A mono/stereo switch on the headphone set is desirable. If you want to use both headphone pieces, flip the switch to mono to let sound come through both earpieces. If you want to use only one headpiece, perhaps to leave the unused headpiece resting off your ear to enable you to hear sounds around you, flip the switch to stereo and only one headpiece will be operative. Some detectors have an internal connection, however, that sends audio into both headpieces. In that case, a mono/stereo headphone switch would be non-functional.

Dual, miniature headphones are commonly used. While satisfactory, they do not block as much external sound as the large padded kind. They are, however, lightweight and comfortable and a quality pair will produce good sound. A coiled extension cord is desirable to keep the cord out of the way.

Headphones help you keep others from knowing what you are doing. In most cases, a person standing within a few feet will not be able to hear the headphone signals unless the sound is very loud.

Since headphone plugs are usually either one-eighth or one-fourth inch in diameter, make sure which size you require. Right-angle plugs are highly desirable because they minimize the possibility of broken plugs, which often occurs with plugs that extend straight out.

That Second Detector

Probably two thirds of active treasure hunters own more than one metal detector. Usually, they have a main instrument--the one they search with most often. They keep on "standby" one or two additional detectors which are usually older models. Should their primary instrument fail, or get stolen, the hunter always has a backup unit.

Many THers have several detectors because they enjoy more than one type of hunting. They may be both land and surf or underwater searchers. In that case they probably need a dry land model and one they can get wet. Many hunters have several models, perhaps a specialized coin hunting type, a deepseeking cache hunting type and a model for electronic prospecting.

Some hobbyists purchase a new detector almost every year as newer, deeper seeking and more capable detectors

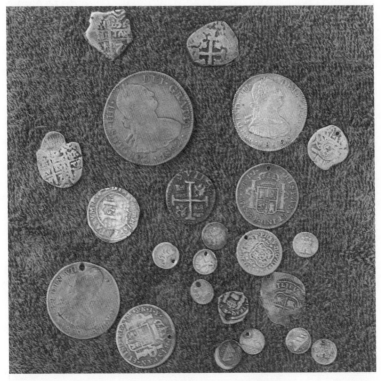

These Spanish coins dating to the mid-1700s were recovered on a beach in Key West, FL. Note holes punched in some of the coins as if they had been strung together for some reason.

are introduced. They know how just a slight bit of extra detection depth can pay dividends.

Some detectors are all purpose; they can perform many treasure hunting and prospecting tasks. All purpose detectors eliminate need for more than a single detector unless the hunter is concerned with primary detector failure. Also, there is no all purpose detector built that can be submerged for surf hunting.

Should you obtain a *second* detector? In the event of primary detector failure--which, by the way, is not likely to occur--a backup detector is necessary. If you don't travel far from home and rental instruments are available, your need for a second instrument is reduced. After you have purchased a surfing model, when you decide to cache hunt or go prospecting as well, you may wish to equip yourself with a different model for more effective performance in those other fields.

A second detector is especially beneficial when there is someone to use it. Perhaps your spouse or other family member could hunt with the second detector, yet be willing to temporarily give it up (or maybe do the digging...?) if the primary detector fails or is stolen. Let me urge, however, that you purchase wisely any and all instruments you buy. Choose reliability no matter how many instruments you need and you may never have to purchase again.

Key Features

In Chapter 8 I will review the basic types of detectors that are most commonly used today for searching beaches and hunting in the water. In this Chapter 7, however, I want to discuss four important features that are common to all detectors. A thorough understanding of each of these features is essential to your success in hunting for treasure of all kinds...especially as a water hunter.

-- *Discrimination*
-- *Pinpointing*
-- *Audio*
-- *Ground Balance*

Of course, each of these four topics is vital in almost any aspect of metal detecting, in or out of the water. Because these topics are so important to the hobby, any time two or more treasure hunters get together, you're liable to hear several different opinions about each of them. So, here are my thoughts on these important subjects:

Discrimination

You can minimize digging and still not miss valuable targets by using discrimination properly. This is especially true on most beaches, where you're likely to find literally *pounds* of trash metal.

It's sometimes difficult for those of us who have been hunting with metal detectors for a quarter-century or more to accept the ease and precise nature of modern discrimination circuits. We remember when any discrimination was considered "too much," and many veterans still urge you to dig all targets. Yet, I must admit that many of these same oldtimers can be found dialing in "just a little" discrimination to permit them to miss some of the trash that now seems to be present in the soil everywhere...and especially on beaches.

Some of the so-called *universal* modern detectors, such as Garrett's Grand Master Hunter CX II feature two basic modes of operation--Discriminate (motion) and All Metal (non-motion). In the Discriminate mode the operator can utilize discrimination controls to designate the type metal targets that are desired. In the All Metal mode, of course, all targets are audio-detected. But, remember this one very important point...in *both* modes the target ID meter continues to identify all detected targets. So, here's a tip...operate in the All Metal mode to achieve the greatest possible depth, and simply read the meter to identify detected targets!

Several Garrett detectors feature dual discrimination controls. They offer multiple selectivity and the ability to reject and accept targets in both the ferrous--iron, or course--and non-ferrous ranges. The two controls split the full range of discrimination between ferrous and non-ferrous. Detection of iron objects such as nails, some foil, iron bottlecaps and small pieces of junk is controlled by one knob. The other control governs discrimination of such non-ferrous items as aluminum pulltabs and aluminum screwtops.

Of special interest to water hunters is the fact that Garrett's Beach Hunter AT4, designed especially for use on the beach and in shallow surf, utilizes this dual system of controls to permit more effective discrimination.

Each of the two controls operates independently. The setting of one has no effect whatsoever on the other. If you wish to detect all ferrous materials, rotate the ferrous control of your detector to zero (fully counterclockwise on Garrett controls). As you advance it back to the right to higher numbers, you will reject more and more ferrous materials. The control operates cumulatively; that is, if you have it set at bottlecap rejection, most nails and some foil will be rejected along with bottlecaps. We urge that you advance this control no farther clockwise than necessary to eliminate the troublesome ferrous junk material in the ground where you are searching.

Operate your non-ferrous control in the same manner. When it is turned fully to the left, few of the non-ferrous materials will be rejected. To eliminate, say, pulltabs, rotate the control clockwise to the manufacturer's suggested setting for them. Keep in mind, however, that there appear to be as many different kind of pulltabs as there are canning companies. Some few pulltabs, especially those that are bent or broken, seem to be acceptable to any detector at any setting. Set your controls for those you are finding just in the area where you are hunting.

Here's how to set those dual discrimination controls-- or that single discrimination control--precisely. Collect examples of all the types of junk you want to reject--a nail,

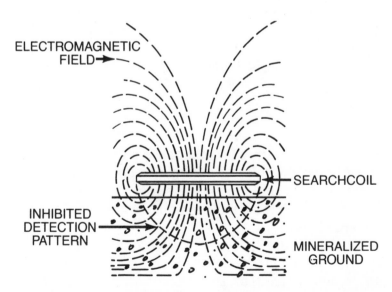

Discrimination control is vital in any detector, especially one that is to be used in or near salt water. Drawing shows how detection pattern can be inhibited by mineralized ground or wetted salt.

bottlecap, pulltab and, perhaps, small pieces of iron trash. Place your detector on a non-metallic, preferably wooden, surface with the searchcoil at least three feet away from all metal. Make certain you are wearing no rings or jewelry on your hands or arms that could be detected. Rotate both control knobs (or only one, if your instrument is so designed) fully counterclockwise to the lowest settings. Turn the detector on and listen for the tone telling you it is ready to operate. Adjust the audio control for threshold sound.

Pass the iron bottlecap across the bottom of your searchcoil about two inches away from it. Your detector will probably make a signal. Rotate the ferrous control to the approximate bottlecap reject position or the setting suggested by your manufacturer, and pass the cap across the searchcoil's bottom again. You should hear nothing more than, perhaps, a slight blip. You may be able to rotate the control counterclockwise back to a lower number and still not detect the bottlecap. Practice so that you can set your control as far to the left as possible because you always want to use the lowest setting that is required.

Using the same technique, adjust the non-ferrous control just far enough clockwise that you do not detect the aluminum pulltab. This should be approximately the manufacturer's suggested setting point, which should probably prove to be your optimum pulltab setting, with the settings necessary for other style pulltabs being both above and below this one determined point. Again, let us stress that you should rotate these controls no higher than necessary to reject the junk items in the ground where you are searching.

Dual discrimination controls such as those on Garrett's Beach Hunter and Freedom 3 Plus offer a greater dynamic adjustment range than single controls. You have more resolution which allows you to set the controls precisely to reject specific junk targets. A most important feature is that you can reject most aluminum pulltabs while accepting the majority of gold and silver rings. When searching for rings in a pulltab-infested area such as a beach, set your non-ferrous control no farther clockwise than necessary to eliminate most of the pulltabs. Rings with a higher conductivity--and, especially, mass--than pulltabs will be accepted. Remember, however, that some rings will fall into the lower, or ferrous, range. Thus, dual discrimination lets you select rings that register both "above" and "below" pulltab rejection. So, don't advance either control any farther clockwise than absolutely necessary.

There is another important reason for setting your discrimination controls conservatively. When a modern detector locates a junk target that you have asked it to discriminates against, it cancels out this junk target with a negative audio response that you normally cannot even hear. As you know, however, good targets generate a positive response which you love to hear. If both positive

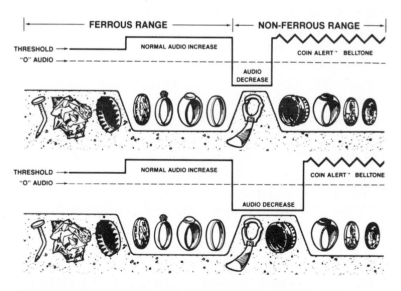

Garrett's multi-range discrimination offers four ranges. Top setting has eliminated junk targets while accepting rings and coins. Below, non-ferrous control has been adjusted to eliminate screwtops.

and negative targets are beneath your searchcoil simultaneously, the two responses tend to cancel one another, and you may miss a good find. Of course, the situation is rarely that simple. Depth of targets, their metallic content, size and many other factors must be considered. So, simply remember this: never use more discrimination than you absolutely need.

Pinpointing

Electronic pinpointing can hasten your recovery of targets and make it far more pleasurable as well. You'll need pinpointing even *more* in the surf than you do on dry land!

Most veteran treasure hunters pride themselves in their ability to pinpoint targets using only the detector's normal search modes. Modern instruments make pinpointing so much easier that we old timers should swallow our pride and take advantage of the electronic assistance available to us. I know that I do! Who knows? The time we save might let us recover that "big one" that's always just behind the next wave.

Of course, you should check the Owner's Manual of your detector for proper understanding and use of its pinpointing function. But, a button or trigger somewhere on the detector will usually activate pinpointing circuitry. After you have detected a target, move the searchcoil off to the side, press and hold the Pinpoint touchpad (or switch) and scan your target area again. You will notice that signals have probably grown sharper to aid you in locating your target more precisely.

Here's a tip for the ultimate in target pinpointing. Once you have determined the surface location where you believe the target to be buried, place your searchcoil lightly on the ground above it and activate the pinpoint control. Continue holding this control and slide the searchcoil back and forth over the target at the same operating height. You will notice very slight blips when the target is directly beneath the center of your searchcoil. If you can't notice these blips at first, perhaps you have elevated the searchcoil from its level when you first selected the Pinpoint mode. Try the procedure again a few times. Maintain constant searchcoil height, and you'll be amazed at your precise electronic pinpointing ability. Warning: this technique requires practice...but, *practice pays off!*

Here are two methods that might prove helpful if your instrument does not offer electronic pinpointing. After you locate your target, continue moving its coil over the spot while reducing your audio level down almost into the quiet zone. You'll soon find your target signal weakening to a soft audio "blip." Your find will be directly beneath the center of your coil where the loudest signal over your detected metal object now occurs.

The second method is to begin raising your searchcoil higher in the air (or water) each time you pass over the detected target. Once again, signals will get weaker and weaker until you can hear only a "blip." Again, the target will be underneath the maximum signal area. This second method is obviously more difficult because the height of your coil will make it harder for you to locate the exact spot on the ground. In moving water your challenge is even greater.

Rely on electronic pinpointing! That's my advice.

Audio

Because the audio setting is one of the most important adjustments you make in learning to hunt coins with a metal detector, your close attention to this subject is strongly urged. I believe that maximum capability can be achieved only by adjusting the audio volume until you hear just the faintest sound coming from your speaker or headphones. *This is very important!* This faintest sound that you can hear is the detector's most sensitive operating point. It is called your threshold, a common term in all metal detector literature. You will notice that when you set the threshold to a very faint sound and then plug in your headphones, the threshold may be too loud. Simply turn the audio control knobs lightly to reduce the sound level back to your faint threshold level.

Perhaps many of you prefer to operate a detector with what is called a silent threshold; that is, with absolutely no sound coming from the speaker or headphones. If you are determined to use this silent threshold, I urge that you achieve it by setting your audio to a slight level of sound, then backing off just enough to achieve silence. This adjustment insures that you miss the fewest possible targets. Be sure to check occasionally to make certain that you remain at this audio level just below sound. Otherwise, the farther below this level your audio drifts, the more targets you will miss!

For maximum success a treasure hunter should use headphones whenever searching with a metal detector. They are essential in noisy areas, such as the beach and near traffic. They enhance audio perception by bringing the sound directly into one's ears while masking outside noise interference.

Most persons can hear weaker sounds and detect deeper finds when quality headphones are used. They come in several sizes and configurations, the most popular being stereo types that cover the ears. For those detectors without volume controls headphones can offer the control that allow a wide degree of loudness adjustment without degrading the sound quality.

As discussed, you know that reducing sound volume to silent on a detector is accompanied by loss of detection depth and sensitivity. I strongly recommend that detectors always be operated with the audio control adjusted so that

The Sea Hunter offers all features desired in an underwater detector: submersible headphones insure precise audio; sensitivity and discrimination controls help select targets.

just a faint sound (threshold) can be heard. Headphones allow this threshold to be set much lower than with a speaker, giving improved performance. As an added benefit, headphones use considerably less power than a detector's speaker which results in the economy of longer battery life. And, you don't have to take the trouble to change them as often, either!

Ground Balance

It is with mixed feelings that I rewrite this section during the winter of 1989-90. This metal detector feature still remains one of the most important today for treasure hunters--whether it be performed manually or automatically. Yet, it is not so important for most water hunters since detectors designed for this purpose are of the *motion* type (description follows) that features automatic ground balancing.

I must also add here that new detectors such as Garrett's Grand Master Hunter CX II and Master Hunter CX (Computer Express) are causing the very subject of ground balancing--once so important--to become obsolete. Microprocessor circuitry is handling this former "problem" quite effectively. In fact, there is no longer any problem because microprocessor circuitry eliminates ground minerals even while the detector is being used...automatically and continually.

Still, ground balance is an area of considerable concern--and some difficulty--to all users of metal detectors...if we can measure it by the volume of calls received at the factory. And, our dealers tell us that their customers also appear to have problems. Therefore, I feel that it is a subject that must be covered in any book dealing with treasure hunting. After all, this text is designed to be of

His modern detector's microprocessor-controlled circuitry offers automatic ground balancing, but this electronic prospector will still insist on precise manual control.

service to *any* beach, surf or water hunter...no matter *what* type of instrument is being used.

There is still no doubt that ground balance,whether performed automatically or manually, will always be one of the most important features of a metal detector. Many veteran treasure hunters would argue the importance of the depth feature, and some might opt for discrimination. The simple fact remains,however, that without precise ground balance--performed either automatically or manually--hunting with a metal detector as we know it today would not be possible in most soil. Why not? Because most soils contain just too darned much mineralization.

You beginning treasure hunters with a new detector may quickly grow accustomed to the excellent ground balance now available on today's modern automatic detector. You may even take this feature for granted. *Please don't!* Some of the oldtimers are still in awe at the ease with which today's automatic detectors ground balance themselves. These veterans will assure you that ground balance is very important, and as you progress in the hobby, you will soon agree. In fact, there will be many times when precise ground balance will be demanded if you are to achieve optimum results. Learn how to ground balance your particular detector if it doesn't have automatic ground balance. It will probably be as important as anything you ever do after you turn on the instrument and set the audio.

Motion vs. Non-Motion

You should know that there are two detector modes of operation that permit ground balance: motion and non-motion. Before we discuss these modes, let's first understand just exactly what is meant by the term "ground balance." As discussed earlier, there are two predominant ground minerals that concern us. They are wetted salt and iron, and they can be found literally all over the world.

Wetted salt can be found predominantly at ocean beaches but also at numerous upland locales. Iron minerals, generally classified further as non-conductive (not metal) minerals, can be found practically everywhere.

Both wetted salt and iron are readily detectable and cause untold grief to conventional detectors unless some means is available to cancel or "ground balance" them out. The term, ground balance, then is our description of the method of circuitry that enables a metal detector to completely ignore these minerals...to go about its business of detecting other metals as if iron and wetted salt were not even present.

The motion mode of ground balancing has been around several years and is available on detectors from a number of manufacturers, including Garrett's Beach Hunter and Freedom Plus models. It is also available on Master Hunter CX instruments (more about this...soon). As its name implies, the motion mode requires that the detector be continually moving (in motion) to detect objects. This mode is very efficient and quite good for hunting most types of treasure, especially on the beach. Both salt and

Spanish coins found in the wreckage of galleons that sank centuries ago include various "pieces of eight"...often called cobs...including many that were struck at colonial mints in Mexico and Peru.

iron minerals are essentially ignored, permitting the hobbyist to concentrate on finding jewelry and coins without being bothered by detection of minerals. This mode, however, does not provide optimum performance and the deepest detection when the detector is used for prospecting or hunting for relics and money caches.

The non-motion mode (permitting a detector's searchcoil to hover perfectly still) which had previously given the best performance for these other types of hunting was achieved only through manual adjustment of ground balance controls. While such adjustments could be made with relative ease, it has been the desire of Garrett and other manufacturers to produce detectors that are fully automatic.

Our new Grand Master Hunter CX II and Master Hunter CX, each of which features computerized circuitry based on microprocessor controls, offer both motion and non-motion ground balance. The motion mode features not only automatic ground balance but also full discrimination control. Treasure hunters have come to love their performance.

Until now non-motion ground balancing of the Grand Master Hunter was possible only through adjustment of manual controls. Now, the new Grand Master Hunter CX II is equipped with automatic ground balance modes called Fast Track® and Ground Track® that balance out iron ground minerals automatically, even as the searchcoil is scanned. Such ground balancing continues whether the searchcoil is moving or not. Even when the earth minerals themselves change density beneath the searchcoil, the Ground Track circuits sense these changes and properly adjust the detector's ground balancing characteristics while the detector is scanning for targets.

The new computerized Master Hunter models, indeed, are *thinking* detectors, the instrument of tomorrow. But, today there remain in the hands of treasure hunters thousands of detectors that respond to manual ground balancing controls in the non-motion mode. This "how to" discussion is concerned with such detectors and will be important to their operators.

To Ground Balance

The following instructions will apply to Garrett detectors with non-motion (All Metal mode) manual ground balancing capabilities and to most other instruments as well, but you are urged to study the Owner's Manual for your particular detector. Read especially carefully the section concerning ground balance.

Now, to ground balance a detector manually in the field! Begin by holding the detector with the searchcoil away from any metal and about two or three feet above the ground. Listen to the audio as you lower the searchcoil to operating height. If the audio signal grows or fades to any degree, you will require manual ground balancing.

This procedure, of course, may differ from one brand to another. Basically, however, if the audio signal grows louder, turn down the ground balance control dial or press

This beautiful and extremely valuable man's ring featuring a cluster of diamonds is just an example of the kind of treasures that can be found with a metal detector in the ocean surf.

the button on your manual ground balance controls marked minus (-) several times. Lift your searchcoil again, press the audio (threshold) control and lower it again to operating height.If the sound level now decreases, you have made too great a negative adjustment. It will be necessary for you to press the touchpad marked plus (+) a few times or turn up your control dial. Remember that with the dial on a Garrett or other quality detector you are dealing with a 10-turn control for precise adjustment. Don't be afraid to turn it several times! Repeat these procedures until the audio does not change or changes only slightly when the searchcoil is lowered to operating height. When performing this ground balancing procedure, make certain there are no metal targets in the ground beneath your searchcoil.

When searching extremely mineralized ground, we recommend that you operate the searchcoil two inches or more above the ground. You will not lose depth, but will actually detect deeper because ground mineral influence is greatly reduced.

Water Hunting Detectors

This chapter will discuss the four types of metal detectors that are now in greatest use as water hunting instruments. Three of these are VLF (very low frequency) detectors. The fourth type features the pulse induction method of detection and is now used almost exclusively under water. It is one of these four types of modern detector that I would recommend for anyone who seeks to pursue the hobby of beach and surf hunting or to become more proficient in it.

First, let's discuss the three VLF types because they are the most prevalent:

-- Automated
-- Manual Adjust
-- Computerized

Some of you oldtimers may immediately cry out that I've omitted your favorite detector, that wonderful old BFO or TR instrument that's found so many coins and rings for you on the beach. Well, I'll just say two things about those old detectors and promise not to mention them again:

1. They're *obsolete*. Newcomers to the hobby have no business using them. (And neither do old-timers, either! I wonder just how many valuable metal objects those "wonderful" old detectors have actually scanned over?)

2. If you insist on using one of the older detectors, you must already know more about them than I do because I certainly wouldn't try to use one to hunt on the beach...*or anywhere else!*

The pulse induction detectors are discussed separately because this is a different type of instrument than the VLF. Let me state, here and now, that pulse detectors are highly capable detectors. I rate them very highly for most types of treasure hunting, especially on the beach, in the surf or in the ocean's depths. The fact is, however, that the only pulse detectors now being commercially manufactured are submersible models intended for hunting under water. Our Sea Hunter, for example, is protected to depths of 200 feet. Since this is a feature not especially desired by most beach and surf hunters, the pulse induction type of instrument will be discussed separately.

So, let's review the various features of the three types of VLF detectors.

Automated (Motion)

The motion-type VLF detector with automatic ground balance is probably the most popular model generally used today for hunting on the beach and in the surf. First of all, it is easy to use. Added to this are its capabilities for finding coins and jewelry that are almost equal to those of the higher priced detectors. This capability becomes particularly apparent when both expensive and average-priced models are in the hands of a novice. Yet, while most models from reputable manufacturers are capable, some will definitely detect coins and treasure deeper than others.

Of course, various models of the automated detectors are manufactured today. Some offer more features than others, and some are simply better than others. Working with a dealer and trying out various detectors will enable you to determine which model is best suited for your needs.

Automated VLF instruments are often referred to as "motion" detectors since they can be hovered over a target for only a few seconds because of their automatic circuitry. Consequently, slight searchcoil motion is always necessary. Certain models, however, can be scanned much more slowly than others. You must learn the capabilities of your instrument through practice.

Another technique you will have to practice is pinpointing, especially in rough surf where exact location is important. Since hovering over a target is not possible, manual pinpointing will be more difficult for some operators than for others. Electronic pinpointing offered on all the better models overcomes this deficiency. Simply stated, however, pinpointing generally presents no problem with any beach or surf hunting detector because the targets you will be finding can be considered comparatively large.

The automated VLF instrument ranks high among all types of detectors in detection depth. Not only is it capable of reaching to great depths to detect coins, but its extremely sharp, fast-response signal is unmistakable when rings, coins and other such objects are detected.

It would be well to warn against confusing automatic ground balance with the "automatic tuning" feature on some models of older detectors. The tuning feature is concerned only with the audio threshold of the detector and has no relationship to ground balance.

All quality automated VLF detectors will offer some form of trash elimination through discrimination control(s). I urge you to read the section on this feature in the preceding chapter to insure that you realize the full benefits offered by your detector.

I should point out here that many hobbyists find the automated VLF models fairly satisfactory for types of metal detecting other than beach and surf hunting. This is particularly true of those instruments produced by quality manufacturers. In fact, I've used our automated Beach Hunter model for shallow relic hunting. Some hobbyists even report they have found gold nuggets with an automated instrument. If you're interested in a detector that will perform satisfactorily in situations other than beach hunting, however, I suggest that you read on about the manual adjust and computerized models.

Manual Adjust (Non-Motion)

Until the development of the automated VLF detector the manual adjust models dominated the treasure hunting field. They represented such an improvement over the old BFO and TR detectors which had but limited (perhaps, *non-existent* would be a better description) ability to eliminate iron earth minerals and wetted salt. Quality manual adjust VLF's are still highly popular instruments capable of performing all coin hunting, treasure hunting and prospecting tasks. They detect very deeply and are offered to water hunters with an array of desirable features.

Some modern computerized VLF detectors, such as the Grand Master Hunter CX II and Master Hunter CX, already include the automatic ground balancing feature. As I pointed out in the previous chapter of this book, I believe that in just a few years all quality VLF detectors will provide automatic ground balance. In fact, it will be an aspect of metal detecting that hobbyists will finally be able to take for granted! What an improvement this truly is...especially after all the problems that veteran THers have experienced over the years with ground balance.

Today, however, a large number of quality detectors already in the hands of treasure hunters permit the treasure hunter to adjust ground balance manually. All of these instruments will fulfill every expectation of most beach and surf hunters. In addition, the detectors can meet the requirementsof cache hunters, relic hunters and electronic prospectors with ease and efficiency. Since quality VLF detectors are so highly capable, they can be selected and used with the utmost confidence.

I especially commend this type of detector to the individual who is interested in hunting on the beach but already has an "itch" to try out the other types of metal detecting. As noted above, many hobbyists use motion-type automated VLF detectors for tasks other than hunting for coins and jewelry. The simple truth of the matter is, however, that manual adjust non-motion models will generally detect deeper than motion models.

Because of those selfsame "manual" controls from which it gets its name, this type of detector is capable of more precise ground balance. Such precision will rarely be required by the average water hunter. Not so with relic and cache hunters who seek deep targets and electronic prospectors working over highly mineralized ground. They demand absolute ground balance that will enable them to hear faint signals from faraway or tiny targets.

Any kind of pinpointing technique is possible with the manual adjust VLF detectors since they can be hovered over a target at will. Still, the matter or pinpointing is not especially important since modern, quality instruments all offer precise electronic pinpointing circuitry.

The fact is that manual adjust VLF detectors are just a little more difficult to use than the automated VLF models because they have to be ground balanced. At the same time, however, they offer more versatility and will usually provide greater satisfaction in areas of metal detecting other than beach and surf hunting. A manual adjust detector, therefore, can prove to be a valuable addition to your metal detecting equipment.

Computerized

The finest metal detectors available today--and, in the foreseeable future--are instruments with computerized circuitry based on microprocessor controls such as the Master Hunter CX series.

Simply stated, the computerized detector is a *thinking machine*; it performs literally millions of analytical computations almost simultaneously to make circuitry adjustments that were formerly made by hand by the hobbyist. As the searchcoil receives data, it is fed into microprocessor circuitry in digital form and compared with the "mind" of the computer, data that has been stored in the computer at the factory. Thus, knowledge that formerly was required from the operator is now in the computer which permits it to make adjustments that once required manual action.. Not only does the computerized detector make these adjustments automatically, but they are made instantaneously--when they are needed, not when the need for them is finally noticed by an operator.

As the detector is scanned, it continually performs self-tests; that is, it self-adjusts to achieve optimum operating performance for all conditions, including battery condition, temperature changes, ground mineral variations and even the possible aging of electronic components that might cause "values" to change. Target data coming through the detector's searchcoil is compared with the particular requirements dialed in by the operator (such as discrimination) to produce the proper audio and meter indications. False signals, caused by conventional detector "back reading" are eliminated. Even large, surface and shallow objects are properly read on the meter, with the precise audio tone given.

Garrett engineers have known for years that different ground mineral conditions cause different discriminating performance. The Grand Master Hunter CX II and Master Hunter CX have various scanning methods stored in their memory banks. As earth mineralization changes while either of these instruments is being scanned, the detector automatically readjusts itself to use the optimum discrimination method.

Computerized detectors such as those of the Master Hunter CX series permit the ultimate in treasure hunting. No better instruments have ever been devised for the hobby. Greater depth and considerably more discriminating accuracy is possible. Additionally, a computerized detector automatically monitors every atmospheric and ground condition to maintain circuitry at optimum levels. Of course, just as some capabilities that can be achieved with computerized microprocessor-controlled detectors aren't possible with conventional instruments, the capabilities may not be required by all treasure hunters.

But, it has been said that operator "mistakes" can be virtually eliminated with the "thinking" detectors. I know that treasures are already being discovered on beaches all over the world that could never have been found before. "Worked-out" areas are producing vast amounts of new discoveries of coins and jewelry. Because these new finds are ones that were buried more deeply or were masked by trash, they are usually older and more valuable than the objects that had previously been found in the same areas.

Computerized detectors permit professional performance and detection accuracy to be achieved easily by beginners at levels that have tantalized professionals for years. We have truly entered the era of hi-tech metal detector performance. Beach hunting and all other forms of metal detecting will never be the same again!

Pulse Induction

You'll remember that VLF circuitry included transmitter and receiver windings that are electrically balanced. Metal is detected with a VLF instrument when eddy cur-

With the name of its London maker, Gibbs, still discernible, this beautiful vintage-1680 silver pocket watch that was found at a shipwreck site is valued at over $5,000.

rent generation draws power from the electromagnetic field and a metal target causes an imbalance between the windings. Pulse induction is different.

A pulse induction metal detector utilizes only one antenna in its searchcoil, serving both as transmitter and receiver. The transmitter delivers only a short burst of energy. Then, the detector becomes a passive instrument awaiting signals from the secondary electromagnetic field of the target. A most important characteristic of this type operation is that most ground minerals are ignored. The eddy currents generated by earth materials die out prematurely and are not received by circuitry of the antenna. Consequently, there is no need to provide the pulse induction detectors with ground balancing capability.

Audio response of pulse induction circuitry is somewhat slower, with a slight delay discernible between the time the target is detected and an audio signal is produced. This characteristic can make pinpointing a bit more difficult. Most pulse induction detectors feature an audible bell tone. The audio is adjustable for slight threshold, but what the operator hears is the faint ringing of a bell. This was first developed for use in underwater detectors to enable scuba divers to hear the detector's sounds over the noise of air bubbles created by scuba gear. The mellow bell tone sound is very pleasing, however, and many operators even prefer it.

Operating a pulse induction instrument like Garrett's Sea Hunter requires only regulating the audio for faint threshold sound and adjustment of a discrimination control to eliminate unwanted trash. Whenever an acceptable target is detected, the bell sound will increase in volume.

The Sea Hunter and other modern pulse induction instruments are quite sensitive and can detect tiny targets, even small platinum and white gold rings. Earlier models had difficulty with this type of jewelry.

Detection depth is also quite satisfactory with pulse induction instruments. In fact, Sea Hunter operators often tell us that they can detect targets at greater distances in salt water environments than in the air.

Pinpointing is slightly more difficult with a pulse induction detector since its peak audio detection signals are not generated at normal scanning speeds until the center of the searchcoil has passed across an acceptable target. Pinpointing can be improved, however, by rotating the searchcoil as it hovers above the target. After a little practice with this technique, operators generally are able to pinpoint with ease.

Pulse induction detectors can be used with confidence in all types of metal detecting on the beach, in the surf or under water. In fact, they are preferred for general use by many hobbyists and professionals who specialize in water hunting. These detectors can be operated at beach sites with dense concentrations of salt and black magnetic sand. The detector can be operated on dry beaches, then carried

This impressive collection of rings and other jewelry, all found by one treasure hunter in the sands and surfs of California beaches, clearly demonstrates how metal detectors can find wealth

into the surf with no deterioration in performance. It would be well to point out that the only pulse induction detectors now being commercially manufactured are submersible models, designed primarily for hunting under water. Too, I should quickly add that they are not recommended for hunting caches and relics or for electronic prospecting.

Submersible pulse induction detectors, such as our Sea Hunter, can be used to depths down to 200 feet as well as on the beach. Manufacturer's instructions for any detector should be followed at all times...especially concerning submersibility. Some instruments may be designed only for shallow submersion.

You'll notice that submersible pulse induction detectors are slightly heavier than comparable land detectors because of their rechargeable battery requirements. Body-mounted units can minimize this weight problem, however. The only other limitation of this type instrument is the slight problem sometimes encountered in pinpointing. Otherwise, the Sea Hunter or other pulse induction detector--really, your *only* option for searching deep beneath the water--is highly satisfactory as a beach and surf hunting instrument as well.

Detectors for seeking treasure far beneath the sea are specially designed and manufactured to work effectively despite the rigors of the ocean's salt and pressure.

112

Using a Detector

Some detectors will find a coin one inch deep; others will detect that same coin when extremely deep. A most important factor is the expertise and ability of the operator. *You must learn how to use your detector correctly.* Success will come in direct proportion to the amount of time and study you devote to the proper use of your instrument.

Purchasing equipment through the mail, or from someone who won't or can't instruct you can cause you to miss treasure that could have been found with proper training. Your goal should be to find treasure, not to find a metal detector bargain! Getting hands-on instruction from the dealer from whom you purchased your new detector is the first step. Learn from your dealer, then go into the field and practice. Then, return to your dealer for additional instructions if you have questions or if you cannot master basic techniques.

Learn your metal detector! Don't worry--at least first-- about what you are finding. You'll soon find yourself getting better and better. You will become more at ease in using it, and there will be fewer and fewer "problems" that bother you. The quantity of found items will be growing at an accelerated rate. All though your learning and training period and even on down through the years, you must develop persistence. *Never give up!*

Read your Owner's Manual (or instructions) not once,

Author demonstrates proper stance with metal detector that allows him to hunt on the beach or in surf for many hours without unnecessary fatigue or sore muscles.

but several times. The first time through, read it as you would a novel--from front to back. Pay no attention to the metal detector or its controls; simply read the instruction manual. If you have an audio or video instruction tape, listen to it or watch it several times.

Then, assemble your instrument carefully. Take the time to do it correctly. The next step is to become familiar with the various controls. The Owner's Manual should explain each switch and each control, describing to you its function and basic operation. All Garrett instruction manuals are pocket-size, designed to be taken into the field.

When you have adjusted each control, and understand how it works, begin to test the instrument with various metal targets. After you have become familiar with the sounds of your instrument, the meter functions, how the detector works and its response to various targets in various modes, it is time to go out into the field.

Your metal detector may have "set-and-forget" controls. Controls like *tone, audio, manual/automatic* are just that--controls to be set once and forgotten. Once you set them, you rarely should expect to have to change or reset them. If you have carefully followed the instructions in your Manual, you don't have to worry about them now...or ever again.

The beginner should initially consider the *discrimination* control(s) as a "set-and-forget" item. Set it to zero elimination (all-metal detection) and leave it there until you have operated your detector for at least ten hours. In other words, dig all detected targets.

Work smarter, not harder. Each time you receive a signal, try to guess what the target is before you dig. Try to guess its size, shape and depth. Analyze the audio and/or meter signals. Say to yourself, "This is a coin, or this is a bottlecap. It is approximately three inches deep." Then, pay attention when you dig the object. Did you guess right? Great! If not, try to determine why not. The more you do this, the greater your success will be. Use the straight-line sweep method illustrated on this page. Hold the searchcoil slightly above the ground and scan at a rate of about one foot per second. Don't get in a hurry and try to cover an acre in 10 minutes. What you are looking for is buried just below the searchcoil and the sweep you are now scanning. It's not across the field somewhere.

After 10 operating hours, begin using your Discriminate mode. At first don't use too much discrimination, just enough to eliminate from detection the junk you have been digging. After you become comfortable with your detector, it's time to go back over those areas you searched before you learned how to use your machine. You'll be surprised how many coins and other objects you missed. Come back six months and then a year later. Each time you'll find more things, especially at greater depths.

Learn about the other forms of treasure hunting such as ghost towning, relic and cache hunting and electronic

The author takes time from the beach to demonstrate the straight-line, side-to-side method of scanning. This technique covers ground more thoroughly and helps keeps the coil at a constant height.

prospecting. Learn the various optional accessories and searchcoils available for your detector. Keep in mind at all times the idea that detectors are not complicated nor difficult to use. The first time you tried to operate a car it was difficult, but now you drive without thinking about it. The same will be true with your detector. Keep working with the instrument, restudy your manual, contact your dealer or manufacturer and ask for more information. Often, problems are cleared up with one simple demonstration by your dealer or someone who knows how to use detectors.

During your learning period, keep the Detection Depth (or, Sensitivity) control turned to minimum or to the "initial" set point. Scan with the searchcoil about two inches above the ground and scan at a moderate speed. Even in high junk areas which can be very difficult to work the reduced detection sensitivity and moderate scanning speed improve your chances of hearing individual targets rather than a jumbled sound.

Treasure is being found right now in your community and a lot of treasure is waiting for you. Detectors are not magic wands, but when used correctly, they will locate buried and concealed treasure. Maintain faith in your detector and have patience until you have it mastered. *Success will be yours!*

Make A Test Plot

One of the first things a new detector owner does is bury a few coins to see how deeply he can detect them. This test usually results in disappointment. The longer an object has been buried, the easier it can be detected. Not only is a "barrier" to electromagnetic field penetration created when a coin is first buried, but no "halo" effect has been developed. As time passes, coins become more closely associated, electrically, with surrounding earth materials, and the molecules of metal begin to leave and move out into the surrounding soil. Also, it is theorized that in some cases (especially in salt water) the coin's surface becomes a better conductor. All of these phenomena result in the "detectability" of coins increasing the longer they are buried. It is estimated that a coin or other piece of buried metal can be detected at twice the depth or deeper, after a period of time in the soil, compared with the same object when newly buried.

Select an area where you can make your own test plot. Scan the area thoroughly with your detector in the All Metal mode and remove all metal from the ground. Select targets such as coins, a bottlecap, a nail and a pulltab. Select also a pint jar filled with scrap metal, a long object such as a foot-long pipe and a large object such as a gallon can. Bury the objects about three feet apart, in rows, and make a map showing items buried, location and depth.

Bury pennies at varying depths, beginning at one inch. Continue, with the deepest buried about six inches deep. Bury one at about two inches, but stand it on edge. Bury a penny at about two inches with a bottlecap about four inches off to one side. Bury the bottlecap, nail and pulltab separately at about two inches deep. Bury the jar at twelve inches to the top of the jar lid. Bury the pipe horizontally, three or four inches deep. Bury the gallon can with the lid two feet below the surface.

The purpose of the buried coins is to familiarize you with the *sound of money*. If you can't detect the deeper coins right away, don't worry. After a while, you'll be able to hear their signals. After you have been able to detect them all, rebury some out of detection range. The penny buried next to the bottlecap will give you experience in "super-sniping" and will help you learn to distinguish individual objects. It will also be a good test to help you understand "detuning." The jar and gallon can will help you learn to recognize "dull" sounds of large, deeply buried objects. Check the targets with and without headphones; you'll be amazed at the difference headphones make.

The test plot is important. Don't neglect it. From time

to time expand it and rebury the targets deeper and add new ones. This will be a measure of just how well you are progressing and how well you have learned your equipment. Remember to make an *accurate* diagram or map showing location and depth of all objects.

Miscellaneous Tips

When searching near wire fences, metal buildings, swing sets, etc., reduce detection depth (sensitivity) and scan the searchcoil parallel to the structure.

You may also try turning down your threshold and operating in the "silent" tuning zone. A few tests comparing "silent" operation with that using a slight threshold of sound, however, will convince you that "silent" operation is not as effective as threshold.

Learn to use a probe to locate the exact point where coins are buried. This will help you retrieve coins with minimum damage to grass and the target.

More Tips

Coins lying in the ground at an angle may be missed on one searchcoil pass but detected when the searchcoil comes in from another direction. If your detector has a volume control, keep it set at maximum. Don't confuse volume control with audio (threshold) control. You can use earphones that have individual earpiece volume adjustment and set each one to suit yourself.

Never dial in more discrimination than you need; too much may reduce detector efficiency.

If you are working on the beach, set target elimination at about bottlecap rejection. Slight adjustment may be necessary, but you can set the detector to ignore salt water. Pulse induction and modern detectors, however, ignore salt water automatically.

Use common sense. *Think* your way through perplexing situations. Don't be in a hurry. Remember that sucess will come from your expertise, research, patience and enthusiasm...though, not necessarily in that order.

Don't expect to find tons of treasure every time you go metal detecting. There may be times when you don't find anything. But the fun and reward of metal detecting is never knowing what you'll dig up next!

Be sure to check your batteries before you venture out, and check them often. Carry spare batteries every time you go hunting.

Keep the searchcoil level as you scan and always scan slowly and methodically. Scan the searchcoil from side to side in a reasonably straight line (not a wide arc) in front of you.

Do not scan the searchcoil in an arc unless you are scanning extremely slowly. The straight-line scan method (see Page 117) allows you to cover more ground in each sweep, helps keep the searchcoil level, reduces skipping and helps maintain uniform overlapping. You should overlap by advancing the searchcoil as much as fifty percent of its diameter. When the searchcoil reaches the extremes of each sweep, rotate your upper body to stretch out for an even wider sweep. This gives the double benefit of scanning a wider sweep while you get additional exercise. To insure a complete scan of any given area, use string or cord to mark scan paths. The width of your paths can be from three to six feet wide.

When you dig a target, scan back over the hole to make sure you recovered everything in and around it.

Fill your holes!
Pick up and carry off all trash!
Don't destroy property!

Beginner's Short Course

These exercises will help you learn to use your detector and gain confidence in its abilities. This short course is, however, no substitute for study, application, and practice. The following instructions are for any modern metal detector produced by a quality manufacturer.

1. Assemble the detector according to your Owner's Manual, using the smallest diameter searchcoil (three-inch to four-inch minimum) you have.

2. Hold the detector with the searchcoil about four feet in the air.

3. Turn the detector on and reduce detection depth (sensitivity) to minimum.

4. Adjust the audio control to achieve a very low sound. This is your threshold level. Depending upon your type detector, you may have to hold a switch in the depressed position while you make this adjustment.

5. Select the All Metal (no discrimination) detection mode.

6. Adjust the ground balance (elimination or cancel) control knob (if your detector has one) to the "center" position.

– If it is a one-turn control, rotate the knob to the half-way point or

– If it is a ten-turn control, rotate the knob either direction ten turns. Turn the knob five turns in the opposite direction. This will be the center point.

7. Lower the searchcoil to a height of about two inches above the ground. If you continue to hear the faint threshold sound, begin slowly scanning the searchcoil over the ground, keeping a constant height. (See *Notes*, below.)

8. Where the audio increases, a target is buried in the ground.

Notes

If the ground is extremely mineralized, the mid-point ground balance adjustment (Number 6 above) may not permit effective operation. The audio threshold level may change as you lower the searchcoil to the two-inch height. If that occurs, you must adjust the ground balance control. Refer to your Owner's Manual and my comments on this subject in Chapter 7. Remember that each time you make an adjustment to the ground balance control, or whenever the threshold sound level changes because of minerals, temperature change, etc., you must press your retune button or switch, if your detector has such a control. Modern detectors retune themselves instantly and automatically.

Initial "Preset" Indicators

All Garrett detectors have initial *preset* points clearly indicated. If your detector has such markings, it will be easier for you to learn the instrument. Set all knobs and switches to the preset points. These adjustments are for average soil and operating conditions. Any controls without initial preset points should be set according to the instructions given above.

Health Safeguards

Within the past three decades, metal detecting has become a very popular activity. People of all ages roam parks, ghost towns, beaches and gold mining areas in search of treasure. Some individuals occasionally complain of pains after they have used metal detectors for long

This varied collection of objects, all discovered by a group of Canadian beach and surf hunters, illustrates the many types of "treasure" that detector hobbyists enounter near the water.

periods of time. Such complaints usually come from those who are just beginning the hobby and swing their detector some 10 to 12 hours the first day out. On the next morning the naturally wake up with a good care of sore muscles. After a few days, soreness disappears and off they go again.

Although the instances are rare, some hobbyists suffer from what is known as "tennis elbow." This is a perfectly real condition--an injury to the tendons of the elbow--whose medical name is epicondylitis. The condition is characterized by mild to sharp pain at the side of the elbow. It is believed to be caused by a gradual weakening of muscle tissue. Repeated muscle strain without time in-between for the muscles to repair themselves, causes the problem.

I have been using metal detectors for more than 40 years and I have never had tennis elbow or any serious problem. I develop more problems from using my gym equipment. The following recommendations are aimed at further lessening the dangers of strained muscles:

– Select the proper equipment, including accessories.

– Strengthen your hand, arm, back and shoulder muscles through an exercise program.

– Before beginning each day's detecting activity, spend a few minutes doing warmup exercises.

– During your metal detecting activities, use the correct scanning techniques and take an occasional break. Stopping to dig a target is usually sufficient "break" time, however.

Let's expand on each of the preventive measure procedures described above. First, adjust the stem to the proper--though not necessarily the shortest--length. If it is too long, you will have a balance problem and your swing will be awkward. If it is too short, you'll have to stoop over to search. If large searchcoils do not give proper balance, use a hipmount kit or armrest.

Select an exercise program that will strengthen your fingers, hand, arm, shoulder and back muscles. You don't need much strengthening, not even bar bell and dumbell workouts. Toning up is of primary importance. As you use your metal detector you'll develop the correct muscles. It's just that at the beginning, and after periods of inactivity, you should protect against strained muscles and ligaments. And, that brings us to the third preventive measure.

Warmup exercises should precede each day's metal detecting activity. A few minutes of stretching and other activity are needed to loosen the muscles and joints and prepare you for a day's work. Begin by observing how cats stretch themselves; then, try to imitate these graceful animals. A brisk walk, a few toe touches, a few arm and wrist curls holding a one or two-pound weight, a few body twists at the waist while standing erect and perhaps a minute or two running in place will get the job done. You can develop your own warmup exercises.

Now, to proper scanning methods:

– Keep a firm footing. Don't ever try to scan while balancing on one foot. This can cause your muscles to make unnatural movements.

– Keep all movements as natural as possible. If you find yourself scanning on steep hills, down in gullies or other unlevel places, keep good balance and take shorter swings.

Proof of the endurance of gold is this lovely band which--when detected and recovered from a depth of several inches--was untarnished and shiny with inscriptions and designs readily apparent.

125

You'll find that it's always best (and usually quite possible) to avoid getting yourself into awkward positions when searching with a metal detector.

– Grasp the metal detector handle lightly, and scan bymoving your arm from side to side. Slight wrist movements are okay when, for some reason, your searchcoil swing is short. But, when you swing the detector normally, use a motion that is natural and one that causes a minimum amount of unnecessary wrist movement. By not "turning over" your wrist, you'll also help keep your searchcoil level.

– Let the entire arm "swing" with the detector. Occasionally, change hands and use the other arm to swing the detector.

– If you feel yourself tightening up, stop and rest. Most likely, however, each time you stop to dig a target, you can rest. Then, you can think of your next detected target as a blessing. You'll get to stop, stoop down and dig. This activity gives other muscles a workout, which will help prevent sore muscles that come from long periods of continuous metal detector swinging without a break.

The Beaches

While attending an International Mining Conference and Exhibition in Sydney, Australia, I spent much of my off-duty evening and weekend hours hunting the beaches which had been, apparently, untouched by metal detectors. My companions and I found coins, jewelry and other items as fast as we could dig, make a recovery and complete the next scan with our searchcoil. Often, I recovered *handfuls* of coins from a single hole. We drew skeptical crowds. After seeing us recover about ten dollars in coins from one hole, someone shouted, "I don't believe you are finding that many coins. You came here last night and buried them!"

Perhaps you are also skeptical? From the moment you discover your first cache of coins or piece of valuable jewelry, you will never again be a Doubting Thomas. The time will come when you find a single ring equal in value to your detector. And, quite likely, if you pursue this hobby forcefully, you'll occasionally make discoveries worth thousands of dollars.

Another rewarding aspect of beachcombing is the joy that comes from simply walking a beach, experiencing the ocean breezes and the sand under your feet while listening to the tranquilizing sounds of surf and seabreeze.

A beachcomber is a person who searches along shorelines for valuable jetsam, flotsam, refuse and other lost treasure. "Keeper" finds can be anything valued by the finder or anyone else. The beachcomber's territory is staked on two parallel sides on many occasions...the shallow surf line and a macadam road. The other two dimensions often seem to disappear into infinity. Digging for treasure on the beach is often as easy as kicking the sand with the toe of your shoe.

The time is *whenever*...day or night...spring, summer, fall or winter.Beach pickings are good almost any time, but you'll learn that certain times are better than than others. At first, you may be disappointed. Your finds may seem to provide small return for your efforts. But, remember, most new ventures begin awkwardly and without reward. Persist you must! Give yourself just a year; you'll be forever "hooked" and richer for your efforts

Beach pickings include coins, rings, watches, necklaces, chains, bracelets and anklets, religious medallions and crucifixes, toys, knives, cigarette cases and lighters, sunshades, keys, relics, bottles, Asian glass and plastic fishnet balls, ships' cargo and other items that will soon fill barrels. And, for the very lucky and persistent hunter, the discovery of some lost pirate treasures of the famed Captain Kidd, or a cache of 17th Century Spanish pieces of eight which were hidden ashore by early day explorers who never made it back to recover their wealth.

People shouldn't wear jewelry to the beach, but they do. Often, they forget they have on valuable heirlooms and diamond rings. Some just don't seem to care one way or the other. But, it makes no difference to the beachcomber because all rings expand in the heat. Fingers wrinkle and shrivel in the water, and suntan oils merely hasten the inevitable loss. Beach lovers play ball, throw frisbees and engage in horseplay. These activities fling rings from fingers and cause clasps on necklaces, bracelets and chains to break. Into the sand fall these lost valuables.

Coins, jewelry, keys and other beach "necessities" are placed on blankets. In a hurry to escape a sudden downpour or just through forgetfulness, the sunbather grabs and shakes the blanket. There go the valuables into the sand. Some items are often immediately recovered, but many are never found except by a metal detector.

Boys and girls play in the sand. Holes are dug and heaps of sand are piled up or made into sand castles. In this process toys, coins, digging tools, knives and other possessions are lost until the metal detector discovers them.

Perhaps, someday, you'll be as lucky as one beachcomber on Grand Cayman whose story was related by Robert Marx in *Argosy* magazine. The beachcomber spotted something shining on the sandy bottom in shallow water. To his astonishment it turned out to be a gold cross covered with diamonds. Without telling anyone, he returned later with scuba equipment and really struck it rich. Using only his hand to fan away thin layers of sand, he recovered a fantastic cache of treasure including a large bar of platinum dated 1521, various bars of silver bullion, a silver bracelet in the form of a serpent covered with emeralds and a large gold ring bearing the arms of the Ponce de Leon family. With no evidence of a shipwreck ever occurring in the area, he believes the treasure--which

Beaches of Florida produced this vast horde of coins during a one-year period for Tom Edds, who certainly demonstrated that use of the proper beach hunting techniques can really pay off!

129

appears to be the booty of a conquistador--was probably buried ashore and eventually washed into the shallow water as the beach eroded.

Research

Chapter 4 lists and describes many of the major and most common sources of leads. No summary or discussion, however, can ever be complete. As you research the various sources, your techniques and abilities will improve. That's one reason why I encourage you to apply yourself aggressively to beach hunting for at least one year before you judge this aspect of treasure hunting. Don't be haphazard and sloppy in your efforts. *Be diligent.* You'll be amazed at your progress and success.

First, begin your research locally. Use every source of leads and information from oldtimers to chambers of commerce. Contact tourist bureaus as well as historical societies. Leave no source untouched in your investigation. To speed up your work, always be specific. Ask for information pertaining to both past and present swimming areas and resorts. Swimming was certainly one of the most popular activities of bygone days. Ghost towns, and there are always a few lying about in ruins, should not be overlooked.

When checking newspapers, pay particular attention to drowning reports which usually give the location, or at least the name, of a particular beach. Review the Sunday or weekend city news columns that announce the joys of swimming and sunbathing at local beaches. Advertisements of beachwear occasionally offer clues to areas of activity.

Author gives metal detector instruction to a group of South American youths who could not believe the treasures they had watched him dig up on their beaches of Colombia.

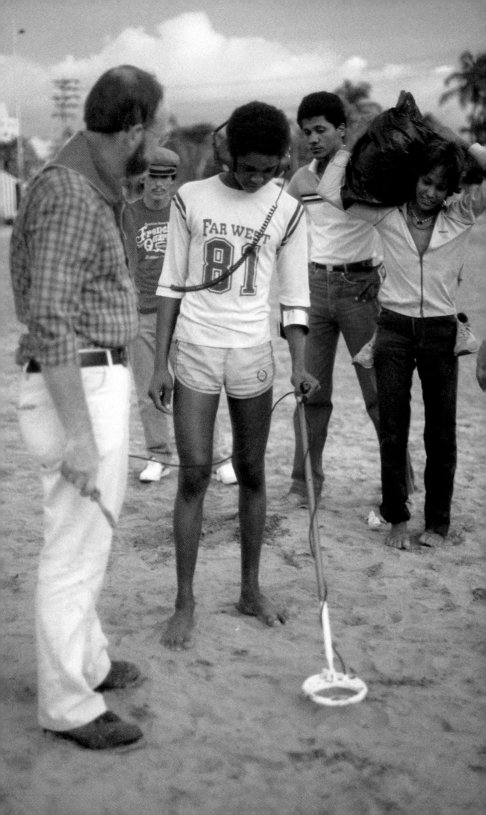

Don't overlook old postcards. Antique shops are often a good source. If there is a postcard collector in your vicinity, pay him or her a visit. Old picture postcards, like those printed in this book, may be reliable *X-marks-the-spot* waybills to treasure.

If you are not a member of your local treasure club, consider joining. The sharing of locations and success stories broadens everyone's knowledge, sharpens skills and increases success rates of members.

Don't be content to work only local beaches. Broaden your scope; it may pay rewards. For example, if you live in northern California, make a study of the history of the San Francisco Bay area. Many ships have gone down here, losing valuable cargoes of silver and gold, much of which has not been found. Violent storms often churn up ocean bottoms and cast sunken treasure on the beach.

Never overlook the possibility of finding flotsam and jetsam washed ashore from offshore shipwrecks. Regardless of a wreck's age, some cargo--especially if it's made of gold, silver, copper or bronze--will probably remain in fair to excellent condition. The principal cargo found in many old shipwrecks is silver and gold from the mines of Mexico and Peru, or gold from California and nearby states. Recent recoveries from old shipwrecks reveal that the typical ship's cargo consisted of cannon, gold and silver coins and bars, and personal relics. Often clumps of silver coins and disks are located. Other items such as English pewter and stoneware are often found. Be quick to take advantage of all opportunities to expand your treasure hunting horizons. You may also expand your pocketbook and require a larger safety deposit box!

A coin is dug from the sand after it was discovered by this XL500 Sea Hunter detector, which finds treasure on the beach as well as 200 feet deep in oceans or lakes.

When researching reports of shipwrecks, don't overlook Coast Guard and Life Saving Service records. Newspaper files and local and state histories are good sources of information. Insurance companies and *Lloyd's Register* may provide precisely the information you need.

Assateague Island, off the coast of Maryland and Virginia, has proven to be the depository of much cargo from ancient ship wrecks. Treasure hunters, scanning the beaches with their metal detectors, have found valuable coins and relics, some of which have "marked" the location of larger treasures. Although much of the island is controlled by the National Seashore Service, portions are completely open to the public. Permission to search with your metal detector can sometimes be obtained on National Seashores. It doesn't hurt to request permission.

These examples of potentially productive areas offer ideas that may help you expand your territory. Treasure hunters often travel thousands of miles in their quest for treasure. You can do likewise, especially if there is a pot of gold at the end of your trail. But, I must stress the presence of considerable local treasure. Find it first; then hit the treasure trail.

As you search records, histories and old maps, be on the alert for clues to landmarks and locations. For instance, the name of a beach led me to the Spanish icon described later in this chapter. Wouldn't a name like *Massacre Beach* cause your ears to perk up? When I began uncovering what looked like human bones at the beach site, I knew the site was worth thoughtful investigation.

Stay alert to current weather conditions. You'll want to search at low tides--the lower the better. After storms come ashore, head for the beach.

When oil spills deposit tar and oil on beaches, there's a good possibility bulldozers and other earth moving equipment can inadvertently get you much closer to treasure. The same kind of earth-moving equipment will be present around beach development work. When pipelines are being laid and when seawalls, breakwaters and piers are being constructed, work these areas of excavation.

Permits

Be alert to regulatory laws and regulations. Quite possibly, most or all your beach areas are open to metal detector hobbyists, but it is possible some areas are regulated. If a permit is required to search a given area, obtain one and operate within permit regulations. As an example, consider the regulations as set forth on treasure hunter Roy Sexton's Niagara Frontier State and Recreation Commission Permit. Its regulations permit hunting all year except during the period May 23 through September 7. No water hunting is allowed, only beach hunting. Hunting is allowed only on Beaver Island State Park and Evangola State Park. Certain digging and archaeological restrictions are enforced. There is no cost for this permit.

Clothing

Although you should always dress comfortably, protect yourself from the elements. Obviously keep warm in the winter and cool in the summer, but I caution you to shade exposed skin areas to prevent sun and wind burn. Skin specialists recommend the use of a high-numbered (at least 15 SPF) sun screen. Use it often and freely. Regardless of the elements, you can protect yourself. This book instructs you in basics, but experience is the best teacher.

In the spring, summer and fall seasons I usually wear shorts or lightweight trousers, a shirt (usually with long sleeves), socks and comfortable shoes or sneakers, a wide-brimmed cotton hat and a neck shield. During early morning and late evening hours, I try to work open sunny areas. During the heat of the day, I work shady areas. Neither heat nor cold keeps me from working all day (8 to 12 hours) in my quest for treasure. I love hot weather, but yet I respect its fury. About one-half my water supply I use to keep my hat dampened. Keeping my head cool and protecting my skin from sunburn permits all-day searching to become a matter of course.

Treasure hunting, or any form of metal detecting must be considered play. But, I don't play when I hunt. The only rule I follow when in the field is to work from dawn to dusk and later, if necessary. Doing less is a gross misuse of time. Develop sound habits, be totally serious about your work and I am confident you'll find twice as much treasure. In fact, the difference between success and failure--separating the men from the boys, if you will--depends almost entirely on dedication to the job at hand.

I never work barefooted, especially in sand dunes. I wear boots and I watch out for snakes. Rarely, do I dig with my hands, but use one or more types of diggers. I use knee pads, at least on one knee. In Chapter 25 I describe various other clothing items and pieces of protective gear.

The arrival of winter weather can signal the start of good beach hunting. Beaches become less crowded and the often violent weather increases its never-ending effort at erosion. As beaches erode, you should be first on the beach every day--the early hunter gets the treasure!

Cold weather hunting, particularly in the North and East and even on Gulf Coast beaches, requires more thought, more caution and more clothing than the same activity in warmer weather. You must keep yourself protected against lower temperatures, fierce winds and persistent drizzle or rain. Adequate protection, however, must not bind or restrict your movements, or else you will tire quickly. My long thermals usually go on first, followed by loose-fitting outerwear. I've found that a lightweight windbreaker suit gives me considerable protection as an outer garment. The top piece has a zippered or button-up front, however, because as I begin to warm up, I first unzip the top piece. With my back to the wind, the unzipped top maintains body heat at the pre-sweat level. As the day warms, I may remove the top entirely.

I wear a Navy deck-watch type wool cap and either a

separate rainproof bonnet or one that is attached to the top piece of my outer rain gear. Gloves are often a necessity; arm's length rubber gloves are a must for cold water work. While working on blustery days, I usually wear rubber boots. Sometimes I'll wear hip waders.

You may ask why I wear rubber boots when I work dry beaches. While they are not needed for dry beach work, I must be prepared when I discover a cut formed by wave and wind action. I never miss a chance to work a cut being formed as long as the water level and the elements permit. If land searching is producing only moderate success, I wade into the shallow water to seek troughs. Even though I enjoy water hunting during cold seasons, I prefer my feet dry. If my feet stay warm, I usually stay warm all over.

I suggest goggles in high winds. If you wear glasses, wear goggles over your glasses, a type which is available from

All of these discoveries, mostly rings and religious medallions, were made by a single treasure hunter who primarily searches the various beaches and surfing areas on the Pacific coast of the U.S.

bicycle, motorcycle or skiing shops. Use goggles that are vented since the vents prevent moisture from forming. Those sold in motorcycle and skiing equipment shops are generally of better quality. Test them by pressing gently outward on the outside corner of one of the lens. If it slips easily out of its socket or rubber groove, don't buy this pair. In the field, the lens will never stay in place. Since lens are usually made of soft plastic, you must treat them with care to prevent scratches.

Always carry extra clothing, including dry socks and shoes. Include small waterproof canvases or paint drop-cloths to protect your car seats and floorboards from water or wet sand. I encourage you to read and study Chapter 29. Take extra special care of your clothing and equipment, or you'll wish you had!

Equipment

Wouldn't it be nice if treasure hunters could always dig holes only in sand? Almost any type digger can be used in beach sand, except your hands. There is too much broken glass. I prefer two types of diggers: a heavy-duty garden trowel and a light-weight pick with a flat blade on one end. Just a quick whack with the pick, and I usually have my treasure. Of course, pinpointing is essential before you start hacking your way down to treasure. Begin by using a trowel or small shovel. As your pinpointing improves, you can graduate to a pick-type digger with a long handle. The long handle lets you uncover your target without kneeling on the ground. See Chapter 22 for more information on my recommendations.

Scoops are reasonably good in *dry, loose sand.* A quick scoop, a few shakes and you have your find. In damp and wet sand, however, scoops are just a waste of time. It takes too long to work damp sand out of a scoop. When you are working surf at the shoreline, however, a scoop can be effectively used. Onrushing waves will quickly clean the wet sand from your scoop.

Occasionally, you may need a strong, thin digger-like screwdriver. A good percentage of my finds are buried in roots beneath trees and tree stumps. Digging becomes difficult amongst the roots, and a strong, thin, rod-type digger is required to loosen the soil. I left one "treasure" on the Caribbean beach of Guadeloupe because I did not have a strong digging tool or saw. A faint detector signal came as I scanned over the roots of a tree stump. As I dug deeper, the signal grew louder, but digging became more difficult. Because the root system was so tangled, I could make only slow headway. My hunting companions were already loaded in the vehicle and were anxious to leave. Still some distance from my target, I saw the need for a stronger tool and filled in the hole. As I walked sadly away, I promised myself a return trip with the correct tools.

And speaking of holes, some treasure hunters leave the holes they dig. *Don't you!* Always, without exception, fill every hole you dig. It takes an extra moment, certainly, but you must do this for the sake of our hobby. And, you don't want someone to step into one of your holes and twist an ankle, do you? I have filled so many holes that I do it automatically. Even in mountainous regions and desert areas, I kick dirt into the holes I dig.

Other gear you need includes a general assortment of pouches, a secure pocket for especially good finds and a place for personal items. I often wear an Army-type web belt with a canteen and an extra pouch or two. If you hunt at night, you'll need a battery-powered headlamp.

Metal Detector Selection

Although much has been said about selecting the proper detector, a few more words of advice are in order. The sand on most beaches looks innocent enough, but the "wrong" type detector can spoil your day at the beach. Depending on ground minerals, some detectors are practically worthless, others so-so, and yet others perfect. A quality automated VLF with discrimination is your best choice. Of course, I'm talking about a *modern detector.*

On iron mineral-free beaches such as those of Florida, any detector--even an obsolete BFO or TR--will generally work well. If your BFO or TR has a discriminating mode, water-saturated sands can be worked easily. With discrimination control set near bottlecap rejection, salt minerals in the water are eliminated from detection.

Manual adjust VLFs give good depth in most beach sands. Unless the circuits are "automated," however, heavy iron mineral black sand beaches may somewhat limit performance. If your VLF has a TR discriminating mode, you should set it at approximately the bottlecap setting. Of course, that setting imposes limitations, especially if you decide to advance the setting to pulltab rejection and dig mostly coins.

I realize that most professional beach hunters will be aghast at that remark, since few professionals use any discrimination unless the beach is truly a "junk yard." Using discrimination, certainly, makes it more likely that you may miss valuable treasures. That's a fact of life. But, there are times when discrimination is needed.

The new automated VLFs have become popular with beach hunters. Many models ignore minerals, including those associated with salt water. Some instruments have an internal switch that cuts out salt minerals. Automated models can be operated from zero discrimination through pulltab rejection.

Pulse Induction instruments operate nearly flawlessly on all beaches. Giving depth, they are a pleasure to use. Generally, they are heavier because of extra battery requirements and the heavier case needed by submersible/land models. One shortcoming of pulse detectors is that small iron pieces, especially nails and hairpins, may not be rejected. I have learned that Caribbean beaches can be a true hairpin junk yard, while U.S. beaches are generally free of them.

On beaches with black sand (iron-magnetite) present, your choice of detectors is narrowed considerably. The old

BFOs and TRs are out of the question because they cannot cancel the effects of the natural iron. Pulse Induction detectors ignore it as do manual and automated VLFs and all modern detectors.

So, a choice must be made: A quality, automated VLF with discrimination is most desirable. These instruments ignore black sand and salt minerals, and you can adjust discrimination control(s) to your desired setting.

If you are determined to use your trusty BFO or TR, take it to the beach and adjust the discrimination control near bottlecap rejection. Then, try it over wet sand. You may have to make minor adjustments to find the correct setting. If the detector's audio cannot be "smoothed out," you are probably encountering black sand.

You should consider purchasing one of the late model automated (sometimes called motion) discriminating instruments. Give thought to buying one of the environmentally protected units. Then, neither rising water, rain, blowing sand, nor storms can send you home.

Metal Detector Notes

If your detector is not protected against the environment, carry along a plastic bag to slip over its control housing. When you set the detector down, sand will have less chance to work into its controls and circuitry.

Always use searchcoil skidplates to extend the life of your searchcoil.

Always, always, always (need I repeat, always?) use headphones for the greatest success. Wind, surf and "people" noise will mask your detector's signals causing you to miss many good targets. Any type of headphones are better than none, but the most desired are those with ear cushions and adjustable volume controls. Coiled cords are preferred along with right-angle plugs.

Since large cushioned headphones can become quite hot, you might try the smaller and lighter versions, even though their tiny cushions may not mask out as much noise interference.

Most searchcoils are submersible (check with your manufacturer, if in doubt), but not all detectors have a stem plug to prevent water from running back into the control housing. To be safe, immediately after using your detector in water, drain the lower stem. If you don't, the first time the searchcoil is raised above the control box, you may have a flooded instrument.

Tides and Weather

Wouldn't it be great if the ocean suddenly receded several feet leaving your favorite hunting beach high and dry? You could walk right out and recover lost treasure so much more easily!

Well, the ocean does recede slightly every day during low tide. Nearly twice a day a full tide cycle occurs--two high and two low tides. Low tides are of greatest interest to you because the water level has dropped, leaving more beach area exposed. A one-half foot drop in tide level can

GALVESTON (Galveston Channel), TEXAS

Times and Heights of High and Low Waters

AUGUST

Day	Time h m	Height ft	m	Day	Time h m	Height ft	m
1	0125	0.7	0.2	16	0038	1.3	0.4
Sa	0724	1.1	0.3	Su	0409	1.2	0.4
	1449	0.2	0.1		0542	1.3	0.4
	2243	1.1	0.3		1607	0.0	0.0
2	0227	1.0	0.3	17	0218	1.5	0.5
Su	0718	1.2	0.4	M	1713	-0.1	0.0
	1545	0.0	0.0				

Shown is a typical tide table that might be available at tackle stores or scuba shops, listing water heights in feet and meters to indicate the times for high and low tides throughout the month.

142

expose an extra ten or more feet of ground distance to the water's edge, allowing you to work not only more dry land but also a greater distance into the surf. Low tides occur approximately every twelve and one-half hours. You should plan your work period to begin at least two or three hours before low tide and continue that long after designated low tide times. That's four to six hours of improved hunting.

You can buy tide tables or get the information from scuba shops, fishing tackle stores, or the newspapers. If you plan to work inlet, cove and river areas, water current data may also be of interest. On some days, especially after a new or full moon, there will be lower-than-usual tides. Take advantage of these times. Also, listen to weather forecasts to learn of prevailing wind data. Strong offshore (outgoing) winds will aid in lowering the water level and tend to reduce breaker size and force. Offshore winds also seem to spread out (thin) sand at the water's edge. This effect could result in decreasing the amount of sand that has built up over lost treasure. On the other hand, incoming waves and resulting larger breakers tend to pile sand up, causing it to thicken and increase in depth. Be alert to the lowest or ebb tides when you can work beach areas not normally exposed. You must get your timing right. Of course, you can work dry beaches during high tides and then be prepared to follow the tide out. That procedure offers maximum work time.

As you follow the tide out, work in a parallel path hugging the water's edge. If your path length is not too long, each return path will be nearly parallel to the preceding one. If your path length is long, each succeeding path will veer outward. Wide searchcoil sweeps can offset these veering paths, however. Be alert to the relationships between locations of your finds. It may be that you'll discover a trough, or other treasure deposit that needs additional scanning or work with a larger, deeper- seeking searchcoil.

Look for tidal pools and long, water-filled depressions.

Any beach areas that hold water should be investigated since these low spots put you closer to treasure. As the tide recedes, watch for streams draining back into the ocean. These "mark" the location of low areas. If you will constantly keep in your mind the vision that only a few feet beneath the sand's surface a *blanket of treasure* awaits, your powers of observation will keep you alert to specific areas to search. After all, that blanket of treasure lying on the clay, gravel or bedrock belongs to *you,* and you are *going to get it.* Continually watch for those low areas that put your searchcoil closer to it.

Weather is a major contributing factor to tide levels, and strong storms and winds can change tides drastically. A storm at sea moving in your direction may rise the normal tide level several feet. When this occurs, wave action becomes so violent it is sometimes impossible (and dangerous) to hunt, even upon the beach. But, the stage is set, however, and you should hit the beach when calm returns.

Conversely, a winter storm reaching the coast with any strength at all can cause lower tides than those listed in the table and an accompanying compression of wave heights is noticeable. The water is often calm. These conditions and the changes they cause is a continuing process that controls sand deposits on the beach and in the shallow water. Storms often transfer treasure from deep water vaults to more shallow locations. For a change in your searching habits, plan a beach search immediately following a storm. If you are among the more hardy individuals, try working during a violent storm. It may be revealing.

Indian John told me of working a Florida beach during a storm. Suddenly, at the water's edge, a gully began forming before his eyes. As it grew deeper, he suddenly saw the unmistakable color of treasure. I don't know how much he took from that glory hole, but he smiles when he relates the story. Before you decide to try your luck during a storm, however, please read carefully the safety precautions that are outlined in Chapter 26.

Keep in mind, that extremes in weather and surf conditions can make unproductive beaches suddenly become productive. Remember that storms play havoc with beach sands. Fast-running beach drainage currents can wash deep gullies in the sand. So, keep your eyes on water movement during such violent weather.

Sand Formations

Both wind and water move beach sand around in a continual process. This process creates *nature's traps* that will hold treasure for you.

Let me tell you of the time when I missed by only a few days what I believe would have been a "gold mine." On a stretch of beach along the eastern seaboard of Italy not far from Pisa, prevailing winter winds blow sand inland, uncovering a harder packed soil. A retaining wall about one hundred yards inland prevents the sand from being blown farther. Before each springtime bathing season, earth-moving equipment is used to return sand to the beach. Quite likely, considerable lost treasure captured within the harder-packed strata could be found during the winter months when the beach is stripped of sand blown inward. During a trip to Europe which included a visit to Italy, I brought to the beach shown below the prototype of a new

The author, right, scans the Italian beach which he discusses on this and the following page. As described, plentiful sand is now on the beach to separate him from "the blanket of treasure" beneath it.

beach/surf hunting detector for testing. We arrived there immediately following the completion of the sand's redistribution along the shoreline. It was obvious the sand was from about two to four feet thick. My chance had been lost!

Another reason for working beaches immediately after a storm is that the beach continually reshapes and protects itself. Sands shift normally to straighten the beachfront and present the least possible shoreline to the sea's continuous onslaught. During storms, beach levels decrease as sand washes out to form underwater bars which blunt the destructive force of oncoming waves. Following the storm, the smaller waves return the sand to the beach.

To understand how sand, coins and jewelry continually move around, consider the relentless action of waves upon sand. At the water's edge, particles of sand form the sand

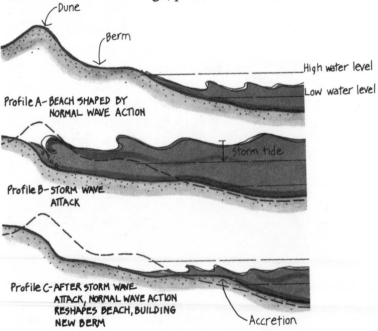

The dramatic fashion in which storm tides can completely reshape sand dunes on beaches is shown in this illustration from a booklet produced by the U. S. Army Corps of Engineers.

146

bank. When a wave comes in, the sudden immersion in water causes the grains of sand to "lighten" and become more or less suspended in the water. The constant churning keeps particles afloat until the next wave comes in. The floating particles are then carried some distance by the force of the water.

In the same manner, coins, jewelry, sea shells and debris are continually relocated, generally in the direction of prevailing wind and waves. As they move, waves and wind shift materials about until a spot is reached where the action of the water is lessened. Heavy objects fall out and become and become concentrated in "nature's traps." So, whenever you find areas with a concentration of sea shells, gravel, flotsam, driftwood and other debris, work them with your metal detector.

As your experience accumulates, you'll one day realize that treasure can be found outside the normal limits of the swimming area. How did this treasure get there? Possibly, at an earlier stage in time, the outlying stretches of beach were actually the swimming beach itself. For one or more

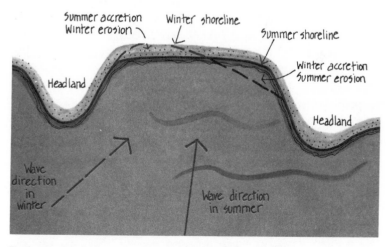

Because beaches continually reshape and protect themselves by sand shifting to expose the least possible shoreline to the sea's onslaught, their contours will change with the winds and waves.

reasons (property disputes, beach erosion, etc.) the "old" beach was abandoned along with its buried treasure.

Another reason for this *mislocated* treasure is natural erosion that moved it. How does this occur? These redeposits do not "just happen" nor are they permanent. It may pay you to consider and attempt to understand these forces that create treasure vaults for you to find.

On your next visit to a beach where surf is especially violent, pay attention! When a wave comes in and breaks near the beach, notice that water has a brown appearance caused by suspended sand. When this wave crashes and water rushes up on the beach, it transports sand and mixes it with other loosened beach sand. If the waves break parallel to the beach front, most of this deposited sand is then washed back into the ocean by the receding water. It remains in suspension in the surf or is deposited near where it came from.

Close observation, however, will reveal that most waves do not come directly in, but rather at an angle that sets up a current. The sand carried by the wave comes in at the same angle of transport, causing the sand to move farther to the left or right of its origination point. Some of the displaced sand remains on the beach and some is washed back into the water at its new location. The result of this action is that sand is transported in the general direction that waves are moving. Understanding this phenomenon is important because this same transport system (via storms and high wind) causes a redistribution of treasure from the point where it was originally lost.

The ability of water to move heavier-than-sand material depends upon its speed. Large waves and fast-moving currents can carry sand, coins, and rings along a

This barefoot THer searching the beautiful white sands of a Florida Panhandle beach is prepared to follow the signals of his Beach Hunter AT4 out into the shallow surf.

continuous path. When wave action slows down, movement slows down or stops. When wave action picks up, movement resumes. Growing shores (perhaps those severely eroded by prior storm action) are "nourished" by material that has been washed away from a nearby stretch of beach. Heavy treasure takes the path of least resistance, being pushed up along the lowest points of cuts and other eroded areas.

As coins, rings and other jewelry are brought into these new beach areas, they become fill along with new sand. Being heavier, they gradually sink to lower levels and become covered. When that eroded beach has become fully "nourished," this buildup essentially stops, leaving your treasure *buried and waiting for you.*

Perhaps you doubt that erosion and resulting treasure redistribution really take place. After all, during your many summer trips to the beach, everything looks serene and you have never seen coins and rings being washed around. Actually, it is usually during fall, winter and spring that weather patterns produce major face-lifting on beaches. Strong winds and high tides do most of the redistributing. Violent storms cause considerable damage. The classic northeasters that sweep up the East Coast not only churn up beaches, but often cause millions of dollars of damage to property. Violent storms cause people to move inland as heavy snow, high wind and beach-grinding tides do their damage. High tides often flood beachfront communities with 10, 15 and sometimes 20 feet of water. Since normal high tides are only three to four feet, you can imagine the erosion forces that are set in motion. As much as 90 percent of the sand on a beach can be washed away during a violent storm. During this

Discovery of this 16th Century Spanish religious icon by the author in the surf of Massacre Beach on the island of Guadeloupe is described on the following pages.

151

erosion process, considerable redistribution of treasure takes place. Unfortunately, some treasure is washed out into the surf areas, but it still may be found by surf hunters.

Since shorelines and beaches are continually being reshaped, you must be observant. One key to success is establishing permanent tide and sand markers. Your marker can be a piling or any structure you can readily observe at any time. Ideally, your water marker will be somewhat submerged during both high and low tides. By keeping your eyes on this water marker, you can determine water height at all times and know if the water is rising or falling.

Your sand marker is important because it is a gauge of sand height. The more of your sand marker that is exposed, the greater your chances of detecting treasure that lies out of reach during those times where sand is being piled up by the winds and waves.

There are high and low sand formations. High formations do you no good except to serve as height gauges when storm and wind activity erode cliffs. Imaginative beachcombers keep their eyes peeled for cliffs that begin to erode. You are interested in their lowest levels where you will find coins and rings as they become uncovered by the action of winds and waves. Eroding cliffs may reveal decades-old settlements and accumulations of treasure and debris. In your research, be alert for references to old settlements or ghost towns. What has been covered for many generations may be uncovered before your eyes today.

Locating the Best Places

When you walk out onto the beach, where do you begin? How do you select the most productive areas? This is possibly the question that I am asked most frequently by beginning beach hunters. Let experience be your teacher. You can pick up ideas from experienced beachcombers, but the final decisions must be based on your experience and your intuition. Experience will teach you of places that never produce and other places that are often rewarding. A knowledge of storm, wind and wave action will often come to your rescue as you study a new beach. I'll tell you of an experience where visual and mental study led me almost directly to an *X-marks-the-spot* location.

I was with a group of treasure hunters on a Caribbean Island. Submerged at the entrance to a cove were numerous old and very large anchors protruding a few feet out of the water. We learned that these anchors had been placed there centuries before to prevent enemy ships from coming into the cove, then serving as harbor for a settlement. This historically active location interested me. One could just imagine enemy ships sailing in with cannons blasting and shore batteries returning the fire. Were ships ever sunk in the harbor?

A short distance away was an area called Massacre Beach. This name stirred my imagination with a scene of brutality so violent that this site should forever be remembered as a place of ruthless killing. What treasure hunter could resist standing on such a beach, visualizing the artifacts that must surely lie beneath its sands? As I studied the beach, I noticed an outcropping of coral protruding a few inches from the water and ending abruptly where beach met the sea. I thought that if there had been a slaughter there, relics might still be trapped by coral that prevented high water from washing it back into the sea.

Also, I thought of sunken ships in the offshore water and of storms that hurled objects from their wrecks onto the beach. I walked over to the edge of the coral and turned on my detector. After only a few scans, my detector sang out with a loud, unmistakable *sound of money!*

At a depth of about one foot I dug into a shelf of solid coral that had become smooth from centuries of water and sand abrasion. When I moved my hand around over the coral and failed to locate a target, I reasoned that it must lie underneath the shelf. I scanned again and heard my

Master Hunter 7 frantically signaling the presence of an object that *sounded* both large and valuable.

Again, I drug my fingers around in the hole and my fingernails caught on something that moved. I grasped the object and lifted it out of the water. It appeared at first to be just a chip of coral. Looking again as I wiped away the sand, I saw that it was a man-made item either carved or cast of metal.

The "item" proved to be a Spanish icon made of pewter. The Virgin Mary was holding the Christ Child in her arms; halo rays adorned the heads. As companions surrounded me to examine my find, I forgot to recheck the hole in my excitement. The next day, another of the group was scanning the area and he found, in the same hole, a Spanish cob dated 1692. This date, plus features of the icon, date the religious relic to a few years prior to 1700.

My study of the area obviously worked in my favor. The name Massacre Beach prompted me to pay particular attention to the site. My knowledge of wind and wave action led me to the imaginary "X."

Beaches protected from winds that cause large waves are more popular than unprotected beaches. For instance, beaches on the west coast of the United States that face south are more protected from wind and heavy surf than beaches facing west and north. Popular beaches are usually wide with fine, clean sand and feature a gradual slope into the water. Many such identifiable sections of "lost" beaches should be hunted. Not all are connected to the mainland. Some are separated by lagoons and marshlands. Some have been converted into bird and wildlife sanctuaries.

Around populated areas many natural beaches have been changed or have eroded as a result of land development. Breakwaters, harbor extensions, jetties and the results of damming or otherwise diverting streams and rivers have destroyed once-popular play area. Search out these long-lost treasure vaults and reap a harvest.

Learn from my success at finding the icon. "Reading" a site requires recognition of key features and the forces that act upon them. Going pell-mell out onto a beach and hunting first here and there is for beginners. You've already begun this fascinating hobby, so slow down now and do it right.

There is a right and wrong way and I hope you'll choose the correct one. As I have said so many times before...*start right and be successful!*

You must begin by being at the right place at the right time. I have given explicit instructions directing you to research sources that will indicate productive sites. Discussions of tides, weather, and beach selection should put you there at the right time. Now, you must develop the skill needed to "read" the site. If you learn which features are important and why, much of the battle is won.

Study beaches carefully to look for "treasure traps," such as the posts and rocks shown here. Note also the long trough at the right and the waterway that connects it back to the ocean.

155

Sharpening your skills and powers of observation are a necessary part of your training. To obtain an idea of what can be accomplished, I suggest you read one or more of my friend Tom Brown's fascinating books relating his training and experiences under the tutelage of an Apache Indian. You'll be amazed at Tom's powers of observation. His ability to see things that others don't will astound you. While his books are not about treasure hunting, per se, they will open your eyes and make you a better treasure hunter. See the *Appendix* for a partial listing of Tom Brown's books.

Some of the following material is discussed elsewhere in this book. For convenience, however, let's draw upon the data one more time. The key to success is learning where treasure traps are located, then searching for them with your metal detector when covering sands are lowest. Certain features demand your attention, such as cuts, exposed shell, rock and gravel, exposed troughs, depressions, shallow pools, accumulations of jetsam, debris and drift wood, gullies, sandbank cuts, exposed clay, bedrock and coral areas and other irregularities in the beach sands. Since nature is trying to help, you will do well to accept the help.

The obvious "other" places to search for beach treasure are man-made spots. Walk out on a beach and observe people at play. Watch children of all ages as they frolic. Then, when they tire of that activity, watch them scoot away. Coins fall from their pockets as they play games in the sand.

Adults have their toys and games too, but they are sometimes more subtle--such as blankets and beach chairs. When people relax, down go coins and other items into the sand. Adults play volleyball, throw frisbees and horse around. When they do, rings slip off fingers, chain and necklace clasps break and jewelry falls into the sand.

Search around trails, walkways and boardwalks. Never pass up an opportunity to scan the base of seawalls and stone fences. People without lounge chairs often camp by these structures where they can lean back. Never fail to search around and under picnic tables and benches. Sure, you'll find lots of bottlecaps and pulltabs, but you will also discover lots of coins, toys and useful utensils. Search around food stands, bath houses, shower stalls, dressing sheds, water fountains and under piers and stairs. Posts and other such obstacles are good traps where treasure can often be found.

Grid Searching

When searching a large section of beach, you should clearly define your area of search and systematically scan every square inch. There are many grid methods to use, some simple, some elaborate. The simplest, perhaps, is to guide on your previous tracks as you double back and forth. This method works if others don't destroy your tracks as fast as you make them.

Using a stick or other object you can draw squares in the sand. Work the first square completely and then draw an adjoining square and work it. Again, like the footstep method, this works if your lines and tracks don't disappear too quickly. You can drive stakes into the ground, or just guide yourself on piers, water fountains, trees and other permanent objects.

Some hunters prefer to walk a path parallel to the water. They then turn around, move about two feet away from the water and walk a return path. Others prefer to start at the high tide mark and scan down to the water. They then turn around and walk a return path about two feet to the side of the first path. This second method has more merit because you can more quickly spot a treasure belt (trough) if one exists.

You'll remember that troughs sometimes form parallel to the waterline. There can be more than one trough and they come in all sizes, often as long as a hundred yards. These troughs are "cut" areas that bring you closer to clay, gravel or bedrock where coins and jewelry accumulate.

157

What happens to these troughs when the tide goes out? They almost always fill with sand. You can sometimes find them if the treasure they contain is not too deep. Walk a scan pattern perpendicular to the waterline. Walk from the high tide mark to the water's edge. Each time you make a find, either remember where the find was made, or mark the location.

After you have scanned some distance down the beach and made several good finds, look back and study where you have worked. Observe the locations of your finds to determine if some pattern is developing. Most may have occurred in a narrow belt running parallel to the waterline. If so, you may have discovered the location of a covered trough where a storm or other wave action has created a treasure vault.

When selecting a stretch of beach on which to walk your grid pattern, try to choose one where you earlier observed a cut formed perpendicular to the waterline. Storms or high waves pouring back into the ocean form these cuts, usually at existing low points such as one formed during a previous storm. Cuts are important to you because they bring you closer to the treasure base and because coins and jewelry washing off the beach are pushed into them by the force of water drainage streams.

After reading the various searching patterns, can you see value in keeping precise logs of your treasure finds? Even with others working the same beach, it is likely that valuable patterns will emerge on the pages of your notebook. These patterns can actually show you where to look to find "hot spots." You may think that with others and yourself steadily working a particular beach, all its treasure will soon be recovered. What's the use in keeping track? You'll learn, if you continue to work the same beaches year after year that they are being replenished regularly by "new" treasure lost almost every day and by "old" lost treasure that periodic storms withdraw from deeply hidden storage vaults.

Scanning Tips

The *eyes* of a metal detector probe deeply to locate treasure buried in the sand. Your detector scans over the ground untiringly to alert you to the presence of metal beneath it. Without a detector your "take" would be considerably reduced. Even so, no metal detector can do it all. You must develop your powers of observation to be alert to what your detector cannot see.

Always watch for clues and for the unusual. Occasionally you'll visually find currency, marketable sea shells and other valuables. But the real value in developing keen powers of observation is that you never miss the signposts that point to detectable buried treasure. The rock outcropping, the gravel that is peeking through the sand, the slight depression or mound and the revealing accumulation of jetsam and debris might mark the location of a glory hole. Remain always alert and be rewarded!

Do not race across the sands with your searchcoil swinging wildly in front of you. *Slow down* and work methodically in a controlled, preplanned pattern. Unless

This handsome and quite expensive twin-diamond-cluster ring found with a metal detector on a Florida beach is just one example of the treasures that await the serious student of beach hunting.

you are in a hurry and want to locate only shallow, recently lost treasure, reduce your scan speed to about one foot per second. Let your searchcoil just skim the sands and keep it level throughout your entire sweep length. Overlap each sweep by advancing your searchcoil about one-half its diameter. Scan the searchcoil in a straight line. This method improves your ability to maintain correct and uniform searchcoil height, helps eliminate the "upswing" at the end of each sweep, and improves your ability to overlap in a uniform manner, thus minimizing skips. Practice this method; you'll soon come to love it.

A word is in order here about "hot rocks." If gravel is on your beach, some pieces may have the mineral content to be classified as a detectable "hot rock." A VLF detector may occasionally get a good reading on rocks and will sound off with a "metal" signal. When you detect the little pests, switch into Discriminate mode and set your discrimination controls to "zero." Then scan back over the spot. If it is a "hot rock," your detector will ignore it, or the sound level will decrease slightly. For more on this phenomenon, study my book, *Modern Metal Detectors.*

Don't ignore loud detector signals. Determine the cause. If it is a can or other large object, remove it and scan the spot with your detector. If you hear a *very faint* signal, don't ignore it. Scoop out some sand to get your searchcoil closer to the suspected target and scan again. If you don't get a signal, check the material you scooped out--you may have detected a very small target. It might only be a BB, but at least you'll know what caused the signal. Remember, your metal detector won't lie to you. When it gives a signal, something is there!

If you search for 30 minutes in one location and do not locate "keepers," move to another spot. Don't become discouraged; go find treasure somewhere else.

During your search near the water's edge, when you begin detecting trash (pulltabs?) in a straight line parallel to the water line, search for another nearby parallel trough. Remember there will sometimes be more than one trough created by wave action. The one closest to the beach may contain mostly light trash. Those farther out can contain heavier treasure items. To locate the second one, start from the trashy trough and walk out as far as you can safely go. Move over about two feet and walk back to the trash trough. Continue walking this grid and if there is a second trough within your grid, you'll find it. As explained earlier, you find it by keeping track of the location of "found" objects. A straight line pattern will develop.

When pinpointing, always be precise. Good pinpointing saves time and lessens the probability of damaging your finds when you dig.

Trash and Treasure

Marine debris has come of age. A committee for Texas Coastal Cleanup believes that plastic trash may be Texas' "Public Enemy No. 1." Fish and sea birds become entangled in plastic six-pack rings; sea turtles mistake floating plastic bags for jelly-fish and swallow them; sea birds peck at plastic pellets and feed them to their young. And, of course, hundreds of other items of trash are discarded on the nation's beaches every day. What can a concerned beachcomber do about it?

Most hobbyists carry out the metal trash they dig because all treasure hunters benefit from its removal. But, what about non-metallic trash? I know none of us carry trash containers around that are large enough to hold the plastic objects and pieces of broken glass that we find in only a few hours. But, let's join in by properly disposing of as much trash as possible. We not only do all beachcombers and sunworshippers a service, but we help safeguard our sea creatures and bird life as well. How about it...can't we join together and help one another?

Additional Thoughts

Various pinpointing and retrieving ideas and methods

have been reviewed. Here are a couple of other suggestions that could increase your take. As part of your beach gear, consider adding a garden rake. When you encounter debris, seaweed and other materials spread over an area you want to scan, use this rake to clean it out down to the sand. Try to place the raked materials where they can be picked up by beach cleaners and not washed back into the ocean. Removal of any overburden will let you scan your searchcoil closer to the ground, giving you extra depth for those deeply buried treasures.

Try exploratory trenching to locate out-of-reach troughs and glory holes. Choose a spot where you have found a concentration of good objects (not items flung from a blanket) and dig, if it's not illegal, a trench about a foot deep. This trench should be wide enough for you to insert your searchcoil in its normal scanning position. Be sure to scan the sand you dig out. The trench length can be as long as you like. If you are digging near a spot where you found several items together, determine whether you are in a natural drainage pattern. If so, dig toward the low side (in the direction water flows) because that is the direction coins and jewelry have been washed. If you are digging a trench to try to locate a trough, dig in a direction that takes you perpendicular to the "line" along which you were previously digging targets. You may have to dig several parallel trenches to locate the trough. Good luck! And...*fill your trenches.!*

Personal Tips

Plan your beachcombing expeditions around current (to the hour) weather reports. Go prepared to withstand the worst.

Don't forget spare batteries. Make a list and review it the day *before* you plan to make the trip. Check all gear *before* you leave home.

Take along a friend, if possible. If you go alone, leave word where you plan to be. Always carry identification that includes one or more telephone numbers of persons to call, including your personal physician. And, don't forget to tuck in a quarter for the pay phone!

Use caution and don't drive on beaches with deep sand. Carry along an extra tow rope and a shovel. You may have to dig some "exit ramps" in the sand to rescue your car if a tow vehicle isn't handy.

Search among crowds if there are no regulations to the contrary, but stay out of people's way. Making the wrong person mad can result in a complaint filed against you. I'm sure you would not want to be the cause of having a beach put off limits to metal detector users.

As I have emphasized, pick up and properly discard all broken glass and bottles.

Do your best to return all valuable finds to their rightful owner. When someone asks you to help locate a lost item, try to oblige. Perhaps you can loan them your detector and

Proving that beach treasure is where and *what* you discover are these coins found in a cluster, with the holes indicating they were once held together by leather or string which rotted away.

teach them just how to use it. You may bring another individual into the hunting fraternity! It's always a good idea to have them stay right with you during the entire search. If they leave, the person might decide you found their lost item and accuse you of stealing it. That has happened. If you don't find the lost article, get the person's name and telephone number--you might find it another day.

Use caution when you handle rings with stones. Often, mountings corrode during exposure. You wouldn't want to lose a two-carat diamond, would you? Examine jewelry with a pocket magnifier. If a stone is loose or the mounting has corroded, keep that ring in a container or at least wrap it to prevent the stone (or stones) from being lost.

We have mentioned your powers of observation. Occasionally scan or just walk along the waterline and observe the sands under the water. You may spot a coin shining in the water. Check the spot with your detector. It may only be a freshly dropped coin, or it could be the top layer of a glory hole.

Learn what stinging jellyfish look like. During high water they often wash ashore and become stranded. Their tentacles can sting long after the creature dies. Bury them if you can.

Specialized Hunting

Be ever on the alert for "sea stories" and legends. Don't dismiss rumors of discoveries...some of them may be true! A major concern when you get active in such specialized areas as legend-tracking is to locate the precise spot where rumors report a particular treasure was last seen. Even if you are certain you know the exact name and location of a beach, remember that they can stretch for miles. They can become severely eroded and they can become covered with mountains of sand brought in from the nearby surf. Spend time investigating these stories. Check with the newspapers, police records, historical societies and local coin shops. Uncover sufficient information to *prove* beyond doubt that the facts you have are correct. Then, you can pursue that tale knowing you are not searching for something that does not exist. And, when you believe you have discovered the location of an unusual treasure, don't put off investigating further. You may be on the trail of your own rich treasure ship!

The Amazing Money Machine

Warren Merkitch named his dry sifter the Amazing Money Machine. Many years ago he perfected a man-powered sifter for beach sands and wrote a book describing the need for such a device, including detailed construction plans. The late treasure hunter, Karl Von Mueller, who owned Exanimo Press, Segundo, CO 81070, printed Warren's book, which is entitled *The Beach-comber's Handbook*. The book, which you can obtain by sending five dollars ($5) to the above address is interesting and well-written, authored by a man who knows what he

These watches and various other lovely objects were recovered by a friend of the author, Alden Fogliadini, who is a steadfast searcher of beach and surf areas in Northern California.

165

is talking about.One reading will reward you with many, many beach hunting tips, any one of which is well worth the low cost. The construction plans and operating instructions alone should sell for much more. The device is a sort of reverse lawnmower sifter that lets you "clean" a wide strip of sand and recover all metal and non-metal objects down to several inches depth. You pull the device through the sand. The rear section rolls on wheels while a front-mounted blade cuts through the sand. A built-in wire sifter lets sand and small objects pass on through, but traps larger objects.

The device can be used effectively on dry sandy beaches and in the surf where the bottom is loose sand. It finds lost treasure and collects shells and even edibles. I saw one being used in an Italian surf to locate edible mollusks. I didn't ask the fellow if he also found treasure, but I am sure he did. In fact, I suspect mollusk hunting was only a sideline.

The joys of beach and surf hunting are truly beyond compare, whether on a beautiful sun-kissed Yucatan shore or in the cold, wintry waters of a lonely Texas surf.

The Surf

There is a place...a treasure hunting place...an "all-weather vault"...where the treasure hunter can do his or her best any day...spring, summer, winter or fall. For the knowledgeable hunter, this place consistently produces the best treasures.

I am speaking, of course, of the surf--one of the "hottest" and newest treasure hunting locations. What exactly is surf hunting? Where does *beach* hunting end and *surf* hunting begin?

Visualize, if you will, the seashore divided into three sections or *zones*. Zone One is the actual sandy beach--the picnic, sunbathing and rollicking area between the parking lot and water. Zone Three is the deep water expanse stretching out as far as the eye can see--strictly scuba-diving territory.

Zone Two, our area of interest, our *treasure vault*--the area between Zones One and Three--is the shallow surf, from the foamy edge of the water to a depth of five feet or more. That's where treasure is kept--coins, jewelry, diamond rings, gold chains, gold and silver religious medallions and crucifixes. And, most amazing of all, access to this vault is free--free to you and free to me. Here's where you should stake your claim. I've staked mine there.

Successful THers who have staked such a claim don't even converse like ordinary coin hunters. When greeting

Treasures in the surf, plentiful and diverse enough to challenge any THer, include this handful of rings, all found in or near the water of beach areas along the Texas coast.

a friend, they don't say, "Hey, I found ten silver coins today!" Instead, they say, "Hey, today's take was ten gold rings!" They don't discuss their treasure in terms of silver ounces; they calculate it in pounds of gold. They keep their finds sorted in large containers. Experienced treasure hunters know that surf hunting offers rich rewards. There are millions of coins and items of jewelry "stored" in the surf's treasure vault. Where people have been, that's where you'll find this treasure; it can't be any easier than that. Try this test. Visit a local park on any warm, pleasant spring or summer day. Count the people you see. How many did you count? Maybe 50? Now, drive to the local swimming beach. Count the people you see. How many did you count? Certainly 50, plus several hundred more! Hundreds more who may lose valuable treasure.

Walk the beach and count the rings, necklaces, bracelets, ankle charms and other valuables you see the bathers wearing. How many are using tanning oil that makes fingers so slick that rings threaten to fall off momentarily? How many young people are horse playing or tossing a frisbee? Their rings and necklaces are likely to be jerked loose any moment. How many swimmers carry their "hot dog" coins in their anything-but-safe bathing suit pockets?

You can be sure treasure will be lost at that beach every day. And, I don't mean "cheap" treasure either. People consistently wear expensive jewelry while swimming. They either forget they have it on, or they don't understand how they could lose it. But, lose it they will--by the buckets and barrels full.

That's one of the truly neat things about surfing: the supply of coins and jewelry is constantly being replenished. If you could somehow locate every lost item in any given surf (which, of course, you can't), next year the treasure vault would be "filled" again. Actually, you won't have to wait a year. Wait until the day following a storm and then try your luck. You'll be amazed how much you'll find that nature has brought up from the depths and deposited in your private treasure vault.

How much surf treasure is there to be found? More importantly, how much can *you* find?

In Chapter 3 you met a number of surf hunters who keep finding enough to come back for more. You met those who have given up all other forms of treasure hunting to devote their full time to surfing. They have proved that the treasure is there. How much you find is up to you. Learn to use your equipment; do your research and be persistent; you won't be disappointed.

Perhaps you have read the two *Walk Across America* books by Peter and Barbara Jenkins. Their adventures were fascinating, weren't they? Well, I received a call from a detectorist who was setting forth on what I believe was to be an equally fascinating but different sort of adventure. He was planning to walk across America and pay his way by surf and beach hunting at every location he came to. You know what? I believe he'll make it and he won't go hungry. He will find more treasure than he'll need.

In addition to the monetary aspects, other rewards come from this activity. You can't help but be healthier at

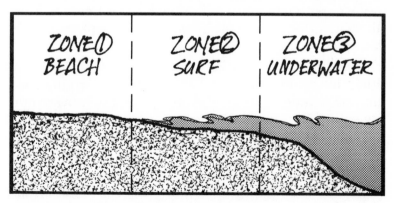

Drawing illustrates arbitrary separation of the seashore into three sections or "zones" where treasure can be found: Zone 1 is sandy beach; Zone 2, shallow surf; Zone 3, scuba-diving territory.

171

the end of a long and vigorous surf-hunting season. I always feel terrific following even a single day in the surf. I have spent weeks searching several Caribbean swimming beach surfs. Following a day's hunting of six to eight hours, all I need to be refreshed and ready for the next day is a hot shower, a great meal and a good night's sleep. You don't fatigue as much when you work surf as compared with working land sites. Especially is this true during hot, 100-degree summer days, provided you take care of yourself. In this and other chapters you'll learn my secrets of getting along with whatever climate is present.

The surf holds *much less competition* than you'll find on land. The ratio of water hunters to land hunters is easily 100 to 1. It's nice when there is little competition. Of course, water hunting requires a few more skills, and there are dangers you won't find on land--such as stinging jellyfish. But, about the only way you'll ever get tangled up with one of those fellows is to work with your eyes closed. There are other dangers and I have discussed them in Chapter 26 which concerns personal safety.

You'll have to learn how to retrieve your finds in three feet of water using a long-handled scoop. At first, you'll feel foolish, especially when you'll make, perhaps, ten tries before you finally come up with your first treasure from the water. But, believe me, finding lots more of them soon becomes easier!

You'll have good days, then bad days when you won't find enough to brag about. Maintain your enthusiasm anyway. Everyone has bad days; so don't sulk over your "poor luck," but, instead, turn your defeat into constructive planning. Make up your mind that you'll do a better job of research the next time you are looking for that really special beach. Stop and review your situation: analyze your site, your timing, and your search methods. And, don't forget, bad days make the good days seem even better!

Well, are you ready to give water hunting a try? If you are tired of those dull everyday park finds, try going after gold in the surf!

Research

The most important advice I can give you may very well be *don't neglect your research!* The one thing, the major thing, that separates successful treasure hunters from mediocre treasure hunters is research. Research is the key to locating the "hot" productive sites that really pay off in old and valuable coins and jewelry. Did you know that through research you can locate beaches most likely to yield high school and college class rings? Through research you can locate the beaches with mostly inexpensive jewelry and other beaches with the most expensive jewelry. Some beaches, you can learn, will contain a predominance of silver medallions and crucifixes. Other beaches will contain mostly gold religious pieces. All this data is available to the diligent researcher who takes time to learn.

Did you know that some treasure hunters plan where they will be hunting one, two or even five years in the future? They know where they are going next, and they allow plenty of time while there. Should their present site prove unproductive, they have alternate sites nearby. They keep meticulous records concerning site location, time of year, water conditions and the quantity, quality and location of their valuable finds. They live with their log as though it were a *Bible.* They correlate one site's data with that of another and plan their trips accordingly. They return to some sites regularly and to some only once a year.

The smart researchers make it their business to know which beaches high school and college students visit and when. They know when young people go there, not only during regular swimming and sunbathing times, but also during their special parties. They know that rich folks and the not-so-rich folks have their own preferred beaches. In areas predominantly Catholic, knowledgeable hunters know they will find religious jewelry. From ethnic studies, they know which beaches will produce mostly silver pieces and which sites the more valuable gold pieces. From their studies, they know where the old, the really old, beaches are. That's where they go in search of the valuable antique jewelry often worth the most when "sell" time comes.

I suggest you reread Chapter 4, especially the sections on Research Sources where I list sources of information and describe the *where* of seeking them out, such as the newspapers, libraries, historical societies, the Department of Parks and Recreation and others. During your research of these sources, you should specifically study the newspaper's recreational and lost and found advertisements. At historical societies you'll review area histories, photographs and postcards. At the Parks and Recreation Department, you'll ask for both new and old maps that locate long forgotten communities and public gathering places.

As for *who* to ask, start with fishermen, oldtimers and even *new*timers, the youngsters who may frequent the old out-of-the-way and often forbidden sites. And, speaking of newtimers, why not start with yourself? Ask yourself where *you* swam when you were young. I can remember five such places where my pals and I swam back during our growing-up days. One place is now an off-limits State Park; another is covered by asphalt; the third place is on restricted private property; the fourth, I've worked and the fifth, well...I am thinking about it. I've done some research. In fact, just today, I was told it is still being used. Not only that, but I learned from the same source the site of a turn-of- the-century community with the location of the general store pinpointed. Maybe, just maybe, I can keep myself at this typewriter long enough to complete this chapter before I head south, down into Deep East Texas.

Clothing and Equipment

Chapter 25 describes the various kinds of clothing and gear needed for the various weather and wading conditions you'll encounter. As your experience grows, you will accumulate your own preferred wardrobe. In cold weather, your clothing and gear should keep you warm, dry and comfortable. One exception is that while a neoprene wet suit won't keep you dry, it will keep you warm, very warm. If you don't care for the initial plunge into cold water, first pour warm water into the suit.

The type equipment you need depends upon whether you work shallow surf or deep-water surf. Shallow surf is defined as water depth that permits you to dig with your hands, a hand scoop, or a tool...in other words, at arm's length. Deep water surfing is hunting in deeper depths from arm's length to about five feet, or the maximum depth you can safely work.

The choice of retrieving tools depends upon soil conditions and your preferences. In sandy areas, a scoop is fast. If the soil is muddy or hardened clay, you will need some kind of digger. In deep water, a long-handled scoop is required to retrieve your finds. During moderately cold water, you'll probably want to search in hip or chest-high waders with suitable underclothing to keep you warm and dry. When wearing waders be alert or else you may bend too far and, suddenly, you've got "convertible" gear: Your waders have been converted to a wet suit! Wearing a waist or chest belt over waders might reduce the amount of water that comes in.

Whatever type pouch (or pouches) you use, they must close and fasten tightly. Water hunting treasure pouches must have a secure flap covering. Some surfers use a sturdy open-weave bag or pouch with zipper or drawstring. Whatever equipment your ingenuity comes up with, keep it in good shape. Don't lose valuables through holes! It's a good idea to have several pockets that let you separate treasure and trash. But, whatever you do, never discard trash without carefully examining every piece. You may have inadvertently placed a good find into the trash pocket. Also, that item that looked so corroded and unrecog-

175

nizable may turn out to be a valuable object. When in doubt about any find, examine it thoroughly, even placing it in an electrolytic bath for cleaning.

In warm weather your clothing should keep you decent yet protected from the sun's rays and other dangers such as sharp rocks, coral and stinging jellyfish. In shallow water you can stand and work or snorkel as you float. In deeper water you'll need a long-handled scoop unless you prefer scuba gear or a floating compressor hooka like Brownie's Third Lung. In strong breaker areas a floating hooka compressor is tricky to use. It's best used in a lake or other calm water areas.

You might try free diving. Others have, and prefer it. Surfers have learned to hold their breath for as long as three minutes. They swim along under water, scanning with their detector and retrieving objects with their hands or a small tool. When they need air, they pop up, take a breath and go back down to continue hunting. It sounds efficient, but requires experience to learn to fully conserve energy and get the most out of each breath. This method has some risk, however, and I do not recommend it.

The following are two amusing incidents related to me by a fellow surfer who prefers to free dive when the conditions are right. Once, when he popped to the surface for air, he emerged in the midst of several youngsters. One frightened youth managed to stammer, "Wh..wh..what are you doing here?" My friend used his best and coarsest monster-of-the-deep voice to answer, "This is my home; what are *you* doing here?" Then he quickly submerged and swam away. Needless to say, he had the surf mostly to himself the remainder of that day.

Once when he was searching the bottom someone stepped on him and quickly jumped back, then cautiously nudged the motionless body with his foot. Suddenly, there was a wild commotion; people began scrambling toward shore. He again had things to himself until a rescue squad came and began dragging for the "body."

Free diving is not for the fainthearted. It requires deep concentration, a will of iron and good swimming ability. Some say there is the likelihood of blacking out. Free divers do not venture beyond neck depth, but there is the possibility of straying into deep water. A good swimmer would have no difficulty, but in case of an emergency, it could become a problem. Free divers usually wear swim fins and goggles or a mask. Some use a snorkel.

Some surfers use a flotation screen; others do not. If you use a converted land metal detector, you'll need a flotation device unless you mount the detector control housing on your body, or on the end of a very long searchcoil stem. The flotation device, of which there are several designs, is constructed with a one-half inch sturdy chicken wire screen. The screen opening should not allow a U.S. dime to pass through diagonally. If you are searching for smaller objects, the screen opening should be smaller. If your flotation device is large or contains your

A surf hunter sent this photo to the Garrett factory labeled simply, "Collection of coins, rings and jewelry found by one detector addict in one summer along the shorelines of Delaware!"

detector's control housing, the screen portion should be hinged to permit rapid dumping of accumulated trash. The float can have recesses for the detector, a water bottle, your lunch and, perhaps, an extra tool or other necessity. Select a tube from the various automobile, motorcycles or bicycle sizes available. Since you are not supporting much weight, the tube does not have to be highway bus or truck size. You should position the screen so that its bottom surface is about one or two inches below the water line. This facilitates quick washing of debris, mud and sand. In fact, when you dump several scoops into a well designed flotation device, surf action should quickly clean the material.

Some hunters have said they prefer to place several scoops of dug material into their screen before they examine its contents and retrieve their finds. This can be efficient if you're using a zippered bag which takes extra time to open and close each time you store a find. If the bottom is heavy silt and mud, it might be quicker to dissolve and inspect a large amount of soil rather than stir through your retrieving scoop each time you make a dig.

An innertube can be punctured accidentally. This is a problem only if your detector housing is mounted on the float. Even then, I think you would hear the air escaping and you could rescue the detector before it gets a bath. Also, the detector has no protection from rain or water splashed by swimmers.

When I work loose sandy bottom sites, I do not use a floating screen. As I start up with the scoop filled with sand and other bottom objects, I immediately begin shaking the scoop. By the time I have it up to the water's surface, most, if not all, the sand has already fallen through the holes.

I don't recommend a land detector for working in deep water. In fact, I can't honestly recommend using a land detector for *any* kind of extended water hunting. It just too easy to become lax and forget momentarily that your detector needs constant supervision. It happened to me once when I was working the water's edge on a white sand beach in Cozumel. Because it was dry where I was working, I wasn't paying strict attention to the wave action. I stopped scanning to dig an object and without noticing, I placed the detector down on the sand too near the water. A higher than usual wave gave my control housing a good bath. That ended all searching for the day with that detector.

You must tether a float to yourself or you'll lose it. According to Garrett's (infallible) Law, the first time you turn your back on an untethered float, it will float straight out to sea. I consider having to manipulate a detector and a long-handled scoop problem enough. Plus, it is not practical to use a float in surf areas when the waves are high. It will be constantly banging into you. And, it will never be where you want it when you need it.

In using a large open-basket screen, you invite thievery. Some individuals are naturally tempted when they see valuables laying in an open screen. A friend, Carl Ratigan, and I were working a Guadeloupe surf while several boys watched. Carl brought up a scoop that contained what he described as "the most beautiful and valuable gold medallion of the week!" A boy reached into the scoop, grabbed the medallion and swam away.

Some have suggested constructing floats completely of non-metallic materials. They say that if you want to make sure no mud balls and other encrustation conceals treasure, you can scan the contents with your detector. While that idea has some merit, it is not the most efficient method. You should hand investigate and closely scan every strange item you discover. And, as I have said, take every "unknown" object home for closer scrutiny.

Your scoop and all other retrieving tools should be ruggedly constructed. You will be putting a lot of force on your scoop each time you make a dig. A plastic scoop may not stand up under the strain. The upper end of the handle should have a screw, lanyard, paint stripe or other marker to tell you at a glance where the scoop opening is located. A looped handle, which is the configuration I prefer, should be curved backward so that you don't have to lean too far forward to tilt the scoop into the required vertical position for proper digging. When you push the handle forward to position the scoop vertically, your hand will be about midway or lower down the handle. Then, you begin your backward pull while sliding your hand upward. You'll also rotate the handle to free the scoop from the muck. As you bring the handle backwards, you'll slide your hand over to the front section and grasp the handle as low down as possible. You then pull the scoop free of the bottom. The low position of your hand on the forward mounted handle section keeps the open end of the scoop in the upward position. Shake the scoop as you bring it up to remove sand and small debris.

Alden Fogliadini is a very successful water hunter. I have worked with him in the Caribbean and witnessed his phenomenal surf finds. A scoop which he manufactures and sells resulted from careful thought and much water retrieving experience. Stainless steel construction allows it to be disassembled easily for packing and transportation. Also, it has three different handle lengths. The midsize handle lets you use it effectively without bending over when you work on the beach or in shallow water. The shortest handle converts it into a lightweight and sturdy hand scoop for shallow water and dry sand sifting. Next to your metal detector, the scoop is your most important tool. Select and use a well-designed, sturdy one for the highest efficiency. Alden's address and photos of his scoop can be found in Chapter 22.

Selecting a Surfing Detector

Chapters 6, 7 and 8 contain discussions about every aspect involved in the selection of the proper metal detector. As mentioned several times, a land detector can be used for surf hunting, but extra length searchcoil cables are usually necessary. Some manufacturers offer submersible searchcoils with nine-foot-long cables. Extension cables are available, but some means are needed to waterproof the connector. Discussed in Chapter 22, the Beach Connection device will keep water out of cable connectors.

When you use a land detector in the surf, you must prevent the control housing from getting wet. Ingenious hunters have devised various effective waterproofing methods. One built a shoulder platform that keeps his detector not only high and dry, but also places the speaker near his ear should he not want to use headphones. Another hunter installed his electronics and controls in a construction worker's hat. I have seen photos of this device and it appears quite functional.

If you doubt whether your searchcoil is waterproof, ask your metal detector dealer or manufacturer. Not all searchcoils can be safely submerged. There are three designations you should become familiar with: splashproof, waterproof and submersible. Splashproof means the searchcoil can safely be used in wet grass and weeds. Waterproof means the searchcoil can safely be used in heavy rain. Submersible means the searchcoil can be safely submerged in water to the cable connector. In terms of depth, submersion is about 30 inches. To insure a searchcoil's water tightness, apply a bead of silicone rubber around the cable where it comes out of the searchcoil.

Most land searchcoils are buoyant. You must add weight to give the searchcoil either neutral or slightly negative buoyancy. A sandbag or a brick can be attached to the top of your searchcoil and some hunters pour specially shaped weights using cement. Others attach lead weights to the stem. To keep from adding extra drag, lead can be poured into the lower stem. Keep lead or other metals at least eight inches above the searchcoil. A weight of from about one to three pounds is usually necessary. I

181

prefer that my detector float somewhat vertically so that the searchcoil "bobbles" near the bottom. This keeps the handle nearby. When I have recovered my find, I need only to reach over and take hold of the detector handle and continue my search. Some users recommend letting the stem and searchcoil float on the surface. This involves extra work and effort because you have to reach up to grab the handle and then force the searchcoil down to the bottom. To achieve the proper "float" and angle, it may be necessary to add buoyancy material such as cork or styrofoam to the upper end of the stem. Tape the cable to the stem at a point near the searchcoil to prevent it from snagging on objects.

No land detector can be as efficient as a submersible detector designed to be used in the water. There are submersible models such as the Garrett Beach Hunter AT4 and the Sea Hunter XL500 that were designed specifically for working under water. Their design prevents water from seeping into the control housing and searchcoils. Both land (non-submersible) and underwater headphones are available for each model.

Your choice of a surf hunting detector should be either an automated VLF model or a Pulse Induction type. The Garrett AT4 features automated VLF circuitry with a unique Dual Ferrous/Non-Ferrous Multi-Range Discrimination circuit. This circuit, described in Chapter 7, lets you select the metal objects you want to recover and rejects those you don't. You can accept most rings while rejecting pulltabs. Automated VLF circuitry needs no ground adjusting. The circuitry ignores black sand, iron earth minerals and salt water--automatically. This type detector and the Pulse Induction are the easiest to use. You simply turn on the power and adjust the audio for silent running or slight threshold.

True Pulse Induction instruments automatically ignore iron earth minerals and salt water. Some models feature the ability to reject such trash items such as bottle caps and aluminum pull tabs. Elongated iron objects such as small nails and ladies' hairpins will be accepted, however, and some rings will be lost when the detector is adjusted to reject aluminum pulltabs.

Discrimination Characteristics

Treasure hunting literature is filled with, perhaps, more "information and recommendations" about discrimination than any other subject. Some say discriminating metal detectors are practically worthless in the water; others swear by them. Actually, there are no "rules" when it comes to target discrimination. Let's review the merits of discrimination; you can make up your own mind.

Discrimination is fully discussed in Chapter 7. We are now looking at discrimination as it specifically relates to water hunting. As you probably know, discrimination is simply a term that detectorists use when discussing certain characteristics or capabilities of metal detectors. Of course, metal detectors will detect the presence of all types of metal because that is the main purpose of metal detection. But, there are many metal objects present in ocean surf that are of absolutely no value to most hunters, namely bottlecaps, pulltabs and similar trash objects. Since the main purpose of most water hunting is the recovery of coins and jewelry, time is wasted when "junk" items are dug. Manufacturers have devised various detection methods (circuits) to measure and compare a target's conductivity with a predetermined value. Fortunately, most good targets have a higher level of conductivity than trash targets. Trash, or low conductivity targets, read as "bad" or "reject." Gold, silver and copper are all highly conductive.

The shape and mass of good targets sometimes cause difficulty. Rings are circular, but--unfortunately--so are aluminum pulltabs. Since aluminum is a relatively high valued conductor, some rings and pulltabs *look the same to metal detectors*. For decades treasure hunters dug many worthless targets to get rings. Detectors with discriminating circuitry such as the Garrett AT4 are designed to indicate with 75 to 85 percent accuracy, the difference between most rings and pulltabs. That accuracy level is *acceptable* to most hunters.

When a detector makes a decision about the conductivity of detected metal, it evaluates the combined conductivity of all metal objects within the field of detection. If, say, a high conductivity ring and a low conductivity bottlecap are lying in close proximity to each other, the detector reads their *combined* conductivity which will be lower than that of the ring. The detector may then read the detected target as *junk*. That's why some hunters say that discriminating metal detectors are no good for water hunting. They prefer to dig all targets, or they have developed a "system" for discriminating that lets them dig mostly good targets. They say that *strong* detector signals mean that the detected target is shallow and, therefore, it must be junk. They tell you to dig only weak target signals. Also, they tell you to ignore double "blip" signals which mean the detector has just detected a nail or a similarly shaped iron object.

The application of the above theories may not improve your treasure/trash ratio any more than using a small amount of discrimination or one of the pulltab-reject detectors. All loud signals may not be junk targets. Often, water hunters dig shallow treasure that has just been lost or that a recent storm just brought up from the deep. Also, a junk object standing on end may produce a weak signal. Any experienced hunter will tell you that a ring or a coin standing on edge can produce a double "blip."

This treasure hunter is well equipped to hunt at the water's edge with a hip-mounted detector, submersible searchcoil and a sturdy scoop with long, double handle.

This is my recommendation: Purchase a surfing detector with discrimination. You can always turn the discrimination off. Then, when you want to use it, just *turn it back on.* In some trashy areas with small iron targets, a slight amount of discrimination will avoid much of the trash and sacrifice little, if any, treasure. Since you will at least spend more time digging better targets, this may swing the balance in your favor. Also, pulltab rejection detectors let you spend more time digging for better targets. Yes, you probably will miss a ring or two. So, obviously the decision is yours. I urge you to *experiment.* Use various degrees of discrimination and keep a record of your finds. Also thoroughly work an area using pulltab rejection. Then, rework the same area using no discrimination. Compare the results. Keep in mind, however, that since an area can never be fully worked, your comparisons will never be 100% accurate.

When I discuss pulltab rejection, I refer to discriminating detectors that permit specifically selected objects to be rejected or accepted. The Garrett AT4 is one such model. Discriminating detectors that do not have this selection feature, will reject a larger percentage of rings whenever pulltab discrimination is dialed in. So, be knowledgeable in your decision making. Discrimination is *not* complicated. Study the earlier chapters. Read your Owner's Manual carefully. Question your dealer or manufacturer until you fully understand the discriminating capabilities of *your* detector.

Additional thoughts on the use of discrimination: Some hunters who use discriminating detectors, will find it very difficult and frustrating to work heavy trash areas. Some of them just refuse to work areas with a great deal of trash,

Using an underwater detector, this surf hunter has no fear of splashing ocean waves and can easily put on a diver's mask to continue his search out into the deep.

preferring more productive sites. I recommend that you not avoid these locations with trash. Start by using only enough discrimination to reject small, rusty iron pieces. If you are still digging an overwhelming amount of trash, dial in more rejection. You may find an adjustment that lets you recover a fair share of good targets without digging too much junk. Also, use a smaller diameter searchcoil. Three to four-inch diameter searchcoils are known for their efficiency in junky areas.

Some hunters will tell you not to use discrimination because you will lose silver and gold chains. It's not just discrimination that causes these items to be lost. It's also the *form* factor. As you have already learned, eddy currents must be generated on the surface of metal for the object to be detected. Since chains have a tiny surface compared to their mass, these items present a poor target for detection. Consequently, you will locate about as many chains using a normal amount of discrimination as you will if you don't use any--especially if the gold or silver content is high. Start your training period using no discrimination. Pay attention to all signals. Especially learn the difference between bell-tone (if your detector has this capability) and regular sounds. Dig all targets and remember their signals. Gradually work with increasing discrimination until you are confident of the full capabilities of your instrument. Evaluate every new site. *No two are alike.* Your efficiency will improve in proportion to your expertise. The following discussion includes another method for successfully working high trash sites.

Searchcoils

Metal detectors are normally equipped with an optimum size searchcoil for general purpose searching. For water hunting this size is between seven and nine inches in diameter. Smaller and larger searchcoils are available for some models. Smaller diameter searchcoils in the three to four-inch range are very efficient in heavy trash areas. Not only do they allow precise pinpointing but your discriminating capabilities will increase since fewer targets can be beneath the searchcoil at any given instant. Consequently, fewer good targets will be rejected. Larger searchcoils give greater depth, especially on larger objects, but pinpointing is more difficult. Also, in heavy trash areas signals will be more erratic and discrimination may be worsened.

If your searchcoil is not light colored, you may want to paint it with a non-metallic white or yellow paint. Its visibility will be enhanced. Purchase skidplates (coil covers) for all your searchcoils. Most searchcoils are tough. I know that Garrett's Crossfire models are! But, considerable sand abrasion can occur under the water. A skidplate prevents holes being worn in your searchcoil's plastic bottom and edges.

Tides and Weather

A section on "Tides and Weather" in Chapter 10 explains the cause and effect of tides and how they can aid the beach hunter. Low tides may be your most productive times since you can work farther out into the surf. Don't forget that swimmers also follow the tides out and take with them jewelry and coins to lose. When extra low tides occur, you may be able to work around platforms and other structures that you couldn't reach before. Around such play areas can be found an abundance of lost items.

Beach hunters know that stormy seasons aid in recovery of older and deeper finds. Winds and churning waves wash sand off the beach and deposit it in offshore bars. As sand is washed off, the beach hunter gets closer to the older treasure. Veteran hunters never pass an opportunity to work a cut or a pool of water. They know as they get closer to clay, gravel and bedrock, their chances improve. If you are only an occasional beach hunter, remember it's *important* to work all cuts and exposed areas immediately. Don't wait until tomorrow or a better time. Most likely, when you return, even if only an hour or two has passed, the cut or wash may be filled in. Even embankments formed in the morning can disappear by evening.

Stormy seasons affect surf hunting because offshore sand deposits increase the distance to treasure. So, if your beach hunting buddy reports a heyday during stormy seasons, your day as a surf hunter is coming during the calm seasons when more gentle waves and winds return sand back to the beach. Be particularly on the lookout for *troughs.* Wave action, wind magnitude and direction and water depth combine to dig troughs that generally run parallel to the beach. These troughs are simply low areas that range in width from a few inches to several feet and can run for hundreds of feet parallel to the beach. They can form near the water's edge as well as much farther out. Troughs are important because they are actually areas of reduced sand buildup.

In other words, in troughs you can get closer to the treasure you are seeking. Some trough extend down to clay. When you find these deep ones, you can sometimes spot treasure by eyesight.

Several troughs can be formed simultaneously. Sometimes, the trough nearest the beach contains lighter trash deposits while troughs farther out contain heavier materials where you are more likely to find treasure.

Occasionally, you may find a glory hole that contains numerous coins, rings and other jewelry as well as heavy debris. At these spots and wherever you find treasure concentrations, work the entire area for several feet around. It may pay you to work your instrument here using a larger searchcoil. You'll get greater depth on a mass of metal. In fact, you should try to work the surf occasionally with these deeper seeking searchcoils. You may detect rich deposits that could not be reached with smaller diameter searchcoils. Watch continually for coral growth and bedrock areas. Treasure can become trapped in holes, cracks and low spots, as well as along the beachside edges of such material.

I encourage you to read *Waves and Beaches* by Willard Bascom. He makes a complex subject very interesting. Bascom has also written another fascinating book, *Deepwater, Ancient Ships*. He tells how ancient, wooden ships that have sunk to great depths can be found in near-perfect states of preservation and how these ships can be raised.

Locating the Best Places

How do you know where to enter the surf to begin your search? Such ability generally comes with experience. Keep track of *where* you find the most treasure and always head there first. But, observe where swimmers spend their time. Where people play, that's where they lose things. Generally, you'll do better in areas that are somehow *enclosed.* People generally do not play outside these enclosures. Of course, remember that where people are swimming today may not be where they swam decades ago. Also remember that treasure can "move" out of these areas. I always make finds near and around boundary chain or rope supports, floats, diving platforms and other permanent objects that protrude above the water level. Search protected areas, especially those enclosed by jetties and rock walls. These formations force people to stay generally within confined areas. Search in swimming areas of inlets and coves. They usually feature calm sea with reduced wave action. My experience has been that people don't like to swim in rough surf or where prevailing winds continually blow. Also, the violent action of the elements generally removes treasure from such places.

Watch where the professionals work. Try to determine why they are working there. If you ask, however, you may or may not get a straight answer.

Observe the surf during high wave and storm action. Watch where perpendicular currents are flowing outward. If there is no debris floating on the surface, pitch pieces of driftwood into the surf and watch their motion. Water, piled up on the beach due to wave, breaker and wind action, tends to flow outward in narrow perpendicular channels which are generally calmer than the wave areas. Treasure more likely will settle in these calmer areas than in areas of heavy wave action.

Work far out during low tide. Work along a path parallel to the shore in water as deep as you can. Then, move in with the tide. Keep alert for sudden, rapid incoming tides.

Bottom Conditions

When you find a clay bottom, shout for joy. Even very heavy objects have difficulty in sinking through clay and other hard packed soils. However, over a long period of time, the sandy bottom of an unused swimming area that has little agitation from waves or people, can become a more compact soil. Even though there may be coins and rings within the layers of this sediment, it is very difficult to dig. I have found only one such place I believe to be loaded with treasure. Someday I may dig it out.

Heavier rings tend to sink deeper than lighter ones, primarily because of specific gravity. Chapter 17 contains a discussion about the settling properties of objects with differing specific gravities. Since glass and pottery made of clay has a specific gravity nearly the same as sand, bottles and similar objects that have been in the water hundreds of years may still be found just on or in the top layers of the ocean's bottom.

When you begin to work a new area, use a blunt probe rod to measure the depth to clay. If the overburden sand is a foot or more thick, you may not have much luck especially detecting deeply enough to locate heavier jewelry pieces. Gravel and shell bottom surf areas may be productive because coins and lighter rings may have become trapped in the shell.

When you find areas where soft sand is piled above bedrock or clay, try to remove several inches of the sand over an area of several square feet. Then, use your detector to locate coins or rings. When you find a good area such as this, you'll know what to do. Remember that in shallow water light wave action causes sand build-up. But, light thin rings can build up with the sand. Heavy wave action results in sand removal near the beach, often exposing rock and gravel areas where you'll find the massive heavy rings. The larger the rock and gravel, the better your chances of finding the heavier jewelry. That's an old trick prospectors use when they are searching for placer gold deposits. Small rocks accumulated along the river's edge, forget it; large rocks, investigate.

Padre Island extends southward some 100 miles from Corpus Christi, TX. Several miles below Corpus Christi are two wash areas called Little Shell and Big Shell. Old-time treasure hunters know of these wide beach areas because failure to respect them often resulted in vehicles getting stuck. Another reason they know of them is because Spanish coins were often found there. But, far more coins were found at Big Shell area than at the Little Shell site.

Some hunters advise working at deeper surf depths; others advise working close to the shore. Actually, both can be good, depending upon the conditions. Treasure can be found in the more shallow water, but, generally, it is true that less trash is found farther out. Don't forget to keep all trash you find and discard it later. Just remember to be observant. Watch the actions of people and the waves. Draw maps and plot your finds. Think things through and continue to sharpen your skills.

Always work *smarter,* not *harder.* Never confuse stubbornness with hard work. But, be persistent. Grid the areas where you work and develop searchcoil overlapping techniques. Use shore-based grid markers such as trees, posts, trash receptacles and other permanent objects. If no one is swimming or sunbathing, drive stakes into the ground on the beach or in the water. Another method to use is buoys. Any watertight plastic container will suffice. Milk, bleach or detergent bottles and antifreeze containers make good buoys. Tie one end of a cord to the handle and a brick or other weight to the other end. The cord length should permit the buoy just to reach the surface. Otherwise, it will move around. If you can drive them into the bottom properly, long poles can be used.

Sides of your grid square should be some 20 to 30 feet in length. When you complete a square, move the poles. You must, however, keep a record of the areas you have searched. When you finish for the day, mark the spot so you can start at the correct place tomorrow. Don't forget to record your finds and their location; it may become very revealing data.

Searching Tips

When you work a popular swimming beach and do not find even pulltabs, someone may have just worked the site thoroughly. Since some hunters dig everything, or at least use minimum discrimination, they will remove everything, including pulltabs.

When working in surfs with violent wave action, always try to stand sideways to the oncoming breakers. You need to present as little of yourself to the body-flattening waves as possible. And don't forget, some waves will be larger than others.

When scanning, keep the searchcoil near the bottom and let it skim lightly over the sand. If you hold the searchcoil very far above the bottom, you will lose detection depth. If you drag the searchcoil through the sand, you will be expending energy you need for a full day's scanning.

Dig all signals, regardless of magnitude! Some users suggest not digging large signals. They reason that large detector signals merely indicate surface trash. But, treasure is sometimes found directly beneath such surface trash. Ed Morris tells of a friend who found a gold ring after he had moved a "loud" tin can.

Retrieving Your Treasure

When working in shallow water (arm's length depth or less), use a scoop or digger, depending on bottom material and density. When the material is light, you can fan it away by hand or speed up the action with a ping pong paddle. Be observant when you are fanning since lighter junk items such as pulltabs can float away with the sand. No loss certainly, but you may just keep detecting them over and over again. When using pulltab rejection detection, however, you'll know that a pulltab can't be that "treasure" you just detected. Keep fanning and watch for a ring or coin to appear.

When working deep water, use one of the following scoop-retrieving methods that have been perfected. First, you must pinpoint the detected object. Then, bring the scoop forward and lightly touch the back edge of the searchcoil. Move the searchcoil out of the way and tilt the scoop forward and press on the butt end of the scoop with your foot. I don't like this method because I don't like the detector's loud squeal when the metal scoop comes near its searchcoil.

After pinpointing a target, some hunters will place their

This beautiful collection of jewelry was recovered by avid water hunter Don Cyr, who now uses an AT4 Beach Hunter detector to search the beaches and surfs of his native Canada

195

foot lightly on top of the searchcoil, then move the coil away. They can place the scoop adjacent to their shoe to achieve correct scoop positioning.

Another method is to place your toe directly against the back edge of the searchcoil. Move the coil and lower your scoop until its forward edge touches your shoe's toe. This places the scoop digging rim (or edge) at the back edge of the searchcoil's detection pattern (see Chapter 5). Then, push outward on the top of the handle until the scoop is nearly vertical. With your foot press down on the scoop.

Still another method is to place your left foot beside the searchcoil and move the searchcoil outward to the right. Lower the scoop until it touches the heel of your shoe in the correct position for retrieval.

Regardless of the method you use, practice until you have achieved perfection…even digging several scoop depths, if necessary. Don't worry if you have to try several times at first to retrieve your object. It comes easier with practice. If you occasionally keep "losing" an item, the object may have been small enough to slip through your scoop holes. I had this problem once when I was digging everything at a beach site in Antigua. The "lost" objects turned out to be ladies' hairpins. Jack Lowry suggested I attach a magnet inside and near the bottom of the scoop to attract iron objects. That's a good idea to overcome that problem. If you get a signal but fail to scoop up a target on the first try, pinpoint it again with your detector. If the target moved, it could be a small object that sifted through the scoop. If you cannot locate it with your detector, it may be a deep coin or ring that was turned edgewise when the scoop contacted it. Try digging deeper to see if you can locate those mysteriously "lost" objects.

Here is a phenomenon you will observe: During a science class, you may have learned of diffraction, or the "bending" of light. This occurs when light passes through a water/air boundary. An underwater object such as your searchcoil will thus appear to be in a different place from where it actually sits. Until you get used to it, this sighting error may cause you to misjudge the location of your searchcoil and scoop.

Don't forget to recheck your holes. Here, you should do as *I say*...not as *I did* with the Spanish icon. As I was recovering it, several people came to see what I had found. In the ensuing excitement I forgot to recheck the hole. Later, one of the others in my group returned and found a nice Spanish coin there.

Final Surfing Tips

On hot sunny days, wear a wide-brimmed cotton hat. Occasionally dunk it in the water and pull it back down over your head. It is surprising how cool you'll be even during temperatures well over 100 degrees. I have worked all day for days on end in very hot climates with absolutely no problems. I wear long-sleeved shirts with the collar turned up. I place a handkerchief under my hat and let the loose end shade my neck.

In a surplus store I found a sun "shield" to protect my neck from the sun that slips right over the bill of a "baseball" style cap. The rear portion flows over the head and down to protect mu neck and ears. The sun simply can't get to me when I wear it.

This shade does have one drawback, however. I wore it one hot summer day in Idaho when Roy Lagal, Wally Eckard, Virgil Hutton and I were searching our own private "Treasure Mountain." While walking down a dusty trail, they suddenly jumped aside shouting, "rattlesnake!" I didn't hear the rattle, but fortunately I saw them jump aside. Cloth over my ears had kept me from hearing the snake's rattle. No one had to tell me to carry the shield in my backpack or keep it pulled back away from my ears during the rest of our expedition.

It's best not to show your good finds to strangers. Let them think you are finding only junk and they will leave you alone. I like little children and you may also, but if you don't want to be pestered by them, don't give them your pennies or other coins you don't want. Every time I relent and do so, I'm soon surrounded by others clamoring for their share. Now, nothing is wrong with sharing or with charity in general, but these boys and girls will distract you. When you're hunting, you should concentrate only on your detector's signals.

Don't let yourself be distracted! Consider the story of the Japanese karate expert. Using only his little finger, he defeated his opponent at arm wrestling. When asked how he did it, he replied that through concentration he directed his entire body power into his finger. Had he concentrated his power over a larger area (his arm and hand) he would have lost.

Occasionally, you'll find unusual items. One surfer found a small bundle of marijuana. Several Spanish coins were secured by string to the outside of the package. Since it was found off the coast of Florida, it may have belonged to an escapee from one of the Caribbean islands.

Ken Schaffer of Virginia Beach found a very unusual item--a microfilm "spy" ring. The ring opened to reveal a slot into which could be placed miniature film negatives. He called in the Secret Service and asked them to examine it. Should you find unusual items, it may be to your best interest to contact the authorities.

One final bit of advice: Remember that you plan to search the surf not for your own valuables, but to recover treasure lost by others. Leave all *your* jewelry at home so some other treasure hunter won't be discovering it tomorrow!

Rivers and Streams

As early travelers moved across America, they encountered rivers and streams that had to be crossed. There were few bridges across streams of any size, much less the mighty waterways. At fords and ferry sites human lives and precious goods were lost, especially during times of high water. Many travelers used the water itself as a means of transportation, first in rafts and canoes. Eventually, barges and steamboats carried vast masses of people.

At countless places along waterways, people camped. Some lost or abandoned personal goods. Others buried wealth for safekeeping and sometimes died or fled without digging up their goods. Lewis and Clark, America's great explorers of the Louisiana Purchase territory, buried caches--several along rivers--some of which have never been recovered.

As volumes of water transportation increased, more goods were lost. Whole cargoes still lie beneath every waterway in the world. Some are of no value at all, but many lost cargoes are worth millions. Additional wealth awaits treasure hunters in streams as the results of collapsing bridges or other calamities of the road. Safes and chests loaded with gold fell into murky waters to be tumbled downstream and, in most cases, lost forever.

Through research, planning and persistence, much of this lost wealth can be discovered. Fords, ferry crossings and bridge sites can be determined. Indian and settlers' communities can be located. I found the site of an old settlement in East Texas and discovered dozens of nice relics on the banks of the Trinity River until the mosquitoes ran me away. Some winter day I'll go back and continue my search.

Sunken rafts, barges, steamboats and other craft can be located. There are numerous sources of information to point these places out to those who take time to search the records.

For over a century steamboats carried people and their goods down the rivers and the tributaries that empty into the Gulf of Mexico. Thousands of these vessels were sunk, scattering treasure the length and breadth of the Missouri, Ohio and Mississippi River valleys. Fortunes still lie along their bottoms.

The cargo vessel, *Berstrand,* sank in 1865 in the Missouri River near DeSoto Bend, north of Omaha, NE, carrying a rich load of mercury. When it was found in 1968 only a small quantity of mercury was found, but two million artifacts, 300,000 of museum quality, were recovered.

In 1820 a newspaper account reported the loss of a keelboat just above Owensboro, KY, at a point then called Haphazard. The cargo of silver and whiskey was being shipped south to pay Choctaw Indians for lands purchased by the Government. The vessel has never been found.

Historians and divers report discovery of wreckage from a 1778 flotilla of 10 ships sunk by the British in the Mullica River during the Revolutionary War. Two of the scuttled ships and possibly three more, were found about ten miles north of Atlantic City, NJ. The wrecks, containing historical artifacts, were found buried in mud and water less than 20 feet deep.

Books

A library of books containing nothing but river wreck locations could be assembled. Thousands of sites of fords, ferry crossings, bridges and communities could be included to point out wealth for treasure hunters to find. And, diving is not always necessary since much of this wealth is either on dry land or in very shallow water.

Fords

Hundreds of thousands of American settlers followed the trails across our continent and forded waterways. As they did, they left wealth behind. They lost treasure in the water, or they buried it for safekeeping during the night but failed to make a recovery the next day. You can locate ford sites by studying history to learn the routes of pioneers. When you search these water crossings, don't overlook the land around the ferry where buried caches and relics can be found. When you find coins, why not notify the local historical society and tell them? Dated coins are a practically irrefutable way to establish historical time periods of a location.

Ferry Sites

Long before bridges came to major water crossings, enterprising individuals presented a solution by providing

Targets that can be found in streams often will be quite different than those discovered in the ocean and on beaches. These projectile points and bone tools were recovered from a Florida river.

ferries to transport man and his goods. Not all crossings were successful. Goods lost in waters many years ago can still be found at that site or downstream where they became mired in muck or were stopped by an obstruction. On both sides of waterways, be on the lookout for lost relics, coins and personal items, as well as purposefully buried caches.

While reading one of J. Frank Dobie's books, I read about a cannon filled with gold that was dumped into the East Texas Neches River upstream a short distance from Boone's Ferry. The story related that a chest of gold was taken across the river and buried among the pines. This occurred in the early part of the 19th century when the Texans and Mexicans were at war. I located this site but found no gold. My brother, Don, discovered a flintlock rifle partially covered by a pile of rocks. At this site embankment "cuts" that guided traffic down to and out of the ferry docks were still visible even after nearly one and one-half centuries. On the west bank a huge tree stump still anchored a rusty steel cable. About a hundred yards west we found a brick road and building foundations which research proved to be the site of a sugar cane-processing mill.

There are many such sites along rivers, waiting to be found. In Chapter 17 you'll find numerous listings and descriptions of these sites and in other chapters you'll learn of treasures that have been found along various waterways.

Swimming Holes

You'll find swimming "holes" in streams and at points along rivers generally in the vicinity of cities and towns. They number in the thousands. Many of those places were

Dry land-type detectors are often used for searching shallow streams, but the THer must make certain his searchcoil is submersible...like all those manufactured by Garrett.

far from attractive and in many cases bathers frequented them not from choice, but because there were no better places available to swim. Diversion, comfort and enjoyment during hot weather were precious and difficult to find.

Dry Land Sites

You'll often find shipwreck and other sites that were once under water now on (or under) dry land. Movement of water continually replenishes waterway sites and makes new ones. Islands can be formed almost overnight. Shifting riverbeds are caused by storms and high water. At points where water slows, sand, debris and other material begin to pile up. As water flows around obstacles, areas are created where sand builds up in bars and islands.

Other dry land areas are created when rivers and streams change their course. Water continually seeks the easiest downhill path. Floods and erosion cause whole sections of rivers to move around. These locations can be found by talking to oldtimers and by studying old maps.

River Hunting

Shallow rivers with gently sloping sand banks are often used for swimming and water skiing. The river need not be wide or deep, but rather one that is slow running. The banks of such a river often have a series of sand bars used for recreational activities and camping. You should work beach areas (on the sand and in the water) and downstream from where activities occur. Deep pools and obstructions are potential collection points of coins and jewelry.

Don't expect submerged objects to be evenly distributed. Current, waterflow, specific gravity of sunken

A metal detector was used to find this beautiful and expensive gold wristwatch that was lost in the water, and--would you believe--it was still ticking away.

205

objects and gravity are the determining influences that regulate distribution of debris. The outside of bends continually wash away while the insides build up with objects that settle out. Heavy objects come to rest in one area while lighter ones settle at a different location.

In clear water you may want to use snorkel equipment to locate good sites. They can then be sounded with probes and worked with a metal detector, air lift or hydrolift.

Remember to work rivers and streams at low water levels whenever possible. Visually search for remnants of habitation such as glass, china, pottery, arrow points and flint chips. Look also for building materials such as bricks, roofing tile, pier posts and other items. When you locate man-made objects, scout the site thoroughly, including any adjacent high bluffs. Usually man did not build in a flood plain, but on high, safe ground.

At a boat loading ramp I discovered a .22-caliber rifle at a depth of three feet. The bore was preserved almost perfectly. Preservation occurred because when the rifle was lost, it apparently plunged straight downward, forcing up into the barrel enough mud to keep it dry.

In areas where you locate surface or shallow remnants of civilization, your search may be fruitful. Where there are no visible remains, valuables may be deep to require a good metal detector or dredge for reaching through sand fill. A probe is a good tool to use for locating bottles, pottery and other large objects.

River searching can be the most tricky of all because there is no such thing a safe, smooth bottom of a waterway. Currents can be tricky and water speeds of up to 40 miles per hour have been measured. There are holes, depressions, logs, limbs, whirlpools and water so opaque you can't see your hand unless you press it against your facemask. River courses and bottoms change dramatically in a single day's time. High water caused by upstream flash flooding, can come crashing down on you. Barbed wire stretches across river and creek bottoms to snag a diver.

In deep rivers are rocks the size of automobiles that roll around on the bottom. Collapsing bluffs trap the unwary. Polluted water can be the source of typhoid and other diseases. Because of the treacherous nature of waterways, great caution and proper safety techniques are mandatory.

Diving, or even wading, can be hazardous. A partner is a must. A tethering rope with a quick-disconnect is a desirable safety accessory. A rope tied upstream lets you swing an arc, and you can let out rope as you work your way downstream.

There are many other techniques such as stretching guideropes across a waterway, using multiple divers and freefloating. Choose methods that best adapt to your situation.

An inflatable life jacket is good insurance. Tether your metal detector to your wrist to prevent its being lost. Work slowly and cautiously and take no unnecessary risks. Watch for boats, barges, floating logs and debris.

Just an example of the many treasures waiting in streams and lakes to be found is this beautiful 10-karat gold tiger-eye ring that was detected in the water by Canadian Don Cyr

In this chapter as well as Chapter 4 research sources are suggested to help you locate fords, ferry crossings, swimming "holes," dock areas and other promising sites along and in waterways. Riverboat shipwreck research sources are suggested. You should search through waterway histories. Check disaster and accident records and river transportation and historical books. Diaries and logbooks are an excellent source of data. And, don't forget the ever-rewarding source represented by historical society libraries. Old charts warned of low water and snags, which are treasure clues today. You may want to begin looking for old shipwrecks at these areas of potential disaster.

Lakes, Pools and Ponds

Lakes are defined as large, inland bodies of standing water. A pool is generally a small body of usually fresh water, often still and deep. It may not be entirely surrounded by land; a "pool" can also be a deep place in a river. Ponds are relatively small bodies of still water formed naturally or by hollowing or banking, the level being controlled by a dam. Throughout this chapter the term "lake" is used unless the use of "pool" or "pond" is required to be more specific or to clarify a point.

Searching in and near lakes can be one of the more interesting types of treasure hunting around water. Three distinct areas present themselves: recreational "beaches," swimming areas and deep water sites.

Similarities between lake and ocean "beach" hunting and "surf" hunting are numerous. The types of lost treasure are generally the same. The types of *deep water* treasure found in lakes, however, often differs remarkably from ocean treasure. Boats and ships are both "lost" in each but the types of craft vary considerably. Also, in lakes there is more discarded and purposefully sunken *treasure* than in oceans because small bodies of inland water are generally more accessible than the ocean.

Experience has taught me that there is considerably more trash discarded in lakes than in the ocean. Also, there are usually more of nature's discards, such as leaves, sticks, tree limbs and even entire trees, to contend with. Ocean surfs can be, and usually are, self-cleaning. Both light and heavier "contamination" will soon be removed by the constant wind and wave action.

209

Not so with the still waters of lakes. Unless man does the cleaning, leaves, limbs and trash lie where they fall or are thrown. Trash accumulates to such an extent that cleaning it to search the bottom becomes a difficult, if not impossible, task. Also, the build-up of sand, silt and mud can force abandonment of planned projects. My story of the lost slot machines, printed later in this chapter, illustrates the problem of lake contamination.

Difficult lake conditions can increase your chances of success. When a task is difficult, fewer individuals will spend time and energy to attempt it!

Lake Beach Hunting

Lakes and ponds were often a focal point of early day community life. They were the favored swimming hole, a source of water, a place for bathing and washing, and a location for picnics. On Sunday afternoons large crowds flocked to lakes to spend a pleasant afternoon. Since many lake sites, formerly on public property, are now privately owned, always check for ownership and regulations. Locate old maps and photos that pinpoint beach areas. Study the beach hunting section in Chapter 10 for a discussion of search techniques. Generally, the same activities that take place at ocean sites also occurred at lake beaches. People lose things in the same manner. At lakes, however, picnics were the rule during early day periods. Time should be spent hunting the outlying regions. Since people generally wore street clothes to picnics, it is more likely that they (especially the men and boys who wore trousers), lost coins from their pockets. You may not find much jewelry, but older and more valuable coins will make up for the difference.

Children have always been provided playthings such as swing sets, slides and sand boxes. Early photos will show where play equipment was located. Try to find photos taken, say, every five years because when old equipment is torn down, it may not be replaced at the same spot.

Be alert to maintenance schedules. Some lakes are

drained yearly to lower water levels for cleaning of swimming areas and replenishing beaches. Lakes are also drained to prepare for winter rains, to poison shoreline vegetation, repair dams and spillways and remove trees and stumps. When the water level of a lake drops only a few feet, beach areas can double in size. The newly exposed areas can be a real bonanza.

Occasionally, I travel to Arizona, specifically to the Quartzsite and Scottsdale areas, to test prototypes of new electronic prospecting metal detectors. While there, I often camp with such friends as Roy Lagal and Virgil Hutton. The campfires burn brightly each night, sometimes until well past midnight. During one of our campfire chats I told the group about my progress in writing this book, and Virgil related this story:

In the days of BFO popularity, he lived in Austin, TX, and normally searched for caches and relics at the various Texas fort sites. Deciding to try his hand at beach hunting, he located the site of an old lake swimming beach area and

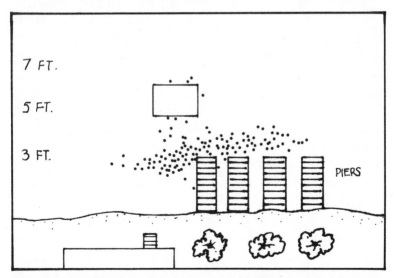

Diagram that indicates where jewelry was discovered in the swimming area of a lake shows many objects near piers with a trail leading out to a floating platform where other items were found.

211

spent one entire winter weekend searching the sands. Apparently, this beach had never been worked with a metal detector. He found so many coins that two or three times each day he had to empty his treasure pouch. The earliest coins dated in the late 1800s. There were Indian head pennies, buffalo nickels, seated Liberties, Barber dimes, Liberty quarters and Liberty Walking half-dollars. He found one large 18-kt. gold Virgin Mary medallion. His jewelry "take" included 41 rings, 16 silver, 17 white gold and 8 gold. There were two star sapphires and a diamond solitaire--a full carat mounted in a gold and platinum mounting, one diamond cluster ring, three ruby rings, three emerald rings and four pearl rings. Also, he found several silver and gold chains, crucifixes and Saint Christopher medallions. He said he often thinks about this lake and wonders if anyone has ever worked the water. That night he began making plans to do just that on his next trip to Texas.

If you live near large lakes, watch for beach treasure cast ashore during storms. Violent storms with high winds can churn up the bottom and hurl things ashore. Watch for bottles, coins, shells, fossils, Indian relics and driftwood. When you see piles of driftwood and debris on the beach, search for valuable articles trapped within. Don't forget to beware of snakes, and stay alert in other ways as well. When you locate coins and other interesting things, consider that they might be from a shipwreck or forgotten cache. Always follow such "leads" through to completion.

I continually stress that hunters, even beach hunters, should fill all holes dug. This is especially important at lake sites because the ground is usually of a harder material that will not be "self-healing" like sandy ocean beach sites. Since some lake sites have considerable grass, good recovery techniques are a necessity. Leaving holes is the fastest way for you and all of us to be permanently barred from sites that only *you* abused. *Fill your holes!*

Searching Swimming Areas

Lake swimming areas can be as productive as the ocean surf. Some lake hunting will be much easier than ocean hunting. And, on the other side of the coin, some lake sites will be difficult. Beaches now being used are the easiest because they are usually kept clean of debris with the bottom loosened by swimmers. Old beaches that have not been used for years are generally more difficult to search. The bottom soil may become hard packed with the passage of time. If the park where the lake is located continues to be a recreational area (but with swimming areas closed), park users will quickly "fill" the lake with tons of discarded refuse.

If there are nearby trees, the area around the lake will gradually fill with leaves, twigs, limbs and even entire trees. Believe me, a swimming area that was once popular and could have been a perfect hunting site can become an almost impossible place to search after it has been closed to the public for only a few years. That's not to say that all abandoned places become impossible to search; it's just that some can be exceedingly difficult.

Before starting work at "your" lake site, make a thorough study to locate all possible swimming areas, past and present. Rely upon maps, photographs, postcards, histories and townspeople both young and old who know of prior activity. Study the shoreline carefully to identify areas that look promising. Gently sloping shore areas, especially with roads that lead to them are promising sites that require further investigation. Use "fish finder" sonar to locate shallow water sites. Concrete foundations and slabs may mark locations where public activities took place years ago.

Be alert to periods of low water. These occur during dry seasons, when the lake is drained and when nearby industry uses water faster than rain can replenish the supply.

Begin your search with a metal detector. Since fresh water does not contain salt, one detector "problem" is eliminated. Ground minerals will dictate the type, or types, or equipment you can use. If the ground contains no minerals, almost any type detector can be used. If ground minerals are present, a modern VLF detector or a pulse induction type will be required. As I have stressed, a water hunting detector is the preferred type, but since there are no breakers and high waves in lakes, a detector that can be used with its control housing mounted on a float will work satisfactorily.

If debris and an excessive amount of bottom fill prevent you from searching, you'll have to resort to other means. You can use heavy duty rakes to clean bottom debris, but raked material then creates a problem. You may not be allowed to rake it ashore. Certainly, you do not want to be raking it back and forth as you search the bottom. Select a site your detector says is "clean," or a site outside the normal swimming boundaries. Place the raked material and other trash there. Check with park officials prior to such extensive preparation.

After you have cleared the bottom debris, make a thorough scan of the site. If you find treasure, the effort will have been worth it. If you do not find treasure, you have some more work to do. Possibly silt has built up the bottom and placed the treasure out of reach of your metal detector. There are several steps you can take. With permission from the park officials or the lake owner, dig an exploratory trench starting at the shoreline and extending out as deep as you can dig. The trench must be wide enough for your searchcoil. Be certain to scan the material you remove from the trench. Place the material where it can be used to fill in the trench when you have finished your test project.

After digging and scanning several trenches, judge the site potential. If it was totally unproductive, you have selected a poor treasure hunting beach. Move to another site and continue your search.

If the bottom is loose and not hard-packed, a surface

suction dredge can be used. Use a two-inch or four-inch size with a wire basket that catches all objects brought up from the bottom. The larger the dredge, the faster your work will proceed. Study Chapter 19 to learn techniques of dredge operation.

At some lake sites you'll find concrete ramps that were constructed for swimmers. One such ramp was provided for early-day swimmers at Dallas' White Rock Lake. Believing the area had never been searched, I located the site and began my metal detector search. After several hours work, I was rewarded with only a few lead weights and fish hooks that were probably lost there only recently. Obviously, other treasure hunters had been there before me! I had expected to find coins and rings in the mud at the end of the ramp. The ramp sloped downward and I knew that all lost articles would gradually slide down the ramp and fall into the mud. Not one did I find! It was disheartening, to say the least, but I was reminded again not to procrastinate. If you learn of a promising site, *don't delay.* Search the site as quickly as possible, or you'll find another truism verified...there are other good hunters who are quite capable of locating hot spots and of using their equipment to locate lost treasure. Well...there is plenty to go around!

Hunting in the Water

Lakes have always been one of the quickest and easiest of places in which people could dispose of or conceal objects of almost any size. Stories of lake treasures abound in every community. Talk to the oldtimers and investigate what they tell you. When I was young, I remember hearing about outlaw loot that was thrown into the Fagley Lake in East Texas. When thieves had to get rid of stolen gold, they tied it in a deerskin and attached a section of barbed wire to the skin. The gold was thrown into the lake and the end of the barbed wire tied to a tree near the lake's edge. There's no record of that gold ever being recovered.

Over the centuries outlaw bands, nervous thieves and

215

even honest but untrusting folk have used lakes as their prime "banking" source. There are many gangster-era stories of bodies weighted with cement, weapons and stolen loot cast from a boat or bridge during the concealment of night. I always keep several treasure stories "going" at the same time. Here's one of them:

In a small East Texas town, two men broke into a business, stole the safe and made their getaway. In pitch darkness they drove to a nearby lake and hauled the safe out on its earthen dam. Here, they tried to "crack" the safe. Alarmed by sounds of approaching cars, they rolled the safe down the steep embankment into the water. That was more than 20 years ago. The safe is probably still there. I've tried to locate it, but I have had no success. The lake bottom along the dam is filled with such a profusion of discarded metal that metal detectors are not effective. By now the safe has probably sunk several feet into the soft earthen dam. Someday I'll find it with probes or other means. It'll be a pleasure to split the contents with the insurance company.

Here's another story to whet your appetite: in 1887 near Great Falls, MT, outlaws robbed a train of $25,000 in gold coins and 25 small gold bars. With a posse on their trail the robbers hastily threw the bars and a portion of the coins into the lake. According to records, the men never recovered any of their stolen loot. One gold bar was found in 1971, but that is the last recorded recovery. This story, which was reported in an issue of *Lost Treasure,* states that those interested in this one should research the area around Haystack Butte and then check the area of the two nearby lakes.

Here's a true story that members of my family have been personally involved in since the year 1919. At that time my late father, Wayne Garrett, was at an age when everything excited him, especially carnivals that occasionally traveled through. Most carnivals in those bygone days consisted of a few horse-drawn rides and side shows, just enough to excite a 14-year-old boy.

My father thought it odd that one tent was not on the midway. There were not even any signs or "teasers" to lure people to it. Their curiosity sufficiently aroused, he and his friends raised the tent flap and crept cautiously inside. What they saw amazed them--tables lined with slot machines stood on both sides of the tent.

Dad heard the whirring of slot machine wheels as people dropped in coins and "shook hands" with the one-armed bandits. Only occasionally did he hear the sound of money as coins fell into the winner's bowl. Dad walked to the nearest slot machine, dropped in a nickel and pulled the lever. Wheels whirred as pictures of lemons, oranges and other fruit blurred past the windows. The wheels stopped, but no coins fell into the bowl. After a few unsuccessful tries, he stopped wasting his money.

Suddenly, a boy came into the tent and ran up to a young man standing near my Dad. He heard the boy say, "The Sheriff's after you!"

Alert for alligators, author edges cautiously from top of dam into an East Texas lake in the search for old slot machines that is described on these pages. Assisting him are John Cross and Gary Lee.

The young man asked, "What do you mean?" The boy said, "He's looking to put you in jail for having these slot machines."

Dad remembers the young man turned sharply and fetched an older man from outside the tent. The two began loading the machines in the bed of a Ford Model T pickup. When they finished, the pair drove through a field, bounced across a gully and onto a dirt road. Dad hopped on his bicycle and pedaled furiously to keep up with the pickup.

Because it was getting dark, the men could not see Dad who could still hear the truck even though he fallen behind. He followed down a dirt road until it turned into a recreational area called Jones Lake. Dad had been to the lake often--why, it was his favorite swimming hole. Pedaling closer, he heard the truck stop and doors slam. Leaving his bike, he crept forward. As he neared the lake he heard a loud splash, then another and another. When he was close enough to see the men, he watched as each man carried a slot machine from the truck to the end of the pier and threw it into the lake. Dad remembers each man made about six trips, meaning at least 12 machines plunged to the bottom.

Often in the following years Dad came and swam in the lake. Each time he thought about the slot machines. One day when he was about 18 years old, he decided to dive down and make a recovery. On his first attempt, he failed to reach the bottom at 10 feet. He hadn't realized the depth of the water in the area off the pier.

Determined to succeed, he dove again, groped around in murky water and grabbed one of the machines. On the next dive he dragged the machine a few feet along the bottom. After several dives, he had wrestled it into shallow water along the lake's edge. He waited until night, then used a crowbar to break into the machine. Only after he had emptied the coin box did he carry the machine back to the pier and return it to its watery grave.

218

For more than 50 years Dad kept the secret of the remaining 11 slot machines. Because of his difficulty in getting just one machine and his fear of the Sheriff, he never tried again. One day, however, as the two of us were driving in East Texas, he told me the story. Drawn like a magnet to the lake, we parked the car and looked the place over. I decided to make a recovery.

Searching for the Slots

My father and my two brothers, George and Don, and several friends, Jim and John Cross and Dave Loveless, met at the lake on a cold January day. Jim's Utah-based underwater salvage company was working under contract near Dallas to dredge a large lake channel. We decided to put his commercial equipment to good use at the East Texas lake site.

To begin the search, we scanned the lake with a Lowrance sonar, making grid surveys of the bottom. Fish were everywhere. At one point, the stylus on the chart mapped a long pencil-like shape on the paper about halfway between the lake bottom and surface. Someone said the mark represented the largest fish he had ever seen on a sonar printout. It may not have been a fish, however, for we knew that alligators have been seen in those waters for decades. The thought of those alligators was to recur because none of us was particularly fond of encountering one. Still, we were determined to find those lost slot machines.

The sonar showed the deepest part of the lake, along the dam, was about 18 feet deep. In many places the sonar drew objects protruding from the bottom. In fact, the whole bottom seemed to be covered with slot machines. Selecting a likely area, Cross donned diving gear to keep his body warm and used a two-way radio to communicate with those on shore. The lake was so dark his hand was visible to him only when pressed against his facemask.

Cross had only taken a dozen steps when he realized he was walking in heavy, knee-deep silt. He continued to walk

219

into deeper mud, reaching six to eight feet as he neared the area of the present-day pier. Cross made his way through the mud by walking on the solid clay bottom. He discovered that the lake bottom under the pier was littered with junk of every size, shape and description.

Because visibility was zero, Cross walked slowly across the bottom until he bumped into something. Then he would reach down, feel the object and try to determine its identity. The first dive produced no slot machines. A Garrett Sea Hunter Pulse Induction metal detector was used wherever it could be forced through the mud. In the "junkyard" beneath the pier, dozens of metal objects caused the detector to sound, but none of those resembled a slot machine.

As Cross widened his search area from that of the first dive, he reported back, "I've found a motorcycle." Digging through the silt with his hands, he felt the frame and spokes of two wheels. We determined the machine was not worth the trouble of pulling it free of the mud. As Cross resumed his search, he marveled at the huge quantity of bottles scattered across the bottom. His second search also produced nothing.

Later, Cross' brother, John, took up the search and began a circular grid search using the detector and feeling his way as he went along. He found fishing poles, spears and more bottles. "I've found something," he said suddenly. "I'm standing on top of it in mud that must be eight feet deep. The object is rounded and is roughly the size and shape of a slot machine."

In his excitement, he turned upside down, diving head first into the mud. Working with his hands, he began to uncover the object. We were certain he had found the first

For her lake hunting this young woman has chosen a Beach Hunter AT4 metal detector, uniquely equipped for shallow submersion when the search takes her into the water.

220

of the 11 slot machines. But as the object emerged, it turned out to be a large piece of concrete. A park attendant later said park personnel had broken up an old concrete building and had thrown much of it into the lake.

Disappointed, but undaunted, he continued his search to find a wooden boat and what seemed to be the bed of a large wagon, about four feet wide and eight feet long. In the thick mud his energy was soon depleted and the lost slots were still as lost as ever.

While the divers were in the water, several of us worked the lake's edge with metal detectors. I knew the lake had been used for swimming for 60 or 70 years and I believed many coins, rings and jewelry might be there.

The mud along the banks, however, was at least two feet deep with tremendous quantities of tree limbs, broken wood, concrete and other junk strewn along the bottom. After about an hour we gave up our search for valuables. The only way to recover anything from this lake I thought, was to drain it and sift through tons of mud and debris.

The next day Cross and I, wore dry suits to work along the steep slope of the dam. He found numerous rotted posts sticking up out of the mud, confirming a theory we had about the location of early day piers. The most remote old pylon was 18 feet deep. Burrowing through the mud another 10 feet, he finally reached hard-packed clay. Searching was difficult here too because of the vast amounts of junk. At one time Cross felt something bump into his back, not once, but twice. Remembering the "alligator" seen on sonar, he suppressed more than a twinge of fear.

I concentrated my search in the water along the dam. I made two passes along the embankment, searching with my hands as I pulled myself along on my stomach through

Using a hip-mounted beach hunting detector designed to "take a bath," this lake hunter has no fear of venturing into the water as far as she can wade in her quest for treasure.

the muddy water. At one point well into a dive, I reached forward to pull myself along and grasped a rounded object. As I reached my other hand forward, I lost my balance as the object started moving. Reeling backwards to escape the "gator" I could imagine before me, I accidentally flipped over and began sliding uncontrollably down the steep embankment, down to the bottom of that 18-foot-deep-hole. When I finally stopped, I was tangled in a rat's nest of air hose, safety line, tree limbs and other junk. After a few anxious moments, I righted myself, untangled my line and climbed up the underwater incline. I knew there was nowhere to go but forward; so, I cautiously pulled myself along the bottom back into shallow water.

At one point, I again grabbed a rounded object. This time, however, I realized I had a tree root in my hand.

Continuing our underwater search throughout the morning, we found an endless amount of objects, but no lost slots. Near the end of the second day--cold, tired and alligator-jumpy--we decided to "call it quits." We packed our gear with visions of slot machines full of buffalo nickels still haunting our thoughts.

As we talked later, we theorized that Dad's pier, circa 1919, could have been anywhere along two different shores of that lake. We believe that if the slot machines are still there, they most likely rest on the clay bottom beneath a combined depth of 20 feet of water and thick, suffocating silt. And, the way we see it, they may be guarded by several hungry, but financially secure, East Texas alligators. I am continuing my search, however, developing new methods for locating not only these slot machines but the booty of lost swimmers and other underwater treasures.

Recently, I received a letter and photographs from Pete Petrisky, owner of Deep Six, who had read my "slot" story in *Skin Diver* magazine. Petrisky and local diver, David Terry, owner of Scuba-Tec Dive Shop in Lufkin, did considerable research on the site and made numerous dives to locate the slot machines. He found hundreds of bottles and other of man's relics, but not the one-armed bandits.

Modern, efficient scuba equipment provides the underwater searcher with unparalleled opportunities for taking extended excursions into the aquatic world. Submersible metal detectors, surface suction dredges and other equipment provide the diver with tools for finding treasure. All that is needed are a few hardy, imaginative and determined individuals to venture into the underwater realm to locate sunken treasure where it is known to exist. Treasure that can be recovered consists of everything valuable from coins to jewelry, to outlaw loot, to sunken boats and ships. You can go after it, if you wish, and you'll mostly have it all to yourself.

Underwater lake hunting, however, is not a cake walk. The visibility, more often than not, is true "zero." Sand, silt, muck, clay and vegetation--tree limbs and, even, whole trees--cover the bottom. It's a grope-and-feel operation. But, of course, your metal detector can be the key to unlock the doorway to success.

You can expect difficulty in maintaining a grid search, but the process can be improved by weighting PVC tubes in a grid pattern. The tubing can alert you to the limits of your search area as you feel your way along it.

Another grid search method is to anchor floats at strategic points. Occasionally, during your search, you surface to take a bearing. Murky water lake searching is more difficult than night diving in clear water with lights because of the flaring, blinding effect of the light. You'll be tempted not to wear gloves because they restrict your sense of feel. Don't give in to this temptation because lake bottoms contain more broken glass, fish hooks and other dangerous objects than any other body of water. Searching river bottoms with bare hands is dangerous, but not nearly as much as working lake bottoms, especially near the shore or along piers.

Searching under piers and docks can be profitable but it is not without its dangers. Around piers you'll locate coins, knives, jewelry, tools, new and antique bottles, chairs, bicycles, sun glasses, fishing tackle, fishing poles, radios and cameras and pound after pound of lead and tin cans. You can expect to occasionally be snagged by some fisherman and run over by a boat if you aren't careful.

When diving, always keep alert for overhead boats, as well as submerged fences fishing lines and nets and trees upon which you can become snagged. Poor visibility usually even increases the complexities of lake diving. Strict adherence to buddy diving is necessary. Safety rules and procedures are discussed in scuba training manuals.

And, speaking of buddy diving, murky water, coins, jewelry and the like reminds me of a newspaper clipping I received from Ted Conard of Cache Inn Metal Detectors of Kent, WA. An article in the local *News Journal,* tells of treasure diving in murky lake depths by a buddy team, Gary Robbins and Loraine Peterson. "Ever since I found a gold ring...I guess I've had gold fever," said Robbins. "I'm hooked too!" Loraine quickly added. The pair had made 25 dives that summer in nearby Lake Wilderness. On Loraine's first dive she found a coin purse that contained numerous coins including a "Walking Liberty" silver dollar that she said must have been "mad money" that was lost nearly four decades ago.

They have found countless coins that date back to the 1920s and numerous tax and transit tokens from times "back when." They use a Garrett Sea Hunter with audible and visible light indicators. "When we make a find," Robbins said, "we get a light beep--sort of like a pinball machine racking up scores!"

For many years, William Houghton and fellow divers Brian Simpson and Richard Myers (state police troopers) have been bringing up treasures from one of Pennsylvania's recreational lakes. Houghton estimates that before their job is finished, they will have found one thousand rings, plus many thousands of other pieces of jewelry and miscellaneous lost items. Already, they have recovered nearly half of the rings they estimated could be found.

For a century this lake has been used by persons seeking the fun and enjoyment of recreational waters. And, apparently, all during those 100 years, people have been losing their treasures. One day, Houghton, a scuba diver, decided to try his luck with his newly purchased Sea Hunter underwater metal detector. At a water depth of about six feet, he heard a faint detector signal. He dug 18 inches into the loose sand and retrieved a beautiful gold ring. "You're digging through the sand and all of a sudden it seems to spin right into your hand," Houghton said. "I could read the inscriptions and design. It was about as shiny as when it was new. There was just no tarnish."

These silver coins that were all recovered by a single North Texas treasure hunter from area lakes illustrate how silver coinage is generally not corroded by minerals present in fresh water.

227

Since then, the Houghton team members have found a wealth of treasure. But, they don't claim one piece of it. They plan to return every item possible to the owner who lost it. Already many pieces have been returned. Working with Jeanie Craddock of the local school system, they catalog every item and then begin a search of school and other records. Ring initials sometimes indicate the original owners. The group contacts high schools and colleges to obtain yearbooks and arrange meetings with reunion committees.

The heaviest rings have been found in about 18 inches of mud. Other items found include Indian arrowheads, a Belgian-made shotgun dating to 1830, an antique ice-cutting tool, champagne glasses and 450 tear-shaped whiskey bottles. Many of the unusual and historical items are being placed in a museum. Congratulations are in order for William and team members for the great work they are doing in enhancing the reputation of all treasure hunters and metal detector hobbyists. They are recovering and returning prized possessions to their owners and helping to establish a museum so that locals can enjoy viewing "treasures" from the past.

Ocean Sites

Considering the vast amount of wealth lost in the ocean, it seems likely that a good percentage of all treasure hunters have *dreamed* of going after their share. Of those who think about it, however, probably no more than five percent ever get their feet wet. Searching for underwater treasure requires greater skills and rewards. If a land searcher spends a thousand dollars for equipment and other necessities and finds $10,000 worth of treasure, the net profit is $9,000. If a water hunter spends $10,000 and finds $100,000 in treasure, net profit is $90,000. Even though the ratios are the same, the amount the water hunter banks is considerably more.

Let's assume, probably correctly, that there is at least 100 times more sunken treasure than buried treasure. Let's assume, also, that there is one water hunter for every 100 land hunters. By doing a little multiplying, we come up with a "success potential" ratio of 10-thousand-to-1, which indicates that the water hunter is considerably more likely to find treasure. I know that there are arguments against this kind of reasoning. These arguments are based primarily on the common assumption that it is always easier and less time-consuming to find land treasure than underwater treasure.

Now, in some situations that might be correct...casual coin hunting in a park and relic hunting in a ghost town. In situations where large treasures are at stake land hunting is not necessarily easier nor faster. I think what this condenses to is simply that the *thoughts* (or fears) of water hunting and the required skills and equipment (scuba gear, etc.) that is mandatory keep most people *safely* on land...and away from vast treasures that could be theirs.

What are underwater treasure-recovery dreams made of? First, there is the discovery of a bronze cannon buried in the sand and refusing to surrender to the corroding effects of salt water. Next to it a hand slowly and carefully fans the sand to uncover an ancient pirate's chest. Just a slight tug and the lid swings up to expose thousands of gleaming golden doubloons! While we all know that it "ain't hardly that easy"...isn't it nice to dream?

Treasure is scattered *everywhere* on the ocean floors of the world. Largely unexplored regions hide many fortunes which can be claimed by those with determination to seek them out. In fact, man has been seeking sunken treasure for thousands of years. Down through the centuries records explicitly record attempts by divers to recover sunken treasure.

Other than wartime, most ships meet disaster in shallow water. Reefs or shoals have ripped the bottom out of thousands of ships, spilling cargo into shallow water. Along the coastline of numerous Central and South American countries shallow reefs parallel the mainland. The remains of numerous vessels lie hidden in the ever-growing coral that relentlessly strives to conceal these sunken riches.

We explored one such wreck site off South America that was visibly marked by a stack of more than a dozen coral-encrusted cannon, shown in the photograph on Page 235. It was strange to see these cannon stacked like cordwood, almost totally concealed by coral growth. How did the cannon become stacked like that? Perhaps the vessel was transporting cannon barrels and the seamen had stored them in one location on the ship. When the ship struck the razor-sharp coral reef, it broke up and quickly sank to the bottom. Over the ensuing decades the wooden ship succumbed to the teredo, leaving the ship's cannon cargo lying exposed on the bottom. There were no other

230

visible signs of the ship except for an occasional cannon-ball.

When we scanned the bottom with our metal detectors, it was a different story. The "eyes" of the detectors pierced through the coral to locate hundreds of metal objects that human eyes could not see. Using rock picks to hack our way through the coral, we discovered more cannon balls, various pieces of iron, and numerous pieces of eight. Sometimes the silver cobs came out in clumps of coral. When the detector indicated that the detected metal object was larger than a single coin, we would hack out large chunks of coral. Later examination of these pieces of coral

After using a Sea Hunter detector mounted on the Scubamate attachment to locate a gold escudo, Robert Marx will now search the adjacent areas carefully for other coins and relics.

revealed numerous cobs that had been bound together by the rock-like growth.

Because of the growing amount of publicity that was given to numerous major discoveries in the early-to-mid 1980s, I hastened to complete the first edition of this book. Metal detector manufacturers experienced surges in underwater detector sales immediately following televised reports of treasure hunters who had struck it rich under water. These increased sales proved that many treasure seekers are poised to strike. They need only the excitement...the proof that is generated by discovered treasure!

Even though numerous treasure-laden shipwreck sites have been found, there are many others...just waiting. For every one found, a thousand others beckon us to the bottom of the sea.

Site Selection

Not every vessel that sank carried recoverable wealth. Even the famed Spanish galleons carried little treasure on their trek westward to the New World. On the other hand, eastbound galleons contained fortunes in hard money treasure. Records show that many of the ships that traveled from California around South America to the United States' eastern seaboard never reached port. These ships carried considerable wealth dug from the ground by California's gold-seeking 49ers and the hordes that later joined them. History reveals that many vessels went to the bottom carrying, not treasure, but relics well worth the cost of salvage. During World War II thousands of ships sank. Most were loaded with war equipment, but some carried surprising quantities of recoverable wealth.

How to Find Your Share

There are two ways you can find your ship--your sunken treasure...by accident or through a systematic, organized search following clues tracked down in research. There is a joy in success either way, but your chances of accidentally finding wealth are almost *zero*. Certainly, there is the human desire to dash into the deep, make a few scans with your metal detector and hit the jackpot. There is something about human nature that causes each of us to think, *I will be the one*. I can be successful *without* any research.

The successful treasure diver is the one who follows a few simple rules that have been established by successful individuals. The first rule is selection of a ship worthy of your time. This ship must truly exist--strange as that requirement may sound. It must not be simply a figment of someone's imagination. Its cargo must be valuable and it must be recoverable. Never believe everything you read or hear about "your" ship. Some of the information contained in magazines, books, and maps may be accurate. Or, none of it may be correct. You must get the facts yourself. You must do your own research. It's your money and time, and no one will search for the truth as you will.

Among the many shipwreck reference sources, you should consider Robert Marx's *Shipwrecks of the Western Hemisphere 1492-1825,* Adrian L. Lonsdale and H. R. Kaplan's *A Guide to Sunken Ships in American Waters,* and John S. Potter Jr.'s *The Treasure Diver's Guide.*

Before attempting to recover any shipwreck, you must clear one mental hurdle. You must *believe.* You must believe 100% in yourself and your ability to succeed. Following through completely on such a vast venture as recovering the treasure from a shipwreck can be such a costly, time-consuming, costly, energy-draining and--oh yes, *costly*--venture. Research, search and recovery efforts, expensive equipment, legal battles, hazards of diving, uncooperative weather, timetable maintenance and energy-absorbing work must all be encountered and overcome.

Long before your search ends, you'll want to throw in the towel and call it quits. If you begin by believing in your success and if you reinforce that belief daily, you'll keep progressing toward your goal. Consider Mel Fisher's success slogan which he uttered daily as he spurred his divers on to success against all odds and hardships. *"Today's the*

Day!" That battle cry, and his belief in it, brought him success that will live forever in the annals of treasure hunting.

Your selection of a ship can begin with tips from friends, divers, fishermen or oldtimers who may have gotten the information from other oldtimers. Then, you must gather source material about your shipwreck from books, logs, governmental records, histories, contemporary newspapers and other sources, including maritime archives, museums and libraries. If you can find confirming data (not material someone has *copied* from someone else) from two or three sources, you can be reasonably certain the story is worthy of further time and consideration.

After proving beyond doubt that your ship *exists,* the second rule is to establish absolute proof that precious, recoverable cargo was, indeed, aboard it. Ships' manifests and other data must record the existence of gold, silver, platinum or other non-perishable commodities.

Next, is the cargo *truly recoverable?* What if, for instance, you could locate one of the sunken Spanish freighters that brought millions of dollars worth of mercury to Mexico's mine owners? When the ship sank, perhaps the hull broke up and the cargo was strewn over the ocean bottom. The quicksilver, likewise, would be strewn over a wide area where it quickly displaced all other lighter ocean-bottom elements as it settled in thousands of cracks, crevices and other low areas. Such a cargo could not be recovered economically. Your only chance would lie in the good fortune that the mercury was transported in rugged, non-perishable containers. And, speaking of non-perishable containers, consider for a moment the hundreds of submarines sunk during World War II...each loaded with one million dollars worth of mercury ballast!

Pinpointing the Site

Before attempting to search any unknown area, you should review hydrographic and oceanographic data. You

234

should learn water depth, the location of reefs and other shallow and hazardous areas, and the directions of prevailing winds and currents. This, and other useful data, can be obtained from charts published by the U.S. Hydrographic Office and the U.S. Coast and Geodetic Survey. Sailing directions and coastal pilot books indicate areas restricted to military use, fishing grounds, shipping lanes and other data that indicates the feasibility of carrying out work such as you plan.

There are two methods for pinpointing a wrecksite. You can search a probable area after having narrowed it down as much as possible through research, or you can continue research until you have it pinpointed exactly. Both methods have been used successfully. The wisest course of action, as proved by those who have searched successfully, is to exhaust all research methods and sources--then, add a little thinking and reasoning--before setting out to scour the bottom of an endless ocean.

It is estimated that up to 99% of all ships lost in the Western Hemisphere were lost in waters less than 30 feet

Because the wooden ship long ago succumbed to the ocean and its creatures, a coral-encrusted cannon may be the only evidence of a shipwreck where considerable valuable treasure lies waiting.

deep. Most of these wrecks lie on sandy bottoms. Even though any lost ship will be difficult to locate, those in sand are easier to excavate. I know from personal experience that coral encrusted shipwrecks are extremely difficult to excavate...so frustrating, in fact, that dynamiting the site often seems the *perfect solution*. Dynamiting is, of course, hardly a perfect, or even a logical, solution. But, after a very difficult day of hacking through coral encrustation, dynamiting just *feels good* to contemplate.

Locating by Name

While I have not located underwater sites using just the name of the site, I have been directed to land-based treasure sites such as Robber's Roost in West Texas, Outlaw Canyon in Central Idaho, and Massacre Beach and Battery Street on Guadeloupe. John S. Potter, Jr., in his book, *The Treasure Diver's Guide,* tells of places discovered using place names. Chameau Rock put Alex Storm on the track of *Le Chameau,* and Thetis Cove was named after *H.M.S. Thetis.*

Locating by Sight

If you are thinking about hopping into the ocean and discovering an ancient shipwreck by quickly spotting its hull, superstructure, and, perhaps, even its *mast*, forget it! You won't find these unless you discover a one-in-a-thousand vessel that was, by some quirk of nature, quickly preserved under protective sand and silt. Then, the day before you dove, it would be necessary for a record-setting hurricane to blast a path through the area, leaving your ship uncovered. *Not likely!*

The remains of most old ships are scarcely recognizable as ships. Most wood will have succumbed long ago to the ocean's elements and creatures. Some assorted objects made of metal may remain, but they will probably be hidden or otherwise covered with sand, silt or marine growth. Nature seeks to return all man-made objects to their natural state--wood and similar organic substances, back to the soil whence they came...metals, like iron, back to magnetite or other ferrous material.

Marine growth begins to camouflage stubborn objects, even cannon, so that even the trained eye may not recognize it for what it is. Wooden ships lost in sand, mud or silt may be the best preserved. The ship's structure and rigging may have become buried before the wood was completely devoured by shipworms. In either case--burial in sand, mud or silt or total encrustation by coral--ship locating will be difficult. More recent shipwrecks with iron hulls may be more easily located since the hulls generally remain intact and their size prevents them from being so totally covered. Such a ship's tall and massive superstructure, providing that this ship came to rest in an upright position, will usually enable it to be spotted from a great distance.

Should you be so fortunate as to learn that the area of your search is clear water, an aerial search should, perhaps, be your first step. Aerial surveying can be accomplished by using an airplane or helicopter. A balloon or hang glider towed by a boat is a less expensive alternative. By hang gliding slightly off center, the boat's wake will not obstruct vertical viewing. Slow towing speed into the wind so you can hang glide more slowly and using polaroid glasses will improve your ability to see into the ocean depths. Scanning in the early to mid-morning or from mid-afternoon to evening may be the best time. While the sun's vertical rays are needed to illuminate the bottom, reflections can be blinding. Also, angled sun's rays may cast shadows that enhance ship's components and other objects that protrude above the bottom.

Be ready to document sighting with your camera (with polaroid lens filters) and to mark or pinpoint the site precisely on navigational charts.

During several successful attempts to locate underwater wreckage, we used the "shark line." Divers with scuba or snorkel gear were towed behind a boat. This method permits a large area to be covered thoroughly and quickly. There is, however, some danger in using this method, as the name implies. Also, fast towing causes rapid depletion of body heat and increases the likelihood of your face mask being pulled away.

Two simple methods to facilitate visual sighting, especially near shore, are snorkeling by fin-propelling yourself over the surface or by floating on a surf board with a built-in view window. During all visual sighting attempts, keep one or more small buoys with you. When a promising site is spotted, drop a buoy to mark the site. Make sure its anchor line is long enough to reach the bottom. Another method is to slip off the board (or release the tow line) when a site is located. Your life vest, will help you conserve energy as you await the towing boat's return. Using a self-propelled, underwater vehicle provides even greater freedom and can increase your coverage by as much as ten times. Under some conditions, headlights will enable you to search at night or when visibility is bad.

You should develop an eye for spotting unusual features that mark the site of shipwreck. Watch for anything unusual--especially, straight lines. Unlike the handiwork of nature "topside" where trees grow vertically in straight lines, underwater growth is anything but straight. Linear or symmetrical man-made objects like a cannon or anchors can be spotted even when encrusted with coral or half-buried in ocean bottom materials. Large marine growth or mounds of sand and mud should be investigated. Mel Fisher's divers spotted a large mound lying in an otherwise flat bottom area. Curious, they scanned the mound with a metal detector and the instrument rang out with a multi-million-dollar *sound of money!*

Ballast is often found lying in a heap near remains of a

Author dives in the Red Sea off Teran and the Sinai Peninsula with a Sea Hunter detector capable of locating relics that will validate events described in the Bible.

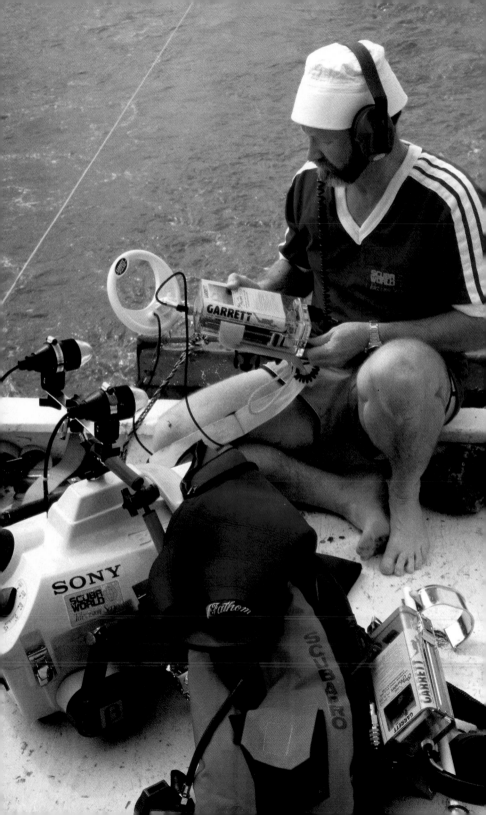

wreck. Over the years this heap has steadily grown larger as sand and silt and, in some areas, coral have covered the stones or other ballast materials. It must be noted, however, that not all ballast piles mark the location of ships.

When large quantities of heavy goods such as gold and silver were loaded aboard, it was sometimes necessary to throw ballast overboard. Robert Marx has discovered ballast piles with no ship's remains anywhere around. Upon excavating the site he found numerous man-made objects, but theorized that as unneeded ballast stones were pitched overboard, other useless objects were also discarded. Large anchors are often found lying on the seabed. In most cases, anchors mark the site where a ship was, at one time, in trouble. Ships' captains often rode out storms by casting out anchors in the hopes they would securely hold and prevent the ship from bring driven into shore. Reasoning follows that the anchor's direction may point to a shipwreck.

In one of Bob Marx's books he tells of divers who found a large anchor. They swam in the direction it was pointing and found another anchor pointing further onward. A short distance along the same route they found yet another anchor, and then yet another--all pointing in the same direction. Near shore, the divers found the remains of a valuable cargo ship.

The applications of tools is described in the following paragraphs. The function and use of these and other tools is described in Chapters 22 and 23.

In clear water, the underwater sled has its advantages. You can skim along at any desired height above the bottom. Close skimming improves your ability to identify small objects and other ship's components when they are

A meticulous survey of his equipment is completed by the author before he dives into the Caribbean off the coast of Cartagena to locate and film long-lost Spanish galleons.

covered by marine growth. Higher level skimming lets you see an area in greater perspective. Unusual straight line and other man-made geometrical objects can be better spotted when viewed in relation to a large area of natural features and growth on the ocean's floor.

On sandy bottoms you can utilize a blaster to remove tons of sand and debris quickly. Too much engine speed, however, can cause such a downward rush of water that everything, including cannonballs, will be swept away. Don't forget, too, when the blaster is being used, an entire perimeter around a spot being blasted will build up as materials settle back to the ocean floor. Such buildup will occur primarily along the route of tidal flow.

Video documentation can be helpful. Underwater cameras can be attached to submersible arms on the underside of your vessel or controlled by underwater robots propelled and guided by an umbilical-cord device.

When sonar equipment is used, large objects like ballast piles and ship's structures can be easily spotted. Liquid crystal and strip chart paper recording sonar devices provide quality, high resolution imagery. Expandable ranging allows you to "zero in" on suspicious sites and get remarkable bottom detail. Permanent paper recording provides data for later study. It is important to indicate careful positioning information on the recordings.

Metal detectors offer "x-ray" scanning to help locate submerged metal objects. Surveying methods available to you are (1) submersible searchcoil scanning or (2) submersible, self-contained metal detector surveying.

Complete metal detector short courses are given in Chapters 5 through 9. Metal detectors will detect single objects as small as a coin to a distance of 12 inches or more outward from the searchcoil's bottom surface. A mass of coins and other metal objects can be detected to a distance of 4 to 6 feet. Larger objects like cannon and anchors can be detected to a distance of about 8 to 10 feet.

Submersible searchcoils allow you to remain topside

while searching. These searchcoils are constructed with electrical cables and harnesses that allow underwater scanning to depths of 50 feet. The electronics are kept above water in your boat or other craft. The searchcoil is lowered to the bottom and then raised a few inches. As you guide your craft along a prescribed course, you profile the locations of metal on the bottom. Since the cord harness is made of white or yellow nylon rope, a diver can quickly follow it to the bottom to investigate the cause of a detector's signals. In shallow water, rigid poles can be attached to the searchcoil. This method provides better control over the searchcoil.

Submersible Metal Detectors

Submersible self-contained metal detectors feature electronics, controls, indicators, batteries and the searchcoil mounted within a specially designed, submersible, water-tight housing. A suitable handle arrangement allows the searchcoil to be maneuvered over an area to be searched. Indicator lights, a visual indicator (moving pointer or liquid crystal) and an audible device (usually dynamic speaker-type headphones or a piezo electric crystal) are the detection-alert devices that report the presence of metal to a diver.

Self-contained batteries that can power a detector for 10 or more hours are usually rechargeable. There are several types of circuitry as explained in Chapters 5 through 9. Some models are stem-mounted, while others are convertible. The control housing is designed to be attached to the stem (stem-mounted) or belt-mounted to waist, arm or leg. When the housing is body-mounted, a short handle attached to the searchcoil allows the coil to be maneuvered over the search area.

Metal detectors are valuable tools. They penetrate sand, mud, clay, marine growth, stone, rock and other non-metallic substances. Metal detectors can be used to locate wrecksites and objects such as the coins vital to dating a wreck. They can find non-corrosive metals containing inscriptions that will identify the vessel and define the parameters of its site. They can lead a treasure hunter to gold, silver, pewter, bronze, brass and other metallic treasures and help to check a "cleaned" area to make certain that all treasures, ship's rigging and other artifacts have been recovered.

The initial search for the site can be conducted by a diver (or divers) scanning an area according to a search-grid network. Since searchcoils will not "reach out" laterally, they must be scanned directly above as much of the target area as possible. Because most ships carried considerable metal, however, even a cursory scan of an area can often locate a wrecksite. Any grid-search method described in this chapter can be used, but the expanding circle method provides the most uniform searching pattern. A cord or rope is wound around a suitable spool. The spool is anchored and the diver slips his hand through a loop in the end of the cord. The diver then swims around the spool, scanning the detector searchcoil ahead. As the rope unwinds, it guides the diver in a controlled expanding circle. See Pages 337-8 for construction data and additional details on this type of guide-rope device.

Metal detectors with a built-in discrimination system

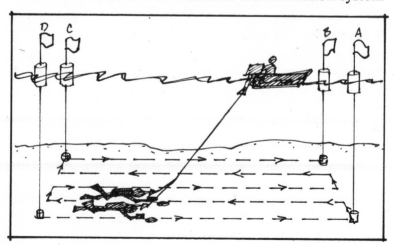

are more versatile than non-discriminating types. For quickly surveying a site to locate only coins and other non-ferrous objects, the discriminating type should be used. This is a fast method to determine if the ship's cargo included treasure. Since non-corrosive metals survive longer than iron objects, identifying stamps, insignias and other markings were usually affixed to these metals. Locating such pieces can hasten identification of the wreck.

A metal detector can speed up almost any search for a shipwreck with concealed treasure. When a sonar device locates a ballast pile, a quick scan with a metal detector will reveal whether metal objects are concealed within the ballast.

When a sunken ship is totally or even partially encrusted and there is not time for a complete excavation, a discriminating metal detector can locate only non-ferrous objects, such as coins, jewelry, navigation instruments and dinnerware. A metal detector with interchangeable searchcoils can be used another way. With a small searchcoil you can detect and precisely pinpoint smaller

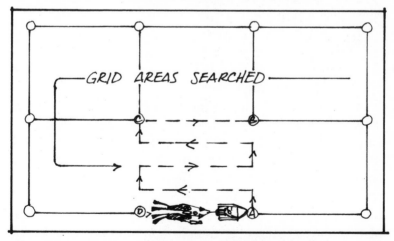

GRID AREAS SEARCHED

The above diagram and its three-dimensional depiction on the facing page illustrate a method of "buddy system" grid-searching that uses marker buoys to insure total coverage of a suspect area.

objects to speed up retrieval. Although not particularly necessary in sand, precise pinpointing in concrete-like coral can minimize hacking and chiseling. When most non-ferrous shallow objects have been recovered, a larger, more deepseeking searchcoil can locate bigger objects at greater depths.

Should you be fortunate enough to find your ship in sand, the first phase of recovery work will require only your hands. Slowly fan the sand away to create a cavity. As lighter materials flow away, heavier items such as coins, jewelry, china and other objects with a higher specific gravity will remain in place. In currents you may need to anchor yourself over the spot by holding an anchor rope, or grasping an underwater object. Don't try to hold on to coral unless you wear gloves; the glass-like substance can penetrate skin to cause pain and swelling. A ping pong paddle or a child's bounce-the-ball paddle makes fanning easier. A water jet can easily remove silt and light overburden.

Specialized Instruments

If funds allow, specialized instruments can aid in your search for a shipwreck. Described in Chapter 23 are magnetometers and gradiometers, side-scan sonar, sub-bottom profilers and robot and manned submersibles. If it is known or suspected that your ship contained a considerable quantity of large iron objects such as cannon and anchors, a magnetometer will locate the magnetic mass by sensing the increase in the earth's magnetic field concentration. Of course, iron objects such as steel drums and other discarded iron trash will also create a detectable concentration of the earth's field, causing you to spend time investigating false leads.

Side scan sonar and sub-bottom profilers are capable of revealing remarkable detail of sunken objects. These instruments are not infallible, but they permit scanning a wide swath of ocean floor. Manned robots using video scanning were used to locate the *Titanic*. Their value remains unquestioned, not only when used in the original search, but also during all phases of surveying, mapping, and excavation.

Whether visual or electronic scanning techniques are used, grid-search methods are essential. Haphazard searching wastes time, money and resources. Many grid-search methods have been developed over the years.

Site Identification

Now that you've found a wreck, is it really the one you have searched for? You must be certain because an extensive conglomerate of ballast, cannonballs, perhaps a few cannon, cargo, countless pieces of copper, lead, iron, bottles, pottery and tons of mud and silt (and perhaps tons of forbidding coral growth) will be found at most old shipwreck sites. You will be spending, perhaps, months and years excavating the site. What a pity it would be if the wreck contained not one ounce of treasure!

These beautiful gold coins and unique toothpicks, also made of gold, were part of the cargo that was recovered from an old shipwreck discovered off the western coast of South Africa.

247

You must always determine beforehand whether any other salvage has been carried out. Possibly, the salvage data can help establish the ship's identity. Coins and ingots provide conclusive evidence, but these may not be encountered until later in the site excavation process. The ship's dimensions, number of decks, type of sheathing used, country of origin of cannon and hundreds of other clues are important in identification. Barry Clifford was able to identify his shipwreck immediately and without a doubt. He discovered what he believed to be the *Whidah*, a pirate ship that sank off the coast of Massachusetts in 1717. From the site he pulled a large bell which had the ship's name clearly cast into its side.

Surveying and Mapping

Before proceeding to excavate, the site should be surveyed and mapped. Aside from archaeological considerations, much useful data can be obtained. Your task will be easier if the ship is not scattered over a wide area and if the ocean bottom is sandy. In heavy coral areas, your job will be much more difficult and require hand chisels, sledge hammers and, possibly, pneumatic tools.

Determining the size of area over which a ship's remains are strewn will help plan future excavation since more time may be needed if the wreck is not contained in a small area. You'll need to know the type equipment needed. Your lease should clearly define the extent of your site. It is important to know the ship's orientation by determining bow and stern. You may want to excavate the stern first. The richest treasure, plus the private wealth of officers and passengers, can usually be found here. Silverware, china, and other more valuable artifacts are also more likely to be found in the stern section.

Site Excavation

If you've made it this far, congratulations! Excavation has finally begun, and you're much closer to your bank's deposit window. Excavation methods range from simply plucking a gold escudo out of the sand to managing giant airlifts and blasters. Select and use those that best suit your salvage job.

A "center" of the wrecksite may contain most of the ship's cargo and other valuable artifacts. Try to establish an underwater grid system and keep it in place throughout your entire project for documenting the exact location of discoveries. The grid method is the most widely used on both land and underwater excavation sites. A grid pattern, built of non-metallic pipe (if metal detectors are to be used) is generally built on a compass alignment basis with equal size squares of five to ten feet. As objects are excavated within each square, their location is indicated on a corresponding chart.

Much simpler and less time consuming is an azimuth circle system. Such a circle is mounted on a brass rod and

These Spanish weapons from a centuries-old shipwreck include unusual types of guns, including the slender small-caliber cannon barrel and three larger cannons, and a sabre.

249

driven into the bottom near the center of the wreck site. If the wreck is scattered over a large area, it may be necessary to place an azimuth circle at several points. The azimuth circle is aligned with magnetic north. A small chain or non-metallic, non-stretchable rope), with distance calibration marks along the entire length of the chain, is connected to the center of the brass rod with a collar to permit the chain to be rotated 360 degrees. When the chain is stretched to the object to be mapped, compass bearing on the azimuth circle and the distance to the object are recorded.

At sites where the bottom is uneven or with considerable marine growth and possibly large mounds of covered ballast, ship's cargo and various debris, standard grid techniques may not be feasible. In such cases, you can devise a "floating" grid network. Such a network should be securely anchored and be kept aloft by air-filled containers.

The various small personal tools you may need include a flashlight, hammer or sledge, chisel, crowbar and geologist's pick. Various floats, pouches, net bags and large containers will also be needed. Lifting big or heavy artifacts requires lift bags and other buoyancy devices.

Miscellaneous Sites

There's a parallel between learning this business of treasure hunting and the way in which a tree grows. First, from the fertile earth pops a single bud that develops into a tree trunk. Then the trunk sprouts limbs. These limbs branch out and grow. Two branches bud into four; then four become eight...sixteen, thirty-two and more. Followed by the leaves. They pop out all over.

That's the way it is with treasure hunting. It keeps growing and growing...there's no end. Think about it. The earth, comparable to research, is a gigantic source of treasure leads. Out of research grows the trunk which is the foundation of treasure hunting. Each branch splits into two or more leads, then four, then eight and so on. Then, when you start finding treasure, it's like tree leaves popping out all over.

At first, 40-plus years ago, I knew nothing about treasure hunting. Then I began to learn. I studied material on the subject, which, although scant, represented *what was known at that time.* I'd go into the field to practice what I'd learned. I'd try to find treasure. I'd talk with other treasure hunters. There were times when I thought that surely, with so many people running about with metal detectors, there would soon be no more treasure to find. Well-meaning friends cautioned me against starting a company to design and manufacture metal detectors. They predicted that there would soon be so many people hunting that all the treasure would be found, leaving no demand for metal detectors.

The truth is, there is already enough lost, buried and

251

sunken treasure sufficient for treasure hunters even if the world runs another *thousand* years! Let me give you just a few reasons. First, people are getting smarter. They are learning to do their research. They are finding where the more difficult treasures are buried and they are uncovering new leads that point to heretofore unknown treasure. Second, treasure locating equipment is getting better. Detectors are becoming more powerful; treasure can be detected deeper. Treasure that couldn't be found yesterday because of inadequate instruments will be found tomorrow when new, improved detectors are made available. Thirdly, there is a *tremendous* amount of treasure being lost and buried every day. The supply is being *regularly replenished!* But, that shouldn't be surprising. After all, the treasure *you* are finding now was lost or hidden in the past by someone.

Is there any reason to expect people to stop losing or hiding treasure? Certainly not. Since man first walked the earth, he has dropped things and hidden and buried them for safekeeping. Lost treasure and treasure hunting is mentioned in the *Bible*. This business of treasure hunting will continue as long as man walks on the face of the earth.

At every turn, I learn of buried treasure. People who know I am a treasure seeker bring me tales of wealth. When I visit foreign countries, the story is the same. People want to spin me a yarn about buried treasure. In Mexico, for instance, I believe there's not one adult who doesn't know of a buried treasure. Throughout Mexico's turbulent history there have been so many revolutions, political upheavals and difficult, uncertain periods that it became almost automatic to bury or hide what little you did have to prevent someone from taking it.

Until just over a century ago, Comanche Indians made a yearly Harvest Moon trek from north of the Rio Grande River deep into Mexico, plundering, raping, killing and taking hostages as they went along. Mexicans soon learned to hide their valuables in anticipation of the onslaught that was sure to come. When the savages came, many people who buried wealth were killed or taken captive with the secret of their treasure lost forever...lost, that is until it is found by accident or until some enterprising treasure hunter comes along to discover it.

Now, after hearing all of that...do you believe there are an unlimited number of places in your area to find treasure and an unlimited supply of treasure to be found? In this chapter I have listed and described many *uncommon* water locations where treasure can be found.

The remainder of this chapter is divided into four sections:

Bridge and Bridge Sites
Waterway Sites
Ocean Sites
Miscellaneous Sites.

I expanded some listings to include additional data and, stories about site possibilities designed to set your mind to work.

Rune Fordal, left, and Arne Adolfsson of Visby, Sweden, worked at a depth of some 15 feet in an old harbor on the island of Gotland to excavate the *Lubecker*, a warship lost in 1566 near Visby.

Bridges and Bridge Sites

There are many kinds of bridges, including vehicle, pedestrian and railway. And, there are many specific types of bridges, including earthen, covered, open and those built specifically for activities like sports (fishing and diving) and tourism. Bridges are permanent landmarks. They are interesting and there are *plenty of them!*

When an individual hides something, he plans to come back for it. Naturally he must have a way of remembering where it was hidden...a special object, tree, structure or landmark to mark the spot. The person on the run must quickly select a place with a landmark that will easily be remembered.

Bridges fit the requirements perfectly. And, if I might interject another thought, so do city limits, county lines and state boundaries. For, it is the very physical nature of a bridge that makes it easy to remember and to find. An elderly gentleman kept his fortune in silver dollars buried in a field just off Highway 94 in East Texas at a point east of the Neches river bridge. Research indicates that Jesse James hid at least one cache near a railroad bridge just northeast of Garland, TX, where the Garrett factory is located. Also in Garland, during the Depression, workmen took up a collection of pennies. The fruit jar in which they put their coppers was placed in wet cement as a bridge was being built on Saturn road, midway between Miller Road and Kingsley road, near our plant

An extortionist, fleeing from the F.B.I., stopped his car on a West Texas creek bridge and hurriedly disposed of incriminating evidence that the F.B.I. wanted. It was the typewriter on which he had written an extortion letter.

Just name it, and it probably has been hidden, discarded or lost either in water beneath or near a bridge. Robbers have on many occasions dumped loot that was too heavy or "too hot to handle" by throwing it off bridges. Thousands of weapons have been so discarded.

Near Reno, NV, lies a large safe filled with gold and

other valuables. It was being transported to higher ground just ahead of a raging river torrent. A weakened bridge collapsed under the weight of wagon and safe. Down it all came. Where the safe lies today under tons of sand and rock is anybody's guess. George Mroczkowski and I have searched for it and believe we have the safe's resting place narrowed considerably. Through research and interviews George was able to pin down the site, and continued investigation is underway.

According to researcher Michael Paul Henson, 40 percent of covered bridges in the eastern United States are connected in some way to a treasure. He also states that sightings of ghosts are also often connected with bridges. Covered bridges are safe shelters in times of inclement weather. They make perfect meeting places and locations for midnight gatherings. Many a traveler has spent the night under one. When searching these sites, look in the water both beneath and downstream from the bridge. Use your detector to search for caches and weapons hidden within the covered portion. And, don't forget to check the approaches for buried treasure.

Waterway Sites

Canals: Beginning in the 18th century and until the coming of the railroads, canals of all sorts played an important part of the American way of life. In Europe, canals and waterways have been used by man since he built the first floating apparatus. Searching is specifically suggested at those places are where canals enter and leave communities, mills and taverns. Bridges and dredging sites should be investigated. As canals fell into disuse, they became the dump grounds for a community's trash. When you search these areas, expect to find coins, tokens, weapons, bottles and other interesting relics.

Channel Dredging Operations: Don't miss these--much of the work has already been done for you. When giant scoops tear huge mounds of mud and muck from river and channel beds, you can count on the fact that there will be many valuables in this discarded matter. Search where the material is placed. You'll find bottles, an occasional weapon and coins. Should you hit it lucky, you may also come up with some cache of outlaw loot or valuable relics. Try to keep track of the dredging operation. Should you locate coins, relics and, perhaps, some nice treasure, make a note of where it was located in the waterway. Search that spot under the waters of the canal as soon as possible.

While on the subject of dredging, let's discuss another type. In placer gold country some old recovery operations included the dredging of potentially productive river sites. At locations where gold in paying quantities has been found, operators with dragline equipment are still dredging literally turning stream bottoms upside down. All recovered material is run through classifiers that exclude pieces of gravel larger than a certain size from ore processing equipment. The dimensions of the classifier screens are determined by the size of the gold nuggets expected to be found amongst the gravel and the limitations of the processing machinery.

As the oversize gravel is diverted, it travels along on conveyor belts and is dumped in piles along the waterway. In case an extra large nugget is diverted, a spotter sits near the conveyor belt exit to stop the machinery. Not all such nuggets have been spotted. They can slip off the end of the conveyor belt. Sometimes the spotter goes to sleep. Also, oversized mudballs can conceal gold and prevent it from being spotted.

To give you some idea of how electronic prospecting can pay off, consider the story of Roy Lagal, life-long prospector and treasure hunter. He has spent considerable time working old gold camps, bedrock areas and placer diggings. Along the highway near the Liberty Cafe

This collection illustrates the many different kind of interesting--and valuable--objects just waiting to be found in the "blanket of treasure" beneath the sands of beach and surf.

in Liberty, WA, a well-known gold-producing site, he worked dredge piles. While he probably won't tell you the total amount of gold he has found, he will tell you that the largest nugget he found weighed seven *pounds!*

Consider, also, that dredge piles have long been a favorite place for picnickers. There are several reports of picnickers who spotted large gold nuggets just lying on top of the dredge piles.

There are many other productive sites located along waterways. While I could expand upon each of them, I will simply try to list the most important prospective sites in the following paragraph:

Steamboat landing sites; mouths of waterways, conjunctions of rivers, islands, Indian campsites, Indian trail crossings such as the two Comanche war trail crossings in the Texas Big Bend area, recreational boat docks, picnic areas, sites near settlements, fishing spots, water control operations and many, many others.

Ocean Sites

Chapter 14 discusses underwater ocean hunting and points out numerous places to search. In the following section I suggest several other possible locations along the seacoast where treasure can be found:

Rock and Coral Outcroppings: These places are natural traps where treasure can be found. One of my most valuable treasures is a 16th Century icon I found at a coral outcropping. Read the full story in Chapter 10.

Pirate Coves: Especially check inland for buried pirate treasure. Relic hunting should be excellent in these waters.

Channel and Port Dredge Areas: We've covered dredg-

An Italian diver prepares to take a Sea Hunter detector down beneath the azure surface of a Mediterranean cove in his search for objects lost in the water.

ing in several sections in this book already. Refer to them for ideas.

Dry Harbor Sites: In some ports you've got lots of dry places to search. While touring southern Maine a few years ago, I visited some of the waterfront areas. I noticed the water had receded far out during low tides. There were dozens of potentially good sites exposed.

Beachcombing Sites: There are many places along the ocean's coasts that are known as treasure beaches. A peculiar quirk about winds and currents is that all kinds of debris floats ashore at certain beach locations. You'll find fish net floats, lots of rope, ship riggings, furniture, bottles, crates of cargo and goods, clothing, small boats and other vessels, plus an unlimited supply of other goods. You'll have to seek out these places but they do exist.

Shipwreck Sites: These are the good ones--the ones that pay off. As we have discussed, when you start finding clues such as valuable coins and relics on the beach, you can suspect that a ship wreck may lie just offshore. It's up to you to do the rest. Two men found one such wrecksite. The Mother Lode was about fifty yards offshore. The pair used a dragline bucket which they carried out in a boat. A steel cable connected the bucket with a four-wheel-drive vehicle. The retrieval method they used was to drop the bucket offshore and use the jeep to pull it in. Their recovered treasure filled a bank vault.

If you want to read a truly fascinating story, look for Lieutenant Harry E. Rieseberg's, *The Sea of Treasure.* Read "The Search for the Golden Jacket's Treasure." This is the story of the *Golden Jacket*, which was driven by a hurricane in 1702 onto a shallow offshore rock outcropping. The ship disintegrated and its cargo, including over one million dollars in gold and silver, plus other coinage, was lost in the shallow waters. Occasionally, coins from the ship are still found on the beach.

Lieutenant Rieseberg describes the moments before the shipwreck...the hurricane's fury, monstrous waves, roaring waters, screaming winds, exploding whitetop breakers, the breaking up of the ship's oak timbers and the pitiful screams of the crew. It's the most vivid account of what takes place during a shipwreck I have ever read.

Miscellaneous Sites

As you should believe by now, the list of places where treasure can be found has no end. Here are a few more for you to ponder:

Natural Springs: Don't overlook these treasure sites. They have been used by man since the beginning. You'll find treasure both in the springs and buried around them.

Wells and Cisterns: These are perfect places to discard junk or to dispose of something that best not be kept. You must use caution around these holes in the ground. Never work them alone. Watch for snakes and be on the alert for crumbling and falling bricks and stones. I should mention outhouses here. If you find one, it will probably pay you to dig it out. While we are on the subject of outhouses, consider this one. I won't give you all the details, but research based on folklore indicate that Pancho Villa hastily threw a large treasure into a community outhouse built near one of the entrances to an old, deserted city in the southern area of the state of Chihuahua. The massive walls and buildings of this city still stand along Mexico's Batopillas river.

Old Swimming Holes: Before concrete swimming pools, the storied "ole swimmin' hole" was the place to go on a hot summer day. It might have been a natural sink hole fed by cold spring water or just an oversized hole kept full by a running stream. I used to swim in one such creek, complete with rope attached to a high branch. You'll find these all over your area. Some that used to be free and wild have been taken over by park board, with a small fee charged for admittance. Talk to oldtimers or write to the chambers of commerce in your area of interest. Request a list of old natural swimming hole site locations. Ask if metal detectors are permitted to be used.

Waterfalls: There aren't a lot of these around, but if you know of one, investigate it by all means. It's easy to visualize that heavy items flowing over a spillway may very well be accumulating at the base of the waterfall. Waterfalls attract people, so they would become natural places to discard something which was to be forever hidden from sight. Waterfalls are romantic places, so why not throw in a coin in exchange for luck or a down-payment on a wish? In gold country waterfall sites could possibly be gigantic, fantastically wealthy placer concentrations free for the taking.

Other sites include natural sinkholes, watering holes, abandoned quarries, mineral-spring bath areas (spas), health resorts (search for caches of people who hid their wealth but didn't get well to recover it), baptismal areas, ceremonial pools, dredge boat dumpsites, beach cleaning dumpsites, produce wharfs, fresh water cisterns and wells, and swimming pools.

Swimming Pools: If you are a good swimmer, you may want to dive to the bottom of every swimming pool you can find. Especially check motel and hotel pools. Carefully search by eyesight for dropped coins, lost rings and jewelry. You could get lucky and receive a reward--others have. All you'll need are your swimming trunks--unless you want to risk arrest--and a snorkel, mask and pair of flippers. Also, take a two-foot long set of tweezers or other device for retrieving items that have fallen through the strainer. These drain-plug strainers are often constructed with two-inch diameter round or square holes.

Watering Holes: Ojo de Leon, nine miles west of Comanche Springs in West Texas is known for its great depth. In the 1800s a wagon master reached Ojo de Leon with a wagon wheel that had rattled almost to pieces. He cast it into the water for soaking, but the wheel disappeared from sight. He could not reach it even with a grappling hook. Since this depth may have prevented everything else from being recovered, it may pay an enterprising person to devise some means for cleaning out this, or other similar watering holes and springs.

Harbors: Deepwater ports must surely qualify as the world's richest depository of sunken relics and wealth. I was in the Navy for four years and even though dumping was against the rules, I witnessed tons of debris, ship's gear and other objects being thrown over the side. When ships tie up alongside docks, refuse bins are provided. But, when ships anchor in a harbor, there are no refuse bins. All trash and garbage must be stowed until the vessel puts out to sea. You can imagine how much unwanted waste can accumulate in a month's time!

Surplus, obsolete and wornout gear must be disposed of. The order to "get rid of it" comes down to the seamen and get rid of it they do…right over the side…in port or out at sea. A group of divers made over one hundred dives

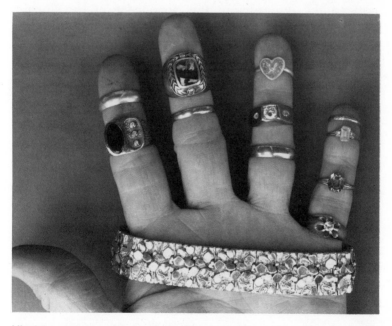

All of these finds were made by Don Littlejohn of Fort Worth, TX, an avid metal detector hobbyist who searches swimming areas and other miscellaneous water sites in North Texas.

in an Argentina harbor. The United States Navy has a 100-year lease on the base. The divers found "treasure" during each dive. Among the boatloads of gear they found were hundreds of three-inch and five-inch brass gun casings. The divers stated that at certain sites, in every direction they turned there were brass casings. The sites were a veritable gold mine of brass. They found ships's rigging, brass portholes, porthole storm covers, a USN bell complete with clapper and hundreds of cups, bowls, plates and other dishes, plus buckets full of kitchen utensils. One of their most prized finds was a brass 1944 Mark V Deep Diving Helmet with breastplate.

Recently while talking with a friend, he told me about witnessing a remarkable find made in the Virgin Island harbor of Charlotte Amalie. He was walking along the beach when several men pulled ashore in the boat. He noticed the underwater detectors were of the Garrett brand. He asked the men if they had any luck and told them that he knew the man who manufactured the detectors they were using. The divers showed him several relics and asked that he "tell Mr. Garrett about this." They then pulled a cloth bag from underneath the boat seat. The bag was filled with gold coins!

War Relics

My first exposure to hunting sunken Civil War relics occurred in Louisiana in 1968. Friends invited me to search for battlefield relics near Natchitoches. One member of the group was particularly interested in a small creek that trickled through the woods. At one point where it widened into a body of water about six feet across, a tree had fallen over the span. The relic hunter walked slowly across it, skimming his searchcoil over the water.

"I just got a faint signal!" he shouted. After a few seconds digging with his shovel he reached into the water and raised a mud-caked cannonball aloft. He pitched the cannonball onto the embankment and made another detector scan at the same spot. He grinned and dug into the mud again. With a whoop he brought up an identical cannonball. To this day, I distinctly remember the water depth to be arm's length. The right sleeve of his short-sleeved shirt was wet.

Why were there two cannon balls in the same hole? Why were they in the water? There is a good probability that they were purposely dumped. And, there is a good chance there are many more in that hole waiting for someone to come along with one of today's super-deep detectors that can reach greater depths than the old-styled detector my friend was using.

The search for sunken relics may not be an activity all treasure hunters enjoy. But, for those who don't mind extra adventure in their search for the big one, such pursuit can be exciting and profitable. The discovery of a sunken Civil War "time-capsule" containing a wagon load of rare historical treasures is a relic hunter's dream come true...a dream that will live and never be forgotten.

Following is the story of another individual's successful recovery. Deep in the woods of Louisiana, far from any road, a relic hunter located a wagon-load of sunken ten-pound Civil War Parrott shells. It was in a shallow creek that his detector indicated metal. Digging down about a foot he recovered one of the shells, complete with wooden sabot. Excitedly, he laid the shell on the bank and scanned again. Another loud signal told him to dig. Excitement mounted as a second shell was discovered. For over an hour the relic hunter dug Parrott shells from the creekbed. Satisfied he had recovered the entire cache, he sat on the bank thinking about his success. He had spent hundreds of hours searching Louisiana Civil War sites, but nothing had been as rewarding as this effort. He had carefully done his research and had located the site where a retreating army had crossed a bridge, spanning what was then a much larger stream. A private diary revealed that a wagon load of munitions caused the bridge to collapse. The munitions spilled into the water and there was no time for the soldiers to recover the cargo.

Before the relic hunter could load his finds in a vehicle, he suddenly felt a sharp chest pain and became nauseated. His strenuous work in the water and the excitement of his success had been too much. He had suffered a heart attack! Not being a person to surrender easily, he placed a shell under each arm and walked toward the road, leaving the other shells, his metal detector and other equipment behind.

This story has a happy ending. The man reached his car and was able to drive to a hospital. Friends brought out his cache of shells. Today the relic hunter continues his pursuit, becoming as excited as ever when he discovers another historical treasure.

Such success is not achieved without effort, patience-- or a minimum of discomfort. This advice may not be welcome or encouraging in a book written to stimulate water hunting. But it is written not to be discouraging. As a person who has been involved in this activity for forty years, I am continually impressed with people's capacity to do whatever is necessary to achieve success. Certainly, I am not encouraging anyone who has just suffered a heart attack to hoist twenty or thirty pounds and hike out of the woods. What I *am* saying, however, is that effort, coupled with determination, will produce rewards.

Determination like that described above is a trait to be found amongst relic hunters perhaps more than any other group of treasure seekers. Successfully locating battlefield sites and recovering war relics can require enthusiasm not needed, say, in coin hunting. Just about any park or school campus is likely to produce coins. Not so for the relic hunter. Lengthy library research, supported by considerable field reconnaissance, is necessary for any success.

These projectiles are relics of the Civil War found in Alabama's Blakely River near Spanish Fort by Larry McCoy of Mobile, whose careful research and Sea Hunter detector led him to the prizes.

267

One especially good reward for the water hunter seeking relics is the realization that he will probably be the first one to the sites he has researched. You see, only a small percentage of relic hunters are water hunters. The relic water hunter has much in his favor because most relic hunters aren't equipped for water hunting and recovery. Specialized underwater metal detectors and water gear are required. Underwater searching and recovery are much more difficult and time-consuming, but the rewards are rarely matched.

War relics can be found in lakes, streams, rivers and in the ocean...and, on a much larger scale than a couple of cannon balls. Retreating armies would often hastily discard war materials in water to prevent their being used by the enemy. After ferries, steamboats and lake and ocean-going vessels were shelled or set ablaze, they sometimes floated miles downstream before sinking, which makes their discovery more difficult.

All relic hunters are familiar with General William T. Sherman's March to the Sea. He left terrible destruction in his path but failed to discover many hidden fortunes in treasure and buried caches. Well in advance of General Sherman's march, people were alerted to the pending destruction. They fled with as much wealth as they could carry. What they could not carry--gold, silver, jewelry, priceless heirlooms and much more--they quickly dumped in wells, cisterns, ponds, lakes, streams and rivers. Much of this wealth was recovered when the survivors returned to their homes. But, much was never recovered. Occasional finds made by persistent hunters prove that Ante-Bellum treasure still awaits discovery.

As General Sherman's army encircled Savannah, Union naval vessels shelled one of Savannah's lifelines, a bridge across the Coosawhatchie river. Relic hunters have made a thorough search of this site. They have found hundreds of pounds of Civil War shell fragments, plus dozens of whole projectiles including the three-inch

Hotchkiss, 10-pound and 12-pound Parrott, 12-pound Bormann and several rare Navy 3.4-inch Schenkl shells.

In the closing months of the great struggle, as Northern troops began overrunning Southern cities and towns, Confederate soldiers dumped tons of munitions in watery graves. Munitions recovered by today's treasure hunters include 2.2-inch baby Mullane shells, 6-pound and 24-pound explosive balls, 4.5-inch Dyer shells with lead sabots, Rains hand grenades, 3-inch high base reed shells with Girardi fuses, 3.67-inch detachable nose Hotchkiss projectiles and many other type munitions.

Other weaponry to be found at river crossings and bridge sites include Sharps carbines, Enfield rifles, bayonets, Colt revolvers, swords (some with scabbards), bugles, pocket knives, mini-balls by the thousands, religious medals and other personal items, tools, wagon parts and even Civil War era bottles.

Searching "black water" is seldom a cup of tea. Even in depths of only three to four feet, swift currents compound search and recovery problems. Proper equipment and techniques facilitate successful search and recovery at most locations.

At some sites, bridge timbers can still be located. Artillery fragments and relics along shorelines mark locations of sunken relics. Low water is the best time to locate and search potential treasure sites.

Before attempting underwater recovery, an understanding of metal preservation is necessary. Even solid cannon balls, if left unpreserved, will slowly crumble after 100 years under water. Chapter 27 describes processes you can use to preserve most relics you'll discover.

Some relic hunters donate discovered prizes to local museums. This not only increases the historian's knowledge of an area, but provides tangible proof to future generations that no country is free from war.

Locating a sunken Civil War vessel can be very rewarding because such a site is, in reality, a "museum" containing war materials, goods and those personal items necessary for survival 125 years ago. Excavation and recovery using archaeological methods is the only way to achieve full knowledge of the historical site to recover and preserve its artifacts. On Dec. 12, 1862, the ironclad *U.S.S. Cairo* was sunk in Mississippi's Yazoo river. A Confederate torpedo exploded and tore open the *Cairo's* bow. The Union gunboat sank in 12 minutes as the first armored warship ever sunk by an electrically detonated mine. Approximately 100 years after she sank, the *Cairo* was located in 25 feet of water by metal detector searchcoils lowered from a boat. A few feet of mud covered the remainst. A tremendous quantity of relics were found on the craft. So important was the find, the *U.S.S. Cairo* Museum was constructed at the National Military Park in Vicksburg. The *Cairo* is being reconstructed and will be rebuilt exactly as she looked in 1862.

A ship from the long-lost Texas Navy, the battleship *Zavala,* was found by naval historian and novelist Clive Cussler in Galveston under an unpaved parking lot near Pier 29. The uppermost of the 201-foot ship's three decks was about 10 feet below the lot's surface. Cussler and his team, who used core-drilling equipment and techniques to locate and verify the ship, have located 52 other shipwrecks around the world.

One hundred five years after the *CSS Georgiana* sank, she was discovered and identified by Lee Spence of Charleston, SC. The *Georgiana* was attempting to run a Federal blockade of Charleston harbor. Crippled by shell fire, the *Georgiana* signaled its surrender. Using this lull in the firing, the captain ran his sinking ship aground to permit its crew to escape. The furious Union seamen tried to torch the ship, but only the upper part burned. The *Georgiana* was soon forgotten. Spence found its remains approximately one mile offshore near Isle of Palms. Needless to say...to locate, explore and salvage a wreck of such historical significance is an experience of a lifetime.

Bottles and Relics

There's something about searching for bottles...a certain fascination and charm that exists nowhere else in treasure hunting. They have been prized for centuries and even though popularity of bottle-collecting is highly cyclical, today's treasure hunters are finding them to be a stable aspect of the hobby. During times of great popularity bottles, including junkers, commanded decent prices. Even during lulls in bottle collecting, higher valued bottles retain their value or increase as the years pass.

Slowly, but surely, bottle--or glass collecting as it is often called--is increasing in activity and gaining new recognition. Frequently, various treasure, collectible and diver magazines print stories about bottle collecting. As writers divulge good hunting locations, more and more people are become curious to try their luck.

Not only is there value in bottles, there is pride in ownership. "Look at this beautiful bitters I found!" Bottles make handsome and charming displays because the limitless variety of shapes, colors and types permit collectors to fill shelf after shelf with strikingly different arrays.

The beginner soon finds himself advancing from "curiosity seeker" to becoming a died-in-the-wool addict as more valuable bottles are discovered. Bitters, medicine, poison, quick cures, embossed beer/pop bottles, snuff and inkwells are only a few of the many types to be found.

Everyone agrees there are limitless numbers of bottles awaiting discovery. The key, however, to successful bottle hunting is research. When you begin searching, you can find more locations than you could ever investigate!

Obviously, bottles will be found where people once lived or congregated. The more people, the better. To locate these productive sites, a study of history is necessary. Where were towns, military posts and forts, waterfronts, bridges, fords and mill ponds located? Where are other historical sites of decades and centuries gone by? A study of newspapers, maps, historical accounts and other sources will reveal many of them.

Your success will be directly related to research. Don't forget, glass collecting is like "getting an itch." Once you've contracted the bottle bug, there is no escaping its clutches. The continuing thrill of finds keeps you hooked. So, do your research, keep your tools busy, let patience and perseverance motivate you and continue hunting...and finding. The rewards are yours to enjoy.

Productive Sites

Bottles are found in some of the strangest places. The following list is by no means complete. But, these locations will get you started in the right direction. As you gain experience, you'll find your own productive locations:

Old homesites, towns, forts, military installations and industrial plants that were once located along rivers and near lakes and ponds;

Large trash dumps, many of which were located near these water sources:

Fords, ferry crossings
Any kind of bridge
Wells and cisterns
Along rivers, streams, ponds and lakes
Outhouses (dry land searching, but still productive)
Shifted river sites (also dry land searching)
Popular beaches and picnic sites
Old waterfronts in present day cities and towns
Channel dredging sites
Sunken vessels in lakes, rivers and the ocean.

Tips on Recovery

When bottles are lost in water, they become covered in sand, entrapped in sediment or, in the case of the ocean, become encrusted by reef organisms. Bottles falling into and becoming entrapped in holes or near rocks, boulders and in other productive spots, are generally in better condition because they are protected from the elements. Depending upon the type of bottle, pollutants and organisms that attract it as well as its underwater environment, some bottles survive better than others. You'll find bottles that are badly corroded, while others will show only mild film residue. Some will become pitted while others develop a heavy encrustation.

Beginning bottle hunters are often surprised to discover by sight alone a 100-year-old bottle lying right on top of bottom sands. Perhaps someone, while standing on

This 12 1/2-inch-tall Spanish olive jar from the author's collection was found at a 1733 shipwreck site in the Florida keys. Glazed ceramic containers such as this were common on Spanish ships.

a bridge, tossed the bottle into the river. Then 100 years later someone discovers the bottle by eyesight alone. Why was the bottle not buried deeply, perhaps ten feet deep?

Specific gravity and the size and shape of an object have a lot to do with the depth at which it will be found. The specific gravity or weight of an article compared with that of surrounding materials, say river sand, will govern the pull of the earth's gravitational field on that item.

Water, sand and rock motion tends to keep riverbottom materials loosened, allowing heavier objects to sink. Small rounded items like musket balls can more readily sink down through sand and silt than can, say a rifle. The rifle can become snagged on boulders, logs and other objects to prevent further settling.

Since glass, pottery, china and other similar articles are made of various earth materials, such as clay, their specific gravity can be the same as riverbottom sand and mud. The gravitational pull upon man-made objects is the same as upon the surrounding materials. Thus, these particular items don't sink but can be tossed about by water and sand movements.

Of course, nearly anything will sink through fine sand and silt. But, it can only sink so far. Clay and rock bottoms prevent objects from sinking forever. Prospectors learned quickly that the best place to find placer gold was at bedrock level. The gold simply couldn't sink farther. The same with bottles. When you are lucky enough (after considerable research and much hard work, it's really not luck!) to find good hot spots on hard bottoms, you'll be amply rewarded for your efforts. Not only might you find bottles, you may also discover coins, relics, arrowheads and other objects.

Bottles are certain to be found by treasure hunters in some of the strangest locations, and they can be arranged in beautiful displays such as those shown here.

Working Lake Sites

Find pier and dock locations by watching for piling stubs. Study old maps and early photos for long-gone piers, docks and amusement areas. During drought seasons, receding water lines allow construction pilings, bottles and shards to be spotted. Mill ponds are usually shallow or have shallow portions where you can spot bottles while you are wading.

Don't be fooled. Just because you cannot see bottles, that doesn't mean they aren't there. Every lake and pond has its share. Especially will bottles be found in abundance around locations such as amusement and recreational centers, near fishing piers and along dams. To give you an example, when I worked an East Texas lake searching for slot machines discarded in the year 1919, we encountered a staggering number of bottles. Everywhere, at every turn, we found bottles! The mud and silt was eight feet deep in places. Yet, at every level we found bottles. The deeper we went, the more valuable the bottles became. The bottles were there. We couldn't see them from the bank, but we found them when we worked the bottom!

Working Rivers and Streams

Near the ocean rivers rise and fall with ocean tides. For best results in finding good locations, work during low tide. Watch for bottles, shards, broken china and other debris. In shallow waterways work around exposed boulders and sunken logs where bottles will collect. Watch closely at fords, ferryboat landings and old swimming holes and under and around bridge sites. Also, work downstream from these places. At bends of rivers where the current slows, water tends to become shallow. Since bottles more readily fill and then sink at these locations,

Author uses a Beach Hunter detector to search for war relics at an abandoned British seaside fortress on the Caribbean island of Antigua.

look for areas where embankments have washed away. Especially in areas that have been inhabited for many years are you likely to find bottles and relics that have washed into the water from eroding embankments.

Channel/Waterfront Dredging Sites

These sites can be very productive. As draglines do their work, decades of history are scooped up and deposited ashore. If you are fortunate (or persistent) enough to be present during such operations, you can expect to reap rich rewards. You'll find many bottles by eyesight, but as you dig through the reclaimed dredge material your chances of uncovering many other valuables are increased. You'll need standard digging and recovery tools. It is sometimes hard and dirty work, but the rewards can be great.

Working Fossil Sites

As you work bottle sites, you'll occasionally discover fossils. Shark's teeth and the bones of prehistoric creatures are being found in many locations. For instance, off Maryland's Calvert Cliffs some of North America's finest Miocene marine fossils are found. The teeth, some nine inches long, indicate that the ancient sharks may have been larger than today's whales. The best times to search areas like this are in the winter after storms and strong winds have churned up the bottom. And, in many areas, diving is not necessary since finds are made in water two to five feet deep.

Tools and Clothing

Everyone, sooner or later, will develop personal bottle hunting tools because specialized implements such as scoops, sifters and probes are just not manufactured. You can start with traditional purchased items such as shovels, pitchforks and pronged garden trowels. A good set of waders and rubber gloves may be a necessity. Refer to Chapter 22 for tips on various types of specialized recovery tools.

278

Nature's Gold

Prospecting for gold has been a favorite pursuit of man since he found and picked up his first gleaming nugget. Every imaginable technique and method for recovering gold has been tried. This chapter describes popular methods available for successfully recovering gold from mountain streams.

Keep in mind that methods presently being used, except the use of metal detectors, are successful because gold is relatively heavy. Its specific gravity is higher than other elements you'll encounter. That means that gold has the greatest pull exerted on it by the force of gravity. Gravitational pull is the reason why gold can be found in water streams and rivers. Gold settles to the bottom of streams and collects in "traps" while rock and sand tumble on downstream. That's where *you* come in. With the right kind of knowledge on how to locate the gold and the right kind of gear needed to recover it, you can find your share.

Other heavy elements, such as black sand, platinum, copper, mercury (used by early-day miners) and gemstones such as garnets can also be found. They are deposited in streams by the same forces of gravity that act upon gold. The recovery techniques described in this chapter will permit you to find these valuable materials.

It takes training and experience, but you'll soon learn to recognize gold when you see it. There's nothing else like it. It looks like, feels like and acts just like...well, like *gold*. It's heavy. It comes in many different sizes from the consistency of fine powder to chunks weighing a hundred pounds or more.

To understand how gold collects in natural "traps" you must think of a river or stream as being one big sluice box (described later) with natural bedrock cracks and crevices and other traps functioning as riffles. The forces of gravity, water, sand and rock cause gold to act the same way in a waterway as it does in a sluice.

Let's start at the beginning...at the mother lode source high up on a mountain. A vein of gold becomes exposed as rain, wind and earth movement slowly cause surrounding earth to loosen and erode. The vein eventually begins to break up, and pieces of gold tumble, slide and otherwise work their way down the mountain slope. Eventually, over a few million years, give or take an eon, the gold finds its way into a waterway. Forces of gravity and moving water, sand and gravel gradually propel the gold both horizontally and vertically, downstream and lower in the waterway toward bedrock, the rock-hard bottom of the stream.

After gold reaches bedrock, it can go no farther vertically. It just continues its horizontal journey downstream until it reaches a resting place in some bedrock crack, crevice or low spot. As gold settles into these traps, it displaces less-heavy material. Here, the gold accumulates. Over a period of many years these concentrations known as placer (pronounced as plaster with the "t" removed) grow larger. Other heavy objects and sediments such as black sand (magnetite/iron mineral) and even gemstones also find their way into the traps.

Now, not all gold is found in cracks and crevices. Some gold, and lots of it, is still in the process of looking for a crevice into which it can fall. Where is it? Still in its downstream trek. Smart prospectors, however, are like bloodhounds. They know, from experience, the routes gold can take. You too can become a gold bloodhound.

As gold tumbles along, it follows the shortest route. When it reaches a bend in the river it doesn't go way 'round the bend. No, it takes the shortest route and hugs the inside. Because water moves more slowly there, gold is more likely to settle. Gold that doesn't get temporarily trapped at river bends gets stopped at other places such as when it washes up behind (downstream from) boulders and rocks. The water is much quieter and slower there giving gold a good chance to settle. If you'll watch water flow you can see that as it slows down behind obstructions, light and floating debris such as leaves and twigs become trapped in the water's turbulence.

Tree roots and similar obstacles make good traps that will stop gold in its downstream flow. During floods, the extra forces of water can cause gold to become dislodged from these resting places to be thrown around until it again becomes trapped. As a result, gold has been found trapped in roots, moss growing on rocks and in other unlikely places.

Today's gold sleuths use every known clue and possible technique to locate placer gold deposits. They know that gold is heavy and will sink to bedrock. They know it follows the path of least resistance. And, they learn to look for natural obstructions such as boulders where gold can become trapped. Then, when promising locations are found, they use a various and sundry assortment of tools to retrieve the trapped gold.

Following a season of heavy storms and rains, there may be less overburden in stream beds, making it easier to reach bedrock where gold is trapped. Also, high water often dislodges gold from inaccessible spots, adding to the supply available for you to recover.

When you begin prospecting waterways, look for bends in the river and other slow-water stretches. Pay particular attention where a tributary or another stream joins your river. Where larger (and heavier) rocks are found along the banks, it is likely that heavy gold has also settled there. Check also behind boulders and gravel bars. If you find gold, even a few colors, you should suspect that there might be more...lots more. Now, it's time to go to work!

This review of just how gold is trapped in nature's sluice

boxes should give you a better understanding of man-made gold pans, sluices and other devices. Knowing how the "process" works will help you to understand how to use available equipment. *Right?* Certainly!

I'll admit, man-made tools do it on a much smaller scale than nature, but the process is exactly the same. When you shovel an alluvial mix from bedrock and put it into your gold pan, sluice or dredge, you have just taken gold, sand, rock and water and started it downstream in your own private waterway. As you agitate your device and the mix starts down the sluice or round and round in the pan, you are simulating nature's process. Water keeps the mix moving down the sluice until the until the heavier elements (usually gold and black sand) become lodged in your man-made traps. Can the process be more simple? No. As long as you have sufficient water and suitable agitation that causes the gold to settle to the bottom into traps (riffles) that are correctly designed, then you will come up with gold

The Gold Pan

Gold pans (see Chapter 22) have been employed for thousands of years. They have been made of wood, ceramic, metal and plastic. In fact, every conceivable kind of container, including automobile hubcaps, has been used at one time or another. I've used a number of them myself! But, my personal favorite is the *Gravity Trap* gold pan with its patented 90-degree riffles.

Remember, now, that a gold pan is simply a container into which alluvial mix is placed, along with water. Built-in riffles are the traps that stop the gold and keep it in the pan while a swirling and tilting motion causes the lighter sand and rocks to flow off the pan's edge.

The all-important point to remember is to make sure your panning procedure completely *dissolves* the mix, freeing any gold to settle to the bottom. Then, the lighter materials can be washed over the rim of the pan. You should take your gold pan wherever you go. You never know when you might stumble onto a likely looking spot. Just remember (and how could you forget!) that *gold is where you find it.*

One way to find it by sniping. What is sniping? It's just a quick, easy technique of examining a likely looking spot to determine if gold is present. Behind a boulder, for instance, you might scrape away the surface to get down to bedrock and pan your recovered mix to determine if gold is present. In fact, you can check out hundreds of likely places both in the water and at its edge in a day's time as you try to determine which areas are worth further investigation.

The gold pan is your indispensable tool for cleaning up sluices and dredges. The concentrates remaining in these devices are washed from their riffles into a pan where you can quickly recover your trapped gold. Pan the contents until you have mostly gold and black sand left in the pan. Gold can be placed in a container for safekeeping with remaining black sand placed in a larger container for later processing of the fines.

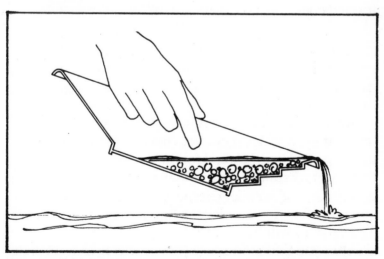

Diagram illustrates how 90-degree Gravity Trap riffles can help trap heavier gold in their sharp right angles while allowing lighter materials to be washed away over the top.

The Sluice

The simplest, full-scale device for placer mining is the sluice box. Like the gold pan and dredge, the sluice is a man-made stream bed on a very small scale. A sluice is a trough with a series of built-in riffles to serve as gold traps. Sluices are of varying lengths, the shortest of which is about two feet. Lengths of 15 to 20 feet are occasionally seen.

A section of the stream is selected where the sluice is placed so that water flows freely through it. Boulders can hold it in place, but its location must be such that the slant of the sluice can be adjusted easily. In this way, water volume and speed can be controlled. If the slant is too steep, gold will be swept over the end. If the slant is less than ideal, riffles will fill too quickly with rocks and gravel.

You can easily shovel several tons of mix through a small sluice in a single day. Periodically, when the traps are filled with concentrates, the sluice must be cleaned. Understanding the correct use of your sluice and gold pan, plus an understanding of how and where placers are formed enable you to operate a sluice successfully.

Sniping

Now, you've read this chapter, perhaps even studied a few other books. So, you are ready to go. You have gathered your gear and scouted an area. But, how do you find gold?

Since you have studied this chapter, you know it can be found at bedrock level. So, you investigate the river banks until you find bedrock and follow it into the water. Then, to find cracks and fissures, you must remove all sand, gravel, clay and boulder overburden. Use shovels, brooms and any other tools to loosen and remove the material. The currents will help you.

After you find cracks, use your crevicing tools to clean them out. Use your pry bar to break open the cracks if you need more space to remove the material. When gold is flipped out, it will sink, not wash downstream...unless the water current is especially rapid. Place all material you remove from the crack into your gold pan for panning. Use your tweezer and sniffer bottle to retrieve flakes and tiny nuggets. If you cannot do a complete job, make plans to use a surface dredge.

Continue sniping by locating all stream obstructions and protruding boulders. These can be worked by digging to bedrock and running a sample of the mix through your gold pan. Scout for tree roots, moss-covered rocks and other traps where gold might be waiting. After you find promising amounts of gold, make your plans for operations on a larger scale.

Surface Suction Dredges

Surface suction dredges derive their name from the fact that they are mounted on appropriate flotation devices that float the engine, pump, sluice box(es) and classifiers on water. The engine, usually gasoline powered, drives a water pump. The pump creates a vacuum which pulls water in through a strainer and intake hose. All of this is pump-forced through another hose to a nozzle where it is discharged at high velocity into a larger intake nozzle. This jet of water creates a vacuum that pulls in a much larger quantity of water through the nozzle intake along with any materials floating in the water or lying at its bed. This nozzle is the business end of the dredge. Thus, it is obvious that a suction dredge is nothing more than a vacuum cleaner that pulls in water, sand, rock, gold, silver and various other materials.

Dredges, measured by the inside diameter of their intake hoses, come in many sizes. They range from approximately one-and-one-half inches up to eight, ten and twelve-inch sizes. The nozzle, however, is slightly smaller, with the suction end always less than the inside diameter of the hose. This is a design feature that keeps large rocks and other objects from becoming lodged inside the hose.

Small two-cycle engines, larger four-cycle gasoline and

even diesel engines are used to power the pumps. The size of the engine, of course, depends upon the size of the dredge and the volumes of water and material it is intended to move

Two basic types of intake nozzles are the power jet and suction nozzle. The power jet configuration gives the greatest amount of suction and lift. This nozzle, however, is not suitable for surface or shallow work because when the nozzle is lifted above the water, it loses "prime" and stops drawing in water. The suction nozzle, on the other hand, does not lose prime, even when held out of the water, but it does not have as much suction as the power jet.

Water, sand, rock and other debris are pulled through and deposited in the riffle tray. Lighter materials--water, sand, rock--flow back into the stream while heavier materials such as gold, silver and black sand are retained in the riffles. The size dredge you select depends upon several factors. If your site is remote, perhaps you should consider a two-inch backpacker model. They are light and easy to set up and operate. Larger dredges are heavier, but they will process considerably more material than a two-inch size. In some areas, governmental agencies allow only the smaller dredges to be used.

The best angle to set your riffle box permits operation with the riffles about three-quarters filled with rock, sand and gravel. Heavy gold will sink down through this material and become lodged in the riffles. If the tray is too flat, riffles will not work because they fill up too rapidly. If the angle slope is steep enough to show more than 50% of the riffles, the angle is too steep and the riffles again can't do their job...this time, because gold washes right over them.

Another factor to consider in selecting a dredge is whether and how often it will be used for other jobs such as coin recovery from a swimming pool or recovery of objects from a shallow sunken shipwreck. Study the manufacturers' literature and ask questions. Get answers before you decide which model to buy.

When you have located a hot spot through your sniping procedures, it is time to set up the dredge. Select a spot where there is sufficient water for operation. The dredge must float freely to insure the riffle tray remains at the proper slant. The pump intake nozzle must have sufficient water for proper operation. Tie the dredge to keep discharge of the mix downstream and away from your nozzle operation. Set a bucket on the river bottom and weight it with rocks to keep it in position. The level of the stream must be higher than the bucket so that the bucket stays full of water. Place the pump intake strainer in the bucket. This reduces the amount of sand being pulled in through the intake, thus reducing pump impeller wear.

If the water is shallow, you should use a suction nozzle. If the intake nozzle gets out of the water, you won't lose prime. When you have sufficient water depth, however, more suction is available with a power jet intake nozzle.

One mistake beginners make is to jam the nozzle into the sand in an effort to make it work harder. This is called "hogging." If you overload the intake, you'll probably have to shut down the pump soon and clean out the hose. Take your time and learn to work the nozzle properly. Work slowly, especially at bedrock level and in other areas where gold is present.

There is much that can be learned about dredge operation, far beyond the scope of this book. I suggest you read, *The Gold Dredge*, by Allen Trees. Study your equipment instruction manual before operating any new equipment. Failure to do so may result in burning out your pump. But, a far more expensive loss may be that of considerable gold because of improper operation.

Another interesting and efficient method of gold recovery is through use of devices called Gold Concentrators. Manufactured by Allen Trees of American Gold Dredge Manufacturing Company, P.O. Box 8932,

Boise, ID 83707, they are essentially for dry land operation. Material is shoveled into a hopper. Water pumped in from a nearby source washes the material, separating the heavier elements from the lighter.

Electronic Prospecting

My books, *Modern Treasure Hunting* and *Modern Electronic Prospecting,* both co-authored with Roy Lagal, discuss how metal detectors can locate gold and other conductive metals. I recommend you study these books from Ram Publishing Company to equip you better for beginning your work with electronic equipment. The proper use of metal detectors in prospecting is the most difficult of all applications to master, but the rewards will surely be in proportion to your effort.

There are several types of metal detectors: namely, the BFO, TR, pulse induction, VLF and automated VLF. Forget the first three when you go prospecting. In this chapter we'll discuss the use of the modern VLF and automated VLF instruments.

As you know, the VLF designation means that the detector operates in the very low frequency radio spectrum of 3 kHz to 30 kHz. It means nothing more, nothing less. Since this type of detector, is a very versatile instrument, properly designed models are appropriately called *ALL*-purpose by users and manufacturers alike. The main feature of the VLF detector is that the disturbing influence of earth iron minerals can be canceled. That is, the detector can be adjusted so that iron minerals are not detected.

Earlier in this book are complete discussions of metal detectors. Here, we will briefly outline their capabilities and as they relate to the basics of gold recovery.

There are two kinds of VLF metal detectors, manual-adjust and automated (motion). Certain models of the manual-adjust VLF are designed to be all-purpose. That is, they will perform almost all treasure hunting and electronic prospecting functions. They can be adjusted to cancel iron earth minerals and they have, basically, two modes of operation, all-metal detection and automated discrimination (motion). The all-metal mode does just that--it detects all metal. The second, or Discriminate mode, allows the operator to adjust the detector to eliminate certain undesirable metal items such as nails, foil, bottlecaps, certain small pieces or iron and aluminum pulltabs.

In almost all electronic prospecting applications, the All Metal mode is used. *Only in areas with a great deal of metal trash is it ever permissible to use discrimination when prospecting...* even then, just the smallest amount needed to reject troublesome pests such as nails or other tiny pieces of iron. Still, some nuggets will probably be lost.

Modern VLF models generally offer a wide range of searchcoils to use. The most important sizes to you, the electronic prospector, are the Super Sniper three to four-inch, the general purpose seven to eight-inch diameter and elliptical searchcoils. The Super Sniper and elliptical searchcoils are necessary when sniping near and under boulders and when searching in tight places for nuggets and placer. Small sizes are also good for ore sampling (highgrading), testing ore samples to determine content.

General purpose searchcoils are, of course, the most widely used. They are good for nugget hunting, ore sampling, sniping and other work. Larger searchcoils such as the 10- and 12-inch sizes should be used only after you have gained detector experience. In some areas, the larger coils are indispensable when nuggets are quite deep or when searching for veins. Since larger searchcoils cover more area, scanning efficiency is improved.

To sum up, modern manual-adjust VLF detectors are the preferred types to use for electronic prospecting because they are the deepest seeking. They have the ability to cancel the earth's iron minerals. They are all-purpose with the ability to perform just about any task. In addition, most manufacturers offer a full range of available searchcoil sizes. You should especially consider elliptical searchcoils since they enable you to be far more maneuverable in rocky streams and boulder-strewn areas.

Several of the new microprocessor models feature automatic ground balancing. This type VLF instrument does not have to be continually moving (like the automated "motion" models) to detect metal. Its searchcoil can be absolutely motionless and still detect effectively.

Automated (motion) VLF ground canceling types, while designed primarily for coin hunting and general purpose work, are not as capable as manual-adjust VLFs. Nevertheless, the newest versions of the automated types are acceptable for nugget hunting and placer sniping. Keep in mind they won't detect as deeply nor detect nuggets as small as the manual-adjust models. Sometimes the automated types do not have as wide a range of available searchcoils. Some models, however, can use the Super Sniper coils and sizes that are slightly larger than general purpose.

Prospectors who are content to locate only larger nuggets can use the automated detectors. Also, such detectors can be used to survey a location and define its productive areas. If a quick scan of a site produces a few large nuggets, it will usually be worthy of closer examination. A manual-adjust or computerized detector can then be used for the deepest and most thorough detection.

Nugget Hunting

To search for nuggets always use the All Metal mode. If you are using a detector with discrimination, rotate the trash rejector control(s) to zero. This is basically all-metal capability. Since manufacturers do not set their detector's "zero" at the same reference point, capabilities of different brands may vary.

Adjust the detector to cancel iron minerals (please refer to your metal detector instruction manual). Automated types ignore earth minerals automatically.

Lower the searchcoil to within a few inches above the ground and begin scanning at a rate of about one foot per second.

In this mode, you'll dig lots of junk pieces of metal. You may tire of digging junk, but at least you'll know that if you pass the searchcoil over a nugget, you've got it. If there is a large quantity of iron junk, switch to the Discriminate mode and dial in just enough discrimination to reject the most troublesome pests, say nails or small iron pieces. Always remember, however, that with discrimination, no matter how little, you run the risk of losing gold.

Occasionally, you may detect what we call "hot rocks." These pests are nothing more than worthless chunks of material mineralized to such an extent that a detector will recognize them as metal. There are methods explained in your instruction manual that enable you to ignore hot rocks. Some practice is necessary, but you can quickly learn to identify them.

Placer Sniping

Searching for placer on dry land or in the water is, in reality, identical to nugget hunting. You may be looking for lesser gold densities since placer is often an accumulation of fine gold particles. Black sand will be present that may look like a detectable hot rock to the detector. This only serves to enhance the ability of the detector to locate placer concentrations. When sniping, you may have better results by using the Super Sniper searchcoil. It is smaller and will more readily detect smaller gold densities. Also, the little searchcoil can be more effectively maneuvered around boulders and into tight places in your quest for gold.

The keys to successful operation of a metal detector for electronic prospecting are

First, learn about the capabilities of your detector by studying your manual.

Second, learn how to adjust your detector by studying your Operator's Manual and recommended Ram books.

Finally, PRACTICE, Practice, **Practice!**
You can't short-circuit any of these three steps and be successful. Believe in your detector, have patience and persevere. Success will be yours!

Tools You'll Need

In addition to your gold pan, classifier, sluice, dredge and metal detector, there are certain small tools you will need in order to operate in an efficient manner.

Sniping tools are available from many Garrett dealers. The short-handled Estwing pick is tough and it is recommended. For heavier work, you may want to invest in a 27-inch Estwing size. It can save you lots of back-breaking effort. A crevicing tool is pointed on one end for digging and cleaning crevices with the other end flattened for scraping. Two sizes of tweezers are recommended. The longer version is good for extracting nuggets from deeper crevices and rocky niches, with the shorter size for the smaller stuff. A suction bottle is a must for retrieving gold from crevices and your gold pan and sluice.

I recommend the Gravity-Trap Gold Pan Kit which contains the world's most popular pan, a 14-inch professional model, a 10 1/2-inch pan for quick sniping and finishing (removing black sand from gold), a classifier for removal of large gravel and a gold-guzzler suction bottle.

Personal items include a snorkel and mask to use for work in shallow water. You may also need a weight belt to hold you in place.

Facing
After locating a likely area with his metal detector, author begins the search for placer gold by panning to locate the metallic substances that caused the detector's signal.

Over
Roy Lagal, known as the father of electronic prospecting, demonstrates techniques in an Idaho river, using the Gravity Trap gold pan which he invented.

Staking A Claim

There are areas available for public use. But, before working a site, determine if it has been claimed. This should be indicated by a pile of rocks, a sign or post. To determine which areas you can work and to stake a claim, check with the offices of the state's Division of Mines and Geology, the Bureau of Land Management, the State Forest Service and the County Recorder's office. You can write to these various agencies to obtain the information you are seeking.

Videos Available

Several new video tapes, produced by Garrett Electronics, cover all aspects of metal detecting, dredging and panning. These tapes are available at your nearby Garrett equipment dealer or they may be ordered directly from the Garrett factory. To obtain the name of your nearby dealer, call *toll free*, 1-800-527-4011 or in Texas, 1-800-442-4889.

Facing
"Working" a stream properly with a metal detector requires careful inspection behind large rocks where nuggets and placer gold might have been washed.

Over
Elliptical searchcoils such as the one shown below are ideal for electronic prospecting, the technique that discovered all of the nuggets shown above.

Dredging

While no studies could obviously be made, it is probably safe to assume that at least half of all coins, rings and other jewelry lost at the beach or pool are lost in the water. Beach hunting, especially the surf, presents treasure hunting's newest frontier. There are numerous other sites where coins and jewelry can be found. Underneath and downstream from bridges, at tourists' stops and along major pedestrian thoroughfares, a multitude of treasure can be found. People cannot resist the temptation to pitch in a coin and say a wish. This practice started thousands of years ago in Europe and continues to this day. Whenever a traveler came to a bridge, he or she would throw a coin in the water and make a wish or mutter a plea to their multitude of gods.

I visited several such sites in Europe. In Rome there is one bridge still carrying pedestrian traffic after two thousand years. I was anxious to get in the water here and try my luck, but being pressed for time, I only worked a short while along an embankment downstream where I found various items of modern jewelry. Upon inquiring about the lost items I learned that flood waters occasionally wash over the bridge where jewelry and souvenirs are sold to tourists. Floods sometimes take these souvenir merchants unaware and wash their canopies, tables and merchandise into the river. My guess is that within the space of one mile downstream from this bridge there must be millions of coins and items of jewelry.

You may scoff at my beliefs, but let me tell you another story. While visiting Bern, Switzerland, I stopped while crossing a major bridge in the heart of the city. Upon looking into the water I was amazed to find it perfectly clear with visibility to the bottom. In the water was a veritable montage of copper and silver colors. I was amazed to discover that I was looking at thousands upon thousands of coins! To this day I can scarcely believe what I witnessed with my own eyes. That river has been a public waterway for two thousand years. Can you imagine how much treasure lies along its bottom? Obviously, I wanted very badly to work there with my dredge, but when I realized that it would be against the law, reluctantly and sadly, I went on my way.

When you consider the thousands upon thousands of pedestrian bridges in the world, you begin to realize just how much wealth awaits the dredge operator. Beneath the bridge at Royal Gorge, CO, thousands of pennies and five-cent pieces have been recovered, as well as numerous rings and wrist watches. Coins found there are thrown by tourists as good luck pieces. The jewelry found is attributed to rings and watches coming off arms and fingers as a coin is flung. Thousands of coins have been recovered with dredges from the Russian River near the town of Monte Rio, CA.

Other lucrative river sites are located beneath and downstream from bridge crossings in Reno, NV, where countless rings have been found. Apparently, many women who have come here over the years for a divorce are so fed up with marriage that they fling their rings into the water in a final show of defiance. Some actually purchase cheap rings to throw away during this ritual of claiming their freedom.

Often, in the various treasure publications, stories are printed about successes of dredge operators in recovering coins, rings, watches and other jewelry from swimming areas.

The vast amount of coins and jewelry lost in the water has been proven many times, not only by users of detectors with submersible searchcoils, but more recently by persons using surface suction dredges. There are submersible dredges, but for various reasons they are not popular. We will discuss only surface dredges in this chapter.

Suction dredges, when used at swimming beaches, will bring lost coins, rings, watches and similar valuables up through the hose to be deposited either on the standard riffle tray or into a basket. The standard riffle tray is not suitable, generally, for salvage because coins cannot be trapped as well as gold. The force of water acting upon the broad face of coins will sometimes propel them right off the tray. I have equipped my own dredge with a wire mesh

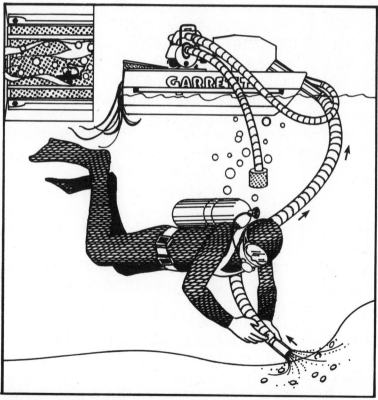

Diagram illustrates how a diver operating a suction dredge can direct it to pick up bottom materials for straining through the wire mesh basket (upper left) located at the rear of the dredge.

basket where all objects pulled from the bottom are dumped. Water, sand and small objects fall through the mesh back into the water.

Two people are needed to operate a dredge most efficiently, one person using the nozzle with the other keeping the accumulated rocks, other debris and, of course, the good finds--coins and rings--clear of the wire mesh to allow sand and water to pass through. Broken glass and fish hooks, among other things, will be dumped into the basket. You are forewarned! Be prepared, especially for an occasional snake which will be pulled up alive through the dredge. If you are successful in locating and dredging some of the earlier swimming areas, of which there are thousands throughout the United States, you could easily pay for your dredge equipment each day of your operation.

Be very careful to keep the rubber tube or float balanced. The float must sit level in the water. If you mount the engine near the edge, the float may tip over or not float level. Also, be extra careful when operating an inflated tube float because if the tube becomes punctured you can guess what happens.

What Size Dredge?

Determine what is the largest sized object you want to retrieve from the bottom and buy a dredge which has a diameter rating at least one-half inch greater. Of course, the larger the dredge, the greater the speed at which you can work. Larger dredges, however, are more difficult to manage. The four-inch size is considered the upper limit for one person to operate.

Some dredges are designed for multi-purpose use. They are suitable for both gold prospecting and for underwater treasure recovery. Dredging for gold is discussed in Chapter 18.

At some swimming sites you may have to go deep into the sand, perhaps two feet or more, before your dredge operation can become productive. But, when you start pulling out silver dollars, halves, Barber quarters, Buffalo and Liberty nickels and Indian Head pennies, your efforts will be rewarded. Some coins will come out heavily encrusted, but others will look like new. Some will be black, some pitted, while others will be worn smooth. The condition depends upon time in the water and upon the soil mineralization and composition of decaying matter. A dredge, especially when used for recovering coins and jewelry in deep water is a two-person operation. The main problem is the difficulty of containing large items or those with a broad surface in a standard riffle tray.

When a wire basket, constructed of one-quarter-inch mesh, is used, only sand and small rocks and debris will pass back into the water. Larger rocks, pieces of metal, bottlecaps, pulltabs and all other items pulled in by the dredge will remain in the basket along with coins and jewelry. Junk items and valuables alike can't get out. Consequently, the basket must be cleaned regularly, depending upon the volume of junk encountered. Here is where the second person is necessary to keep the basket clean while the nozzle operator works.

An extension arm allows you to use the dredge in water as deep as you can wade. You hold the handle end of the extension while you maneuver the intake nozzle along the bottom. You must not "hog" the nozzle by jamming it in the bottom, or you'll quickly fill your hose with sand or mud. One of the best ways to use a dredge, especially in warmer weather is to snorkel. You float along on the surface while you look down into the water and operate the intake nozzle.

Obtaining permission at private swimming holes is a wise course of action. Unless property owners understand what you are doing, they may become irate as they see you creating what they believe to be holes 40 feet deep, while destroying their property. Of course, any holes you make will be only a fraction of that depth. And, in sandy areas your holes will fill in quickly. There might be some slight danger to swimmers who could possibly step into holes, but proper operating procedures will create holes that fill about as fast as you make them. Work in straight lines with the dredge discharge end trailing along behind you. As sand and other dredged materials flow back into the water, the holes are automatically filled.

Dredging causes absolutely no ecological damage in swimming areas. In fact, how could just a little air pressure cause more damage than hundreds of swimmers who spend their day kicking up tons of sand. A dredge operation, however, brings up lots of edible items from the bottom and supplies them to the hungry fish...free of charge.

Underwater Salvage

Who can forget John Wayne's great undersea adventures in the movie classic *Wake of the Red Witch?* He battles a huge man-eating octopus for possession of a chest of pearls. He dons a deep-sea diver's suit and descends to the ocean bottom to recover five million in gold from the hold of a 19th Century three-masted schooner. The ship, precariously perched half over the ledge of a deep chasm, adds frightening suspense as it threatens to fall into the abyss. Thunder, lightning, wind and roaring waves plus other Hollywood excesses forever plant a concept in the minds of movie-goers about the dangers always confronting the diver seeking treasure. It appears that the underwater treasure hunter must surely lead the most exciting, adventure-filled life it's possible to experience...or so the movies would have you believe.

This fine old movie and the other so-called true-life adventure stories have attracted as many men to the underwater world as have the treasures found by real-life salvors like Mel Fisher, Bob Marx, Burt Webber, Barry Clifford and others.

Of course, the real world of today's commercial/treasure salvor bears little resemblance to that of his counterpart on the silver screen or the color TV tube. Fighting the real world of salvage laws, months of separation from loved ones at home, rusted equipment, storms at sea and even modern-day pirates, are the adventure stories these men tell. But, treasures that have been found...or, at least, the promise of treasures to be found are the real incentives that keep these men returning to the ocean depths. And, believe me, there is plenty of adventure and treasure to be found there!

While a chest of golden escudos may be the sought-for treasure, a bronze cannon worth $25,000, a large ship's propeller worth $5,000, an anchor and chain worth $1,000, or just a collection of rare 1800s bottles are treasures sufficient to keep men coming back for more.

There's little glamour in underwater salvage...it's mostly hard work. True, treasure salvors dive for *instant wealth* and, while they might not admit it, for adventure or for the simple reason, "I just had to do it!"

The sport of underwater salvage may not make you rich, but you can add to your income and to your showroom of conversation pieces. Certainly, there is nothing wrong with setting your sights for a Spanish galleon. You should also be prepared for such mundane items as sunken boats and motors, lost anchors and chains, bronze relics and other ships'antiques--and even plain old scrap metal. After all, there's enough sunken wealth to keep you in salvage equipment, compressed air and the necessary square meals that let you continue, perhaps forever, in your dreamers' quest for the truly big one.

The kinds of lost and discarded goods you can locate underwater include boats, motors, anchors and chains, propellers, boating gear, fishing gear and fishnets, rifles, shotguns, pistols, knives, tools and tool boxes, rings, watches and other jewelry, eyeglasses and other personal items, relics and ships' artifacts, golf balls, scrap metal, bottles, stolen loot, contraband, weapons, material (law enforcement) evidence, ships' cargo, aircraft, automobiles and diving gear.

To locate potentially good sites, keep your eyes and ears open. Read everything you can find on the history of disasters in your area. Make it a habit to talk with divers, boat captains and crew, marina operators, insurance agents, local law enforcement agencies and others who may possess knowledge of lost articles, shipwrecks, boat-

306

ing accidents and disasters, downed aircraft and other water related events. Study Chapter 4 for tips on research.

The following is a list of contacts you should develop. Make known to them your abilities and your willingness to search for and recover sunken objects and vessels:

The reclamation departments of the Army, Air Force, Coast Guard, Navy, National Guard, State and local police, Sheriffs' departments, Civil Defense, Flood Control and River and Port authorities.

Equipment

The type equipment you need depends upon the type recoveries you plan to make. In addition to your regular, personal dive equipment, you'll need marker buoys, lift bags (don't use your BC), numerous lengths of nylon line and rope for scanning, towing and air lift attachments and a various assortment of tools including pry bars, metal saws, drag hooks and other items. Depending upon the location of your recovery effort, you may also need a boat, an inflatable, a raft or a floating platform. In many search and recovery activities a metal detector is an indispensable tool.

Other tools and equipment you may need include wrenches, chisels, hammers, wire cutters, tin snips, nails, canvas, come-alongs, block and tackles and flashlights.

Search Methods/Procedures

Review Chapters 10 through 15 for a discussion of various search and recovery methods. In employing search guide ropes you'll have to be able to tie basic knots such as the square knot, half and full hitches and the bowline.

All operations should be carefully planned with every member of your team knowing first aid and safety procedures. Teamwork is the key to successful, accident-free searching, with every team member not only dedicated to his or her job but willing to share the work. Make a thorough study of the water, currents, tides, bottom conditions, weather (forecasts and history) and likely boating

and shipping activities before you work anywhere. Keep safety equipment such as lines and flags ready for instant use. Every team member should know how to use every piece of equipment. This is best accomplished by classroom study and actual practice under the water.

Underwater metal detectors are designed to detect ferrous and non-ferrous metals. These metals can be located even though concealed below and within aquatic growth, bottom soil and rocks, wood and other non-metallic materials. Objects as small as a single coin can be detected to distances beneath the searchcoil of 12 inches or more. Large metal masses such as boats, motors and safes can be located several feet below the searchcoil. The metal detector's capability of "reaching out" into the unknown can make a big difference in the recovery of objects hidden by murky water or buried beneath silt and mud.

Knowing *what* you are looking for will help you select and use the proper equipment. Magnetometers can sense the change in the earth's magnetic field density caused by large iron objects. These instruments are of no value, however, as an aid in locating non-ferrous materials. The metal detector can locate both ferrous and non-ferrous objects. Size, shape and depth can be determined to a degree. Experience is needed, however, to comprehend these parameters.

Before beginning your metal detector search for, say, an anchor chain, try to determine in which direction the chain lies. Then swim at right angles to the chain's orientation. Unless the chain is buried deeply in mud and silt, this method is fast. Locating small, isolated objects is more difficult and requires a precise and comprehensive grid search with the detector.

The racing boat *Liberty* was recovered from Pennsylvania's Conneault Lake by William Houghton and Brian Simpson more than six decades after it sank in 1922.

Should you be called upon to locate a pipeline, a magnetometer can be used, provided the pipe is iron. A metal detector can be used, following the right-angle scan technique. When you are trying to determine pipeline depth, however, the best method is to use a probe. Still, depth can be reasonably well verified with a metal detector. If you know the size of the pipe and can scan it above water, or if there is an exposed section under water, you can calibrate the meter reading for various detection distances. Then take underwater site measurements and correlate your readings with your calibrated readings.

If you understand trigonometry, you can devise other methods for determining pipeline depth.

The use of sonar should not be overlooked. A sonar signal travels through the water and rebounds when it strikes an object. The rebound signals are then reported on a visual screen and/or recording paper. There are numerous kinds of sonar devices including hand-held proximity locators, "fish" finders, sub-bottom profilers and side scan. These devices are discussed in Chapter 23.

Because the treasure salvor often works in black water and in other dangerous environments, direct communications with the surface is important. Should an accident occur such as diver entanglement, then help could be summoned immediately. Chapter 26 contains a discourse on night (black water) diving.

Direct communications are essential and should include discussions of problems and solutions. Topside team members can continually monitor the position of divers by observing the location of air bubbles.

Selling Recovered Valuables

How do you dispose of recovered treasure that you don't intend to keep in your collection? There's a ready market for everything. Chapter 27 suggests sources where you can sell recovered items. The Bibliography includes more references, including publications that will list individuals who collect and buy just about everything.

Marine Archaeology

The metal detector can be eyes that "see" into the ground to locate metal objects of interest to archaeologists. All types of conductive metal, without exception, can be detected. Objects as small as a pinhead can be found. Large objects can be detected to depths of about 20 feet. Metal detectors are so sophisticated they can classify various types of metal into categories and accurately indicate depth. Ground minerals and the ocean's salt water pose no problems. Automatic detectors are simple to use. Just turn them on. Most other functions are accomplished automatically.

Some archaeologists use metal detectors, while others refuse to consider their use. Metal detectors are simply tools, not unlike electrical resistance surveying equipment used widely by archaeologists. So, why don't more archaeologists use this tool that can help them in their work?

Metal detectors have found archaeological treasures that probably would never have been discovered otherwise. A metal detectorist found a bronze head of Emperor Hadrian. A few years later another hunter found a complete, larger-than-life-size, bronze statue of the same man. In England, metal detectorist Ted Seaton used a Garrett detector to find a religious pendant believed to have belonged to England's King Richard III. The pendant was found at a depth of about fourteen inches. It was found alongside a well-worn foot path--probably a site that would never have been excavated by any archaeologist. A most valuable find, it sold at auction for an amount in excess of two million U.S. dollars. Books can be filled with

311

stories of treasures and artifacts found with metal detectors that probably otherwise never would have been discovered. If the use of a metal detector can contribute to historical research, why not use it?

Scuba divers conducting a routine search beneath the emerald-green waters of the Gulf of Mexico about forty miles west of Key West, scanned their Garrett Sea Hunter metal detectors over what appeared to be a large mound of coral. The detectors screamed loudly. The pile turned out to be a mix of ship's weights, pieces-of-eight and ingots of silver as big as loaves of bread. The "mother lode" discovered that day turned out to be one of the biggest caches of sunken treasure ever found--a fortune in silver, gold and emeralds carried by the Spanish galleon, *Nuestra Senora de Atocha,* that sunk in a hurricane in 1622. The value of the treasure she carried was initially calculated at $400 million, but this estimate has been increased.

In addition to its riches of silver and gold that had lain buried on the ocean floor for more than three centuries, the *Atocha* is also proving to be a scientific bonanza. Duncan Mathewson, chief archaeologist for Treasure Salvors, Inc., the Florida-based group of divers and investors that sought the *Atocha,* calls the vessel, "an enormous time capsule, as important as Pompeii, or even King Tut's Tomb."

Mathewson has been diving on historic shipwrecks off Florida and in the Caribbean for more than a decade. He is recognized as one of the world's foremost authorities on shipwreck archaeology. He is a co-founder and chairman of the Atlantic Alliance for Maritime Heritage Conservation, a coalition of sports divers, shipwreck salvors, maritime historians and marine archaeologists. The or-

As part of a 1988 expedition to the Middle East, author uses a Sea Hunter underwater metal detector to seek archeological relics along the floor of the Red Sea.

ganization is dedicated to the conservation of historic shipwrecks and other maritime resources.

Mathewson calls the hand-held metal detector a "very important and effective tool" in underwater archaeological research. "Archaeologists are only beginning to get an idea that they can do serious archaeology with a metal detector," says Mathewson. "I'm trying to get them to understand the detector is not simply an instrument to be used to find the 'goodies,' but it also can be used to help map sites when they really can't do it any other way. If you find a distribution of metal objects on a site and you map that, then you've learned a good deal about the archaeology of the site."

Using a metal detector can also lead to artifacts that otherwise might never be recovered. At the *Atocha* site salvage diver John Brandon found gold links that formed a chain several feet in length. The links had fallen into cracks in the underwater hard pan and were recovered from an area that had been described as "clean" by other salvage divers.

The search method used by the Treasure Salvors team involves the use of large L-shaped tubes called "mailboxes." Two are mounted at the stern of each search boat. Once the mailboxes have been pivoted into place over the boat's spinning propellers, they direct the prop wash downward toward the search site. This not only pushes clear water down to the site to be excavated, but digs a deep crater in the sand. Then, divers equipped with metal detectors go down. They scan the entire area, including the sand berm formed around the hole.

Detectors used by these divers are of the pulse induction type. Each diver merely sets the audio control to his,

Hunting with a Garrett Freedom detector, a hobbyist in Great Britain discovered a religious pendant believed to have been worn by King Richard III in the 15th Century.

315

or her, preferred threshold level and starts scanning. Pulse induction detectors are not affected by ocean salt or black magnetic sand.

A large electrical current is made to flow--to be "pulsed"--into the antenna winding. A powerful electromagnetic field is generated, some of which is "captured" by any metal artifact. Resulting surface currents on the artifact generate a secondary field that flows outward from the metal target.

Even though some underwater detectors can be submerged to depths of 200 feet, divers at the *Atocha* site used detectors at a depth of about 55 feet. But, they have also used them successfully in much shallower waters, such as off the Florida coast of Ft. Pierce, where Spanish galleons dating to 1715 have been found. "The water's depth doesn't affect the metal detector," says Mathewson.

Before recovering any artifacts, divers under Mathewson's supervision lay down grids of non-metallic orange tubes over major finds and exposed portions of the vessel. The grid sections are marked with numbered floats.

Recovered artifacts--from coins to cannonballs, iron locks and sword blades--are sealed in plastic bags and marked with a number for computer coding.

Treasure Salvors maintains an archaeological laboratory at the company's Key West headquarters. A description of each find is entered into a computer. Later, the finds can be studied in relation to one another. Mathewson also supervises photographing, drawing and weighing of each artifact.

Mathewson believes that scientific examination of the *Atocha* and its cargo will provide enlightenment on a wide variety of topics. He notes, for example, that the ship was built in Havana in 1618, a generation after the defeat of the Spanish Armada off the English coast. The *Atocha* could thus shed light on what innovations had been incorporated into galleon design by Spanish shipbuilders. At least five years of investigation and recovery work are anticipated as the minimum time necessary to complete a full examination of the *Atocha* site.

Metal detectors are also being used successfully by archaeologists excavating dry-land sites. A noted professor who teaches historical-site archaeology says that the detector enables him and his students to do a better job of excavating and writing reports.

Archaeological excavation normally begins with the construction of one or more control grids, which are used as an aid in mapping and as a method of recording the artifacts found within the site. It is after grids are laid out that archaeologists call upon the metal detector, sweeping the searchcoil over the square to be excavated. Whenever the detector signals the presence of a metal object, a small flag is planted. No excavation begins until the electronic survey has been completed and the square flagged.

"Using a detector gives us *pre-knowledge* of exactly where every metal artifact is located," the professor says. "We don't miss a thing once we start to dig. The detector increases our expertise."

Not only does the detector enable the archaeologist to find a greater percentage of buried artifacts, it also helps prevent damage to them. "Suppose you're digging a site and you come upon a buried piece of thin metal, perhaps a can that's been down there for 70 or 80 years. A carelessly used trowel could penetrate the metal. But when you know the metal is there, you proceed with caution," the archaeologist observes.

"A metal detector can help make for *safe digging,* too," he states. "If there are buried electric power cables or other objects that are potentially dangerous, you can seek them out and establish where they are before you begin digging."

This archaeologist has been using detectors in his scientific investigations for more than a decade. He tested several different types before settling on the Garrett Deepseeker, a sensitive and stable instrument.

Rick Sammon, President of CEDAM (Conservation, Education, Diving, Archaeology and Museums) International, noted that its members utilize land and underwater metal detectors on their expeditions. CEDAM is a very active professional group of people dedicated to the discovery and preservation of both land and underwater historic sites and shipwrecks.

Metal detectors on many occasions have proven themselves. In Ireland, a metal detector survey was made around the ballast stones of the wreck of the Armada ship, the *Santa Maria de la Rosa*. The survey was made to locate the precise position of the ship's cannon. Numerous targets were located but no detector signals indicated the presence of objects the shape and mass of cannon. Excavation proved the cannon lay elsewhere. On a wreck called the *Kyrenia* a large concentration of lead objects that might have been overlooked outside the excavation area were located with metal detectors.

In 1988 several others and I spent more than a month following the route Moses and the Jews took in their Exodus from Egypt about 1400 B.C. Team leader Dick Ewing devoted years to planning cthis expedition. Mem-

Members of the Egyptian expedition, from left, Astronaut Jim Erwin, Dr. Roy Knuteson, Dick Ewing and Charles Garrett. At right is Ron Wyatt, an explorer who has searched for Noah's Ark.

318

bers of this team, shown on the preceding page, included Astronaut Jim Erwin, Dr. Roy Knuteson and I, who each participated by bringing equipment knowledge and/or expertise into play during the various searches. Irwin's responsibioity was to man various aircraft deploying photography, infrared and other specialized airborne equipment. My responsibility was to handle land and underwater metal detection equipment at the various sites. Our many discoveries will be the subject of future books and videos.

Other Suggestions

An initial survey of a given land or underwater site will locate all metal items down several feet deep. This pinpointing of metal objects helps the archaeologist to determine scope, layout and other characteristics of the site.

A site can be scanned for metal artifacts of all types or just non-ferrous, high conductivity metal items such as those made of copper, brass, bronze, silver, pewter and gold. Since these non-ferrous metals do not corrode rapidly, they may bear visible data that facilitates dating, country of origin, type of cargo or other valuable research information. A complete detector scan of a site with markers placed at each target location helps to establish the areas most likely to be productive. When coins are found, a site can be dated more easily. A simple metal detector survey of a "suspect" area can "prove" the site is one the researcher wishes to investigate. The same investigation can also prove the site is *not* the one to investigate. To some extent, metal detectors can determine when ground-zero has been reached. A complete scan will reveal whether other metal objects (and possibly *nonmetallic* objects) are present below those levels that have already been excavated.

Surveying Known Wrecks

Whenever a wreck is to be studied and excavated archaeologically, it may be desirable to conduct a metal detector survey to proceed in a more orderly and planned fashion. Information can be obtained on the dimensions of the wreck-site, the direction in which remains of the ship are lying, the location of cannon, anchor and other ship's rigging. To accomplish this survey, a non-metallic grid is placed in position. Detectors are used to locate every detectable object which can then be dug or simply size-determined. It is easy for a detector to differentiate between a cannon and a coin or other smaller item. Of course, several metal objects closely associated may appear as one large piece of metal. Iron, however, can easily be distinguished from non-metallic objects. By using these methods, a metal-object profile of the wreck can be developed.

At an underwater site such as the resting place of the *Titanic,* personal artifacts and ship's components are strewn over a vast area. One convenient, simple way to locate most of this metal debris that is buried is to use metal detectors. Approximate locations of each found item could be made or a vast grid network could be utilized. A non-metallic grid network could be set up and metal detectors used to locate every piece of buried metal. Certainly, this would be of great value when there is not sufficient time to completely excavate a site or when murky conditions prevent a photo mosaic.

Rescue Archaeology

Sometimes called *salvage archaeology,* rescue archaeology is a technique used during emergency situations when a site is soon to be covered by rising waters of a new lake or by the construction of buildings, highways and railroads. Archaeologists also use this technique at excavation sites for canals and other waterways.

In such situations archaeologists realize that only a small fraction of the historical relics can be saved; but, even a small part is better than nothing. Thus, compromises are made, as quickly as possible, to recover relics from the site. The metal detector can be the perfect tool

320

to help the archaeologist in this plight. The metal detector will quickly locate all buried metal objects. A marker is placed at each location with a team of people following the detector operators to recover the detected items. One metal detector can keep numerous "recovery" teams busy.

Using *rescue archaeology*, much knowledge of the history of a site can be obtained that might otherwise be lost forever. Residents of a community can be rewarded with the knowledge of a portion of the history of their ancestors. Educational museums can be established for the townspeople. The foregoing discussion about Rescue Archaeology was based on material from my book, *Modern Metal Detectors,* which contained a chapter with case histories and suggestions for the use of metal detectors.

Archaeologist vs. Treasure Hunter

The subject of metal detectors has long been hotly debated. Some archaeologists steadfastly refuse to acknowledge the detector as a viable tool and even seek to brand users of detectors as mere artifact collectors. But, through the efforts of many archaeologists, the value of the metal detector in research is being realized.

I am on the side of *both* the archaeologist and the treasure hunter. In my writing as well as my work in the field I would never encourage or instruct any "treasure hunter" to remove even a single artifact from a valuable historical site. I place historical knowledge far above any monetary value to be gained from artifacts. The treasure hunter should never encroach upon an established or defined historical site. Neither should an archaeologist, as an archaeologist, encroach upon potential treasure sites by imposing general restrictions on locations that represent no value to archaeology.

There are tens of thousands of places where relics and treasures from the past can be found in varying amounts. But, never in ten thousand years can archaeologists locate and excavate them all. Nor, would they desire to! For the archaeologist and historian to attempt to keep the treasure hunter from all such sites is wrong. Not only will all the "historical" sites never be discovered, the passage of time will continue to destroy them along with their artifacts and treasure. Why not let the treasure hunter search for and recover treasure from sites that archaeologists know *realistically* they will *never* work?

On the other hand, historically important sites should not be touched by the treasure hunter. To remove even a single item is the loss of great knowledge about that site and the customs of the people who lived there. Archaeologists are like Sherlock Holmes, veritable detectives of science and history. They doggedly investigate our heritage to provide valuable knowledge about our past. It's remarkable how their investigation and analysis reveals the finest details of life as it took place thousands of years ago. Work is very demanding and thorough. Consequently, they don't need anyone to come along and destroy even a single shred of evidence. They need all the help they can get.

Why can't the archaeologist and treasure hunter work together? It's been proposed and discussed many times. Some critics of treasure hunters strongly oppose any such coalition. To do so, they believe, would confer an unwarranted respectability on the treasure hunter. Instead of recognition, the treasure hunter is often deplored and likened unto looters and thieves. Granted, there are some treasure "hunters" who, without regard to the law or the value of ancient sites, willfully vandalize and destroy as they remove artifacts and treasure. But, are all archaeologists really *clean?* Are there no misplaced artifacts or treasures concealed in home closets and cellars? Never are all members of a profession or calling perfect. Has there never been some minister, banker, law officer, archaeologist or treasure hunter who hasn't "gone astray?"

And what about the thousands of sunken vessels and cultural areas that are never discovevered before kthey are destroyed by erosion? What about bulldozers and earth-moving equipment of developers and builders? Don't they mutilate and completely elminatge countless sites every day?

Well, neither side can win 'em all. Nor, should either expect to! What both the archaeologist and the treasure hunter should try to do, however, is to see the other's point of view and realize that we should work together...at least, not hinder each other. Certainly, working together makes the most sense. It has worked before as proven at numerous sites including the Custer battle site at the Little Big Horn in Montana.

A start would be for each side to learn the true nature of the other's complaints. What are the real objections of archaeologists? And, what is the treasure hunter's gripe? Again I ask...*why won't the two groups work together?* Certainly, each can learn a lot from the other. I believe that if most treasure hunters knew how to recognize a valuable historical site when they found one, they would stay away from it and would direct the archaeologist to the location. It has happened many times. Also, if the treasure hunters knew what was historically important, they would be careful in their recovery work and would supply important site and artifact data to the proper people. Many metal detector hobbyists would gladly, without charge, work with archaeological groups. The archaeologists could achieve many objectives simply by educating treasure hunters on the basics of archaeology and the importance of certain objects.

Since the metal detector *is* an important tool of discovery, archaeologists should benefit from knowing how to use it. Few are the metal detector users who don't welcome the opportunity to instruct others in the use of their equipment. Metal detector manufacturers would offer free training for archaeologists. I would. I have written three times to a Texas state archaeologist and offered such training at no expense to the scientists. Furthermore, I have offered my skills with a metal detector to be used at historical sites anywhere in Texas...free of charge. I am still waiting, after several years, for an answer, yes or no.

What can you, the treasure hunter, do to protect historically important sites and help close the gap between the treasure hunter and the archaeologist? You can start by trying to understand the point of view of the archaeologist. You can become an amateur archaeologist and learn some thing about archaeological methods and techniques. You can acquaint yourself with the background and aims of archaeology. There are several reference books listed in the Bibliography. Try to form a partnership with your local archaeological community, with historical societies, museums and universities. Reach out to them. Offer to work as a site volunteer using your metal detector when and where it would be useful.

Stay alert to the possibility that you may someday discover an important archaeological site. For instance, should you be working a beach or surf area and locate a bronze axe, contact your local or state archaeologist. You may have discovered the site of a ten-thousand-year-old prehistoric settlement.

Learn the nature of the responsibilities of your state's archaeologist. Ask your State Senator or Representative for such information. Obtain a copy of your state's antiquities law and learn what it says. Read it carefully to determine your rights, provisions for licenses or permits and which agency or individual has the authority to issue such documents.

Encourage local archaeological groups, museums and historical societies to establish a central clearing house where you and other amateur archaeologists and historians can turn for information on identifying and preserving important locations and finds. When you make such discoveries, contact this group and report them. Ask if they are interested in the site and joining you in your work. Make your contacts first by telephone or a personal visit, and then by letter. Certainly, you would want proof that you disclosed the location of an important site. Be businesslike, serious and ready to propose a plan. Offer to continue working the site using archaeological knowledge and methods you have learned, and to report data about finds. Welcome the opportunity of having an archaeologist monitor your work. Each time there is a successful encounter between professional archaeologists and treasure hunters, a closer bond is cemented. I know of many persons who have shared their finds with historical groups and federal, state or local authorities. In almost every case, they were made welcome and encouraged to continue working. Also, such contacts resulted in their being granted permits to work in areas otherwise restricted to the metal detector operator.

A metal detectorist discovered several bronze axes in Northern Michigan. He reported the find to authorities. The site has become very important archaeologically. Another treasure hunter, Gary Weicks, found the flintlock mechanism of a Hudson Bay gun. He made contact with DeWitt Bailey of London to obtain data about manufacture and distribution of the weapon. The treasure hunter, realizing the gun's importance, contacted the National Forest Service. He later worked with two Forest Service archaeologists in carrying out a complete metal detector survey, similar to the one at the Custer battle site. The area is thought to be, perhaps a rendezvous site for early-day fur trappers.

To sum up, do not trespass in restricted areas and on known archaeological sites. A British author points out that doing so is stupid, inconsiderate and, of paramount importance, is against the law. This author further compels us "to remember that each time we go out with a metal detector, we are an ambassador for an activity that is rewarding in very many ways. We must face up to our responsibilities as both treasure hunters and citizens. The reputation and future of ourselves and others who enjoy treasure hunting will be secure."

It is my sincere hope that we metal detector hobbyists can develop a rapport with archaeologists and learn from them. There are actions that all of us can take to facilitate this joining of interests. We can become knowledgeable about applicable laws and take an active part in writing and passing good new legislation. We can always remain ready to teach others about treasure hunting and metal detecting.

Most important of all, howver, we should attempt at all times to live up to the Metal Detector Operators Code of Ethics (see Chapter 28). It is the duty of all metal detector hobbyists to remain ever responsible to insure conservation and proper management of the archaeological resources of our nation and the world.

Pouches/Hand Tools

Selecting and properly using correct tools is essential to maximum success in searching for treasure as in any other field of endeavor. If you are wise in your choice of tools and proficient in using them, your rewards should be great.

This chapter describes equipment and tools needed for beach hunting, surfing and underwater recovery. Chapter 23 describes specialized equipment such as depth recorders, sub-bottom profilers and submersible craft. Metal detectors and accessories are described in Chapters 5 through 9. Various "how-to-use" metal detector instructions can be found in other chapters.

Treasure pouches are available in one, two and even three-pocket designs. In the one-pocket style, everything you find--treasure and trash alike--goes into that single pocket. At the end of the day, you must sort through the entire contents to recover "keepers." Even with a two-pocket pouch that holds treasure in one pocket and trash in the other, you should carefully inspect your trash visually before discarding anything.

I recommend that all detected items be placed in a recovery pouch. At intervals you can inspect your trash and discard it *properly.* I emphasize that last word because all of us treasure hunters can help keep beaches cleaner by properly discarding trash. The next hunter (possibly even *you*) will not have to contend with trash. And, even if your detector is a discriminator, remember that reject targets resulting from trash that you have cast aside can diminish good target detector signals.

Some hunters prefer their "treasure" pocket to have a

snap, zipper or velcro fastener. For beach hunting a secure pocket is not particularly necessary unless you often lay down to rest or you have the habit of tossing your pouch on the ground or in the trunk of your car.

Some beachcombers use three-pocket pouches. One pocket is used for trash, one for most finds and the third for more valuable finds. To me, *all* treasure finds are *keepers* and I don't want to lose anything I find. When I find an object of value, I always try to store it immediately.

When I am searching long hours, I sometimes set up a tent where I can occasionally return to eat or rest in the shade. On these trips I place all finds in my stowed gear.

Pouches should be *waterproof* to prevent soiling of your clothes. The fabric should also be rugged and able to withstand lots of weight and rigorous use. A non-fraying cord or other suitable means of securing the pouch to yourself are required. Many pouch styles can be mounted on a belt. I often wear a web belt that holds a canteen, a tool kit and two or more extra pouches for miscellaneous items such as sunscreen, a small camera and first aid kit.

Sometimes, I wear my treasure/trash pouch on this belt. A web belt is versatile and allows you to carry any number of things securely.

The digger or retriever to be used depends upon the beach sands, whether coarse or fine, wet or dry and upon the individual's preference. I prefer a long-handled, lightweight, flat-bladed pick, which with one blow usually dislodges the object. If I still can't find it, one pass with the detector searchcoil tells me where the object is--still in the ground or on the surface. Occasionally, I'll use a wide-bladed trowel with which I can quickly cut a hole and remove the sand and detected object with one circular motion.

Another recovery method for loose sand is to use a cup-size plastic container. Sweep the cup through the sand, then under the searchcoil. If your metal object is in the container, the detector will tell you so.

A great many beach hunters use some sort of garden trowel. When you need to dig deeply through packed ground and tree roots, you'll appreciate a heavy duty digger.

Sand scoops and sifters can be useful at times. When sand is very fine and completely dry, you can use a sifter to scoop up your target along with sand, then shake it and your treasure will be on the sifter. When sand is coarse or damp, however, you'll probably have to shake the sifter for a minute or so to remove all the sand. In damp sand you may never get it all out unless you submerge the sifter in water. In situations like these, a sifter is a waste of time.

You may also be interested in the Estwing long-handled recovery tool. Because the device has a long handle with a digger/scoop, you do not have to bend down each time you make a find. You can drag it through the sand, scoop up your find and pocket it, while you remain standing.

Open-pocket pouches are very risky. I encourage you to use a pouch with a secure closing device such as a zipper,

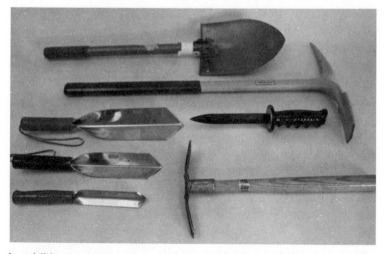

In addition to these many commercial digging tools available to the treasure hunter that can be purchased at most hardware stores are the special implements devised by individuals.

snap or velcro. The trash pocket can and should be the open type because you will quickly become weary of unfastening its pocket every time you recover junk. Opening and closing a treasure pouch each time you find money or jewelry is trouble enough. But you are glad to do it because you are preventing loss of found treasures. Belt pouches with a single, large pocket for trash and a smaller pocket with a fastener are available. Any pouch used in the water must have drain holes.

Some surfers prefer to use a zipper bag or a screwtop plastic bottle attached to a string. The bag or bottle is worn around the neck.

Scoops

When you work in shallow water, you can use a hand sifter to recover detected objects. When you work in water deeper than about 18 inches, you must use a scoop/sifter with an extension handle. There are many designs. I prefer the type with a handle loop shown on the facing page.

There are several reasons why I prefer this loop-handle design. When you are not retrieving a find, you may slip the upper end of the handle loop over your arm for easy carrying. The most important reason, however, is because the handle is very efficient to use. To dig, place the scoop blade at the correct place on the bottom. Grasp the rear section of the looped handle and push it forward. This action places the scoop in a near vertical position for digging. After you have pushed the scoop into the sand with your foot, pull backwards on the handle. Slide your hand down the forward section of the handle loop until you reach the scoop. If the water is too deep for you to reach the scoop, you can make a succession of "jumps" along the handle, each time pulling the scoop farther from

Beach hunter uses the double-handled scoop described on this page and in Chapter 11 to investigate a target that has just been announced by her detector.

the soil. This can be difficult to do with some plain-handled scoops because of their center of gravity. When you pull upward, plain-handle scoops tend to rotate. When loop-handle scoops are pulled free of the bottom, they don't rotate like scoops with a single straight handle. This scoop also comes with two shorter handles as shown in the photograph on the following page.

There are numerous methods you can use to recover detected finds. You must practice to learn exactly where to place the scoop. In the beginning you may have to make a dozen or more tries before you are successful. Even with experience, more than one "dig" is sometimes necessary.

Because light-colored shoes can be more easily seen when you are working in murky water, you'll have an easier time of positioning a scoop at the point of your toe when your shoes are light colored. When shaking sand from the scoop, shake it away from the path you are walking to minimize visibility reduction. Also, when you let water currents clean your scoop, make sure sand washes away from the direction you are walking.

When surfing with a submersible metal detector, a correctly designed long-handled sifter is the only recovery tool you need.

The Beach Connection

Some hunters use their land detectors in shallow water by attaching the housing to the upper portion of their chest or mounting it on a flotation device. This procedure, however, requires an extension cable inserted between the searchcoil cable connector and housing connector. You must waterproof the connector. A waterproofing device I have tested is the *Beach Connection,* which is manufactured by the Beach Connection Co., P.O.Box 175,

Because moist sand will simply clog up a scoop and delay recovery, this hobbyist is using a tool that permits easy digging into a soft beach to find detected objects.

333

Ashland, KY 41105. The device will remain watertight to a depth of about six feet. Number 75-1875 protects connectors with a maximum diameter of 3/4 inches. Number 100-1875 protects connectors with a maximum diameter of one inch. Use the smaller size, if you can, for less bulk.

Various Flotation Devices

Flotation devices are important because most metal detectors can be used in fresh water if the electronics housing remains dry and the searchcoil is submersible-rated to the depth you will be working. Let me emphasize again, however, that non-discriminating BFOs and TRs are *obsolete*. They *cannot* be used in salt water. To cancel the effects of salt water, a detector must have a discrimination circuit adjustable to bottlecap rejection. At this setting, salt water will be ignored. Most automated detectors are capable of effective operation in salt water.

To keep your housing high and dry, it can be mounted

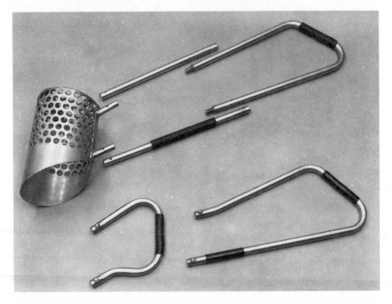

For information on Alden Fogliadini's water scoop whose short and medium-length handles are shown above. write to Aldo's Scoop, 6180 Via Real #1, Carpentena, CA 93013.

on your body, perhaps with a backpack. You must, of course, be able to reach the controls easily.

There are about as many flotation devices as there are people designing them. An automobile innertube or styrofoam device can be easily constructed. PVC tubing makes an excellent float/screen. Monty Moncrief built such a device especially to help me in the prepartion of this book.

It's best to mount the metal detector one foot or more above the water by suspending it from an inverted "L" bracket attached to the float. Remember, however, the housing must not be too high for you to reach the controls, and the cable on your searchcoil must be long enough.

Your sifting screen should float slightly below water level. Submersion in water helps keep it clean. Depending upon the amount of rock, shell and other debris on the bottom, you'll occasionally have to dump the unwanted material. Some means can be devised to hinge the screen for quick dumping. Also, keep it tied securely so that it will remain nearby and not float out to sea. Be sure to build in one or more "pockets" for treasure, trash and other items.

Recovery Equipment/Tools

This section covers hand-held recovery tools, lift bags and other devices. Major equipment such as hooka rigs, inflatables, boats, site-gridding devices and the like are discussed in Chapters 12 and 24.

At some sites, you can just fan your hand and the sand will blow away. At others, you'll need a pick to break coins and other detected items from coral growth. A strong diver's knife should be on your check list. A good sheath mounting location is on the lower leg just above the ankle. A secure locking strap is a must.

Suitable bags or containers should be part of your equipment for keeping the things you find. Nylon netting bags are good. In sandy or heavily silted areas, a probe can be used to pinpoint solid objects.

The Estwing prospector's pick is a good tool. You can fasten it to your wrist with a lanyard. Larger picks may be needed such as the 27-inch Estwing model.

Lift Bags

Lift bags are available in a variety of sizes and shapes. These include pillow bags, buoyancy balls and open-mouth lift bags. Open-mouth bags are not popular, however, because they cannot be laid on their sides without losing air. Lift capacity of bags ranges from 50 pounds to 12,000 pounds. Bags are very strong, durable and lightweight. They can be rolled into a compact roll for storage and easy handling under water. A bag with a 1000-pound lift capacity weighs approximately 10 pounds.

Bags usually are constructed of a neoprene bladder bonded to an outer shell of nylon coated with a layer of polyurethane rubber. This coating is tough and flexible yet highly resistant to abrasion and to most chemicals, particularly gasoline and diesel fuel which are commonly encountered during salvage operations.

Other features of lift bags include inflation and dump valves to maintain buoyancy, as required, and straps or lift points for attaching objects to be lifted. Attaching objects securely permits you to tow them after they have been raised. Air bladders are available without straps for placing inside cars, boats and barges.

Miscellaneous Tools

Grappling Hooks: These can be used to recover objects from cisterns and wells. Three- or four-pronged models come in all sizes. The main disadvantage is their inclination to "stay hooked" to almost anything. If the object proves too heavy or large to retrieve, you've usually lost a hook and some rope.

Magnets: A magnet will attract iron objects, but not non-ferrous metals such as gold, silver and copper. Most magnets have an eye hook or means for attaching a rope. They are rated according to the pull they will exert on an iron object. A magnet will attract iron rust just as it will attract solid iron. Whenever the magnet is not in use, an iron bar should be placed across its open end. Always use care when placing the bar on a magnet. To remove the bar it is usually easier to slide it off.

Probes: In loose sand and lightly compacted soils, probes can be easily inserted two feet or more. With practice, you will be able to determine if you have contacted metal, glass, wood or rock. Construct your own probes with any type of rod material. Slender sizes are preferred, but the rod must not bend easily. A small "bullet" welded on the tip will reduce the amount of drag when you pull the probe from the soil. Only slightly larger in diameter than the probe rod itself, the bullet should be pointed or rounded to facilitate insertion. A suitable, yet solidly attached, handle should be mounted on the upper end.

Spiraling Circle Spool

Various grid methods will insure 100% coverage of an area you are scanning. The *spiraling circle* search, shown below, is a popular method. Use a spool with rope or line wound upon its core. Anchor the spool at the center point of your search area. The spool must not rotate. The preferred method is to spiral outward. Place one of your hands through a loose-fitting loop formed by the end of the rope. Hold the rope and begin swimming around the

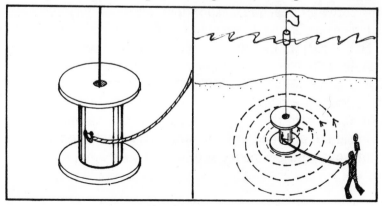

spool as you scan visually or with a metal detector. Swimming in this controlled circle will permit you to search an area without skipping. The amount of "feed out" per revolution around the spool depends upon the width of the path you can effectively scan.

If you wish to "feed out" at the rate of 36 inches for each revolution, the spool core diameter should be approximately 12 inches. Use the following equation for determining your desired spool core diameter:

$$CD \times 3 = FOD$$

Core Diameter...*times* 3...*equals* Feed-Out Distance.

Buoy Markers

Small Buoys: You may need several of these. They can be constructed by attaching lines to bleach or other plastic containers. A brick anchor will serve except in high wind or rough weather. Buoys can be used as site markers or to locate recovery baskets. Then, when you fill a basket, just follow the line topside and haul in your finds.

Diver's Flags: Areas with boat traffic require you to position dive flags to warn boaters. But, don't rely entirely on the flag alone to do the job. Some boaters haven't the slightest idea what a dive flag means. Others may ignore them. So, always approach the surface cautiously.

Underwater Beacon Transponders: In traffic lanes and locations where total secrecy is essential, you can plant underwater beacon transponders. These battery-powered devices transmit a low frequency signal at a given interval. The receiver, mounted in your boat, precisely locates underwater site. Depending on transmitted power, life of your batteries can be several months.

There are many other miscellaneous tools and pieces of equipment that may be needed. Study manufacturer's literature and acquire the necessary items required to improve your efficiency and protect your equipment.

Specialized Locating

Thousands of potentially rich underwater treasure sites have attracted both the professional and the amateur. While not every person seeking sunken treasure strikes it rich, those who do fuel a fire that steadily grows brighter. The desire to find sunken wealth leads men (and women) to search farther and deeper, pushing not only their limits but also those of the equipment and methods they use. Consequently, diving for treasure demands development of improved equipment required by persevering treasure hunters.

This chapter introduces you to some of these inventions. From the simple view-sled to such intricate scientific devices as side-scan sonar/sub bottom profiler and robot and manned submersibles, man's technology has responded to develop whatever new equipment was required to overcome the challenge at hand. Even as you read this chapter, men are continually expanding the limits of underwater exploration as they improve and perfect new equipment that exceeds the limits of today's imagination. Most of the equipment described on these pages was unheard of just a short time ago. Yet, it is now being used daily. Select from it to the extent that your requirements and budget allow. Professional equipment should be used to the fullest extent possible. Let nothing hinder progress toward achieving your goals!

Surface View-Scope

A glass-bottom bucket or view-scope is a simple yet excellent device to permit a visual search in any body of clear water...river, lake or ocean. Constructing a view-scope requires that you bond a round, clear glass plate into the end of a PVC pipe or other suitable tube. Glass shops can readily cut a 1/4-inch thick piece of glass to any diameter you require. Waterproof silicone will securely bond the glass in the proper sized tube. For good visibility, the diameter of the tube should be large enough for viewing with both eyes. A safety sling will prevent loss.

Underwater Photography

Photography can be a useful tool for the dedicated treasure hunting enthusiast. Every good photograph is valuable as a permanent record of data and information that might be lost forever. Before-and-after site documentation can be invaluable and time-saving. By leisurely studying sites you can discover features overlooked at the scene. When a study or reconstruction of a shipwreck is required, grid/photography documentation can help accomplish it. A complete photographic record of finds has many advantages, including its use as proof of posession in case of losses through fire or theft.

Don't feel intimidated by all the technical information on photography. The selection of an adequate camera, a study of its operating manual, an initial training exercise and a basic knowledge of photographic fundamentals are adequate basics. Mastery begins by learning to concentrate on fundamental techniques.

Begin with specific subject selection rather than randomly shooting everything in sight. If you have a plan, a goal to be achieved, you've won most of the battle already. A critical study of your photographs taken as you progress is the fastest means of developing photographic expertise.

Don't be afraid to ask for help. Check out books from your library and study them. Soon you'll be asking yourself what the fuss was all about. There are many good cameras on the market including professional Nikonos models and the Hanimex 110/35mm amphibians. Depending upon water depth and required print quality, you may be able to use one of the waterproof "swimmer's" cameras that do everything except select the subject to be photographed. Also various waterproof camera housings are available. The Helix Company, 325 West Huron St., Chicago, IL 60610, (312) 944-4400, stocks a complete range of underwater cameras and equipment. The Ikelite Company, 50 W. 33rd St., Indianapolis, IN 46208, (317) 923-4523, manufactures a wide assortment of underwater camera and equipment housings.

Aerial Photography

Since 1969 various types of infrared and water-penetrating film have been produced which, when used with polarizing filters, locate from the air those images of sunken objects not visible with the naked eye. These special films have been used to record ocean-bottom detail and to find underwater archaeological sites. Precise location of sites is difficult with aerial photography unless it is near a coastline, or specially placed buoys are used.

Film manufacturers, including GAF Corporation and Eastman Kodak, can provide additional information to those who wish to investigate the use of aerial photography.

Pre-flight groundwork for aerial photography is very important. A marine navigation chart should be used as a graphic planning tool for laying out the area to be photographed. With water depths shown and flight lines can be drawn that enable a pilot to fly your search area. Make at least one dry run over the area you plan to photograph to familiarize yourself with its features for any possible changes prior to actual "picture taking." An excellent source book is *Interpretation of Aerial Photographs*.

A few helpful hints will assist you in the successful use of this type of research activity:

– The camera *sees* what the eye sees...and probably more. However, if water is dirty, deep (50 ft. or deeper), or turbulent, effective aerial photography will probably not be possible.

– Because glare and reflection reduce photo coverage, mid-morning (9-11a.m.) and mid-afternoon (1:30-4p.m.) time periods are best for aerial photography. The afternoon period may be extended during the summer months. A clear day with less than 20% cloud cover is necessary if detail is required in your photography. This is not only because of clouds blocking the view but also because of cloud shadows.

– Vertical or near vertical photography will produce the best results. A helicopter is preferable; it can remain in an almost stationary position. A fixed-wing aircraft should be banked in a slow turn when photographs are being taken.

– A fast shutter speed (1/500 sec. or faster) will reduce image motion caused by aircraft flight and vibration.

– Color slide film usually produces the best photographs. Use a haze filter and *slightly overexpose* for water penetration.

– Check *all* camera equipment and film, and clean aircraft windows prior to take-off.

Surf Boards/Planing Sleds

An easy way to visually inspect large bottom areas quickly is to be towed along the surface. In addition to mask, snorkel and fins it is a good idea to wear a slim-line or inflatable life vest. Towing speed must be slow or water pressures may become too great. Extended towing can also rapidly deplete your body heat and energy.

A surf board with a glass viewing port can be an efficient device when the water is sufficiently calm. Rough weather may cause the view port to bound out of the water, creating visibility problems.

Various underwater sled designs are available. One such model is the Hydrofin, manufactured by Hope Diving Developments Limited, 10 Farndale Avenue, Palmers Green London N 3 TAQ, London, England. This device allows a diver to survey an area precisely in a minimum of time. Using such a device also eliminates the need for massive diver effort. The Hydrofin has a detachable instrument console that will accept a dive watch, depth gauge and compass. It has a camera-mounting bracket and all necessary handles, arm rests and a towing eye. At a speed of approximately five knots a diver can maneuver at will over and around obstacles from surface level down to any practical depth. While its advantages greatly outweigh its disadvantages, the Hydrofin's main restriction is that you must go where the towing vessel takes you. Even then, a simple direct-coupled sound system can be devised to permit the diver to instruct the boat pilot.

A towing sled can be built of PVC tubing and aluminum sheet metal. The device should have a rudder bow plane and water screen. Bow planes permit lateral motion, and a waterscreen lessens water pressure on the face and body.

Underwater Searchcoils

An inexpensive method to locate metal objects under water is to use a metal detector searchcoil. Using the Beach Connection (see Chapter 22) it is possible to connect a submersible searchcoil such as any of Garrett's Crossfire models with waterproof cable of the necessary length. Your searchcoil can then be lowered and maneuvered over the bottom while its electronic housing is kept above water. Objects as small as a coin can be detected. Larger objects such as motors and metal boats can be detected six to eight feet below the bottom of the searchcoil. Maneuverability and coverage is good except in swiftly flowing water. If necessary, the searchcoil can be weighted to improve stability.

With the searchcoil attached to the end of a 10 to 15 foot pole the operator can control and maneuver it from a boat or pier. Various other searchcoils with standard cable length can be attached to a pole for shallow water searching. Just make certain that the detector housing is never submerged.

The Garrett Bloodhound Depth Multiplier attachment can *multiply* (two to four times) the depth capability of the Garrett Grand Master Hunter or Master Hunter 7X on large or deeply buried objects. This searchcoil too is fully submersible and can be used with a cable of virtually any length.

For further information on submersible searchcoils and metal detectors, contact Garrett Electronics, 2814 National Dr., Gar land, TX 75041, (214) 278-6151, Telex 4630163.

Self-Propelled Submersibles

Self-propelled vehicles permit a scuba diver to travel four times faster and ten times farther on a tank of air while reducing air consumption by 50%. These small, self-contained, battery-powered vehicles give you an exhilarating feeling as you glide almost effortlessly along the bottom, maneuvering over and around obstacles. Rechargeable batteries offer a range of up to three miles on a single charge. The units are constructed of high-impact, non-corrosive materials. A headlight improves visibility during cave and night dives. For information on the Tekna diver vehicles illustrated in this chapter, contact TEKNA, P.O. Box 849, Belmont, CA 94002, (415) 592-4070.

The Blaster

The Blaster, also affectionately known as the "Mailbox," was first used as an excavation tool by Mel Fisher. Hampered by murky water, he diverted his ship's prop wash downward to force clear water to the bottom. To Mel's surprise and delight, water velocity also blew sediment away, exposing heavier materials such as ballast, relics and treasure.

There are many factors governing the design and operation of a Blaster...diameter and length, its attachment to the boat, protection for divers, proper boat anchorage, speed of props and length of time operated. An improperly operated Blaster can damage sites and cause treasure to be lost. Excessive Blaster force has cut through coral, propelling cannonballs 50 feet and blasting emeralds as though they were fired from a gun.

Use of Video

The relatively low cost and simplicity of operating video equipment places it within the realm of everyday use by both topside and underwater explorers. Home entertainment cameras and recorders produce superb "viewing" quality.

While the days of film are not over, the arrival of videotape eliminated headaches associated with shooting and processing film. Video cassette recorders utilize magnetic tape, compared with the emulsion film of photography that requires extreme care in handling, developing and processing. Tape is inexpensive and reusable and has near-perfect storage qualities. Editing and assembling your own movies is not that difficult, especially if during filming you plan ahead by allowing ample "on scene" leading and trailing footage. Also, make sure exposures are correct (most cameras feature automatic exposure) and capture sufficient event footage and extra action and closeup takes to enhance the finished product. Home video comes in two formats: VHS and BETA with VHS being the overwhelming favorite. Remember that VHS and BETA tapes and recording equipment are not interchangeable. Your footage can be transferred from one to the other, but image quality usually suffers.

Thoroughly study all equipment. Renting and testing several models is not a bad idea. The more you know about video recording, plus the best possible understanding of your filming and later usage requirements, the better you will be able to select what's best for you.

Panasonic and Sony offer complete underwater systems. Video cameras, recorders, light and batteries are built into especially designed, highly functional and maneuverable underwater housings.

Companies such as AquaVideo manufacture high quality submersible video equipment housings. Free advice and literature is available from Aquavideo, Inc., 5065 N.W. 159th St., Miami, FL 33014, (305) 621-0222.

345

Exotic deep sea equipment such as remote-control cameras play key roles in underwater surveys to locate and explore sunken ships and shipwreck sites. Video cameras provided instant initial viewing of the *Titanic* and its wreckage. A remote-control camera explored the *Titanic* and sent up vivid color footage of the ship and its wreckage to help its discoverers plan later manned-vehicle exploration.

Depth Finders

There are numerous models of depth finders--sometimes called *fish finders*. These instruments can provide information on depths and bottoms. A piezo-crystal transducer encased in a suitable plastic module is mounted on the underside of a boat or on a pole under water. When an electrical current excites the crystal, it expands, sending a shock wave downward into the depths. Any object it strikes, such as fish, logs and the bottom, cause a reflective wave which, when it reaches the transducer, excites the crystal. The resulting current signal is amplified and conditioned to activate lights or recorders and in some cases, audible alarms.

Even the simplest models accurately indicate bottom depth and proximity to large submerged objects. Recording devices like various of the Lowrance models produce paper recordings that provide a veritable road map of bottom contours and reveal submerged objects such as fish, stumps, piers, boat motors...even articles as small as a few inches. Remarkable and exacting data is instantly available for immediate or later analysis. These models are programmable to depths in excess of 1,000 feet. Any portion of the vertical range can be selected to fill full paper height thereby giving great detail of the bottom or of objects protruding from it. Many objects, such as boats and motors, are often outlined with remarkable detail providing instant object recognition. Contact Lowrance Electronics, 12000 E. Skelly Drive, Tulsa, OK, (918) 437-6881 for information.

Magnetometers/Gradiometers

On Nov. 26, 1978, underwater explorer Burt Webber and his *Sea Quest* crew used a cesium magnetometer to discover the wreck of the Spanish galleon *Concepcion* off the coast of the Dominican Republic. An estimated $40 million in silver and gold on board the *Concepcion* highlighted capabilities of the model produced by Varian Associates of Canada.

Magnetic iron and steel objects such as anchors, cannon, cook stoves and parts of ship's rigging cause a local change in the earth's magnetic field. This change, or "anomaly," can be detected by a magnetometer some distance from the magnetic body. The detectable distance and signal strength depend upon the size of an object. The greater the mass...the greater will be the anomaly.

Magnetometers consist of a sensor mounted on a staff. The electronics and display unit are mounted in a waterproof housing. Magnetic field strength is converted to a tone which is fed into the diver's headphones. Changes

This Klein sidescan sonar record of a RAF Wellington bomber that crashed in Scotland's Loch Ness during World War II helped locate the airplane 30 years later, making recovery possible.

in the audio tone are caused by anomaly detection. Even in poor visibility, the diver will know of nearby iron and steel objects.

The gradiometer is essentially two magnetometers, mounted in one instrument that measures the difference in field strength or gradient between two sensor points. The gradiometer is a simpler instrument, in principle, since it is only necessary to measure the difference in field intensity, the absolute value of field strength being irrelevant.

There are four types of magnetometers: cesium, proton precession, fluxgate and optically-pumped. The complexity of optically-pumped magnetometers restricts their general use. Of the remaining three, only fluxgate magnetometers are directional in that they measure the field component through the axis of a mu-metal core.

Magnetometers and gradiometers are available in hand-held, portable and towable configurations which may be towed under water, across ice and through the air. Their development long ago reached the stage where highly reliable systems are commonplace.

Side-Scan Sonar

For more than 40 years, Nessie, the legendary Loch Ness monster, shared the dark waters of its Scottish lake with something equally big and fierce and almost as famous. During World War II, a Royal Air Force pilot ditched a 14-ton Wellington bomber in the long, narrow lake of the highlands of northern Scotland. Records indicated the plane was in the loch, but no one knew its exact whereabouts.

At top is a Garrett Sea Hunter specially rigged in a one-man submarine for underwater searching. Below are police shown recovering a safe found with a metal detector.

In the late 1970s, several teams began systematic sonar studies of the lake using side-scan sonar and the newly developed sonar sub-bottom profiler. They made numerous important discoveries, one of which was the Wellington bomber shown on Page 349. Other "finds" included various other planes, sunken vessels, strange rows of what appeared to be rocks and several "unknowns" that, for all the world, looked just like Nessie, or at least how the creature is *supposed* to look.

Side-scan sonar is a widely accepted tool for mapping topography of sea and lake beds. Scanning hundreds of meters on both sides of a moving ship, it provides an excellent means to rapidly survey any area of interest.

Sub-bottom profiling employs high resolution sonar to profile shallow bottom sediment layers. This is a vertical scanning system compared with the side-angular scanning of side scan sonar.

Both systems are built into rugged, portable and self-contained housings called "tow fish." Side scan sonar beams project outward from the "tow fish" along the sea bed on both sides of a moving vessel. Objects or topographic features produce echoes which are received by transducers. The sub-bottom system transducer projects a conical beam straight down toward the sea floor. Echoes from the bottom matrix excite the transducer which produces signals that can be processed by graphic recorders.

Illustrated on the following page is an artist's conception of the Klein Hydrdoscan side-scan sonar/sub-bottom profiler technique. My friend Martin Klein, president of Klein Associates, has just sent some information on their

These underwater explorers can enjoy the freedom of diving without bulky tanks, since their air needs are being supplied by a floating Brownie's Third Lung.

new sonar system with a high resolution thermal recorder, the System 590 Klein Digital Sonar. The heart of this new system is a new Model 595 Graphic Recorder. Some of the features include image correction, record expansion, so-

Concept of the Klein Hydroscan side-scan sonar/sub-bottom profiler technique shows conical sonar beams projecting down from the towfish to produce a precise topo map of the ocean's floor.

phisticated annotation and ease of operation through menu-driven controls. The system includes the unique Klein Simultaneous Dual Frequency 100 kHz/500 Side Scan Sonar Towfish, which allows a new level of versatility in detection, classification and signal analysis. The 595 will also work with all existing Klein side-scan sonars, sub-bottom profilers and microprofilers. For additional data contact Klein Associates, Inc., Klein Drive, Salem, NH 03079, (603) 893-6131.

Sea Floor Mapping

The sea floor-mapping system of Environmental Equipment Company produces a "plan view" map of the seafloor's topographical features, all appearing in the correct size and shape. Analogous to aerial photographs of land areas, the seafloor images are accurate maps depicting the size, shape and location of such various natural and man-made objects as shipwrecks, downed aircraft and similar lost objects. Further information can be obtained

Note remarkable three-dimensional detail in this side-scan sonar record of *Vineyard Sound Lightship,* which sank off the coast of Massachusetts in 75 feet of water in 1944.

from EG&G Environmental Equipment, 151 Bear Hill Road, Waltham, MA 02154, (617) 890-3710.

Robot & Manned Submersibles

Whether it be a wrecked steamboat, a downed aircraft or a sunken luxury liner, it doesn't stand much of a chance of staying lost any more. The *Titanic* was pinpointed when a robot submarine captured it on film and videotape. A submarine then carried researchers below to make extensive surveys of the sunken liner.

Robots and manned submersibles are becoming more important in man's exploration and conquest of the depths. The *Alvin,* a research submarine operated by the Woods Hole Oceanographic Institution in Massachusetts can take a two-man crew to depths of about three miles

For further information on the Beaver Mark IV 2000-foot submersible, contact IVC Canada, 900 One Palliser Square, 125 Ninth Ave. S.E., Calgary, Alberta T2G OP6, (403) 263-1680.

While preparing this Second Edition, I read of a small, deep-water robot used to locate the wreck of the *Edmund Fitzgerald* almost 100 fathoms below the surface of Lake Superior. When the 730-foot Great Lakes ore carrier disappeared in a winter gale in 1975 with the loss of all hands, Canadian balladeer Gordon Lightfoot began singing of it. The tragedy became a legend. Yet, its actual fate was never known until it was spotted by cameras aboard a submersible from the research ship *Grayling* nearly 14 years later in the summer of 1989.

Never has man gone so deep and been able to do so much with metal detectors while there. It's intriguing to think about using today's high-tech equipment...exciting to the mind to think about what tomorrow may bring in apparatus designed to satisfy the determination of treasure hunters to get there, regardless of where and how deep *there* really is.

Scuba/Snorkel

The selection of scuba and personal equipment is based on the function and use of each component in relation to your need for it. A thorough knowledge of each piece of gear as it relates to equipment technology will help you select the most suitable and best equipment for you. Your selections can determine the level of enjoyment and success you will experience in the water.

Visit your local dive stores. Talk with divers and instructors. Visit dive clubs, read and review *Treasure Diver, Skin Diver* and other diving magazines. There are numerous styles of each piece of equipment. New innovative gear is announced in almost every issue of dive magazines. You'll want to purchase the latest equipment that meets your dive requirements and adapts to your present gear.

Personal diving equipment can be categorized in three distinct categories:

Fundamental,

SCUBA (self-contained underwater breathing apparatus),

Accessories.

Fundamental Equipment

This type of equipment is required for shallow dives, such as beginner diver familiarization, exploratory surface/shallow water dives and recreational diving. All pieces should be selected based upon need; that is, will you be shallow diving? Or, will you venture into the depths with *scuba* gear? Fundamental equipment includes face mask, snorkel and swim fins.

Face Mask: The mask is your window to the underwater world. The space between your eyes and the glass allows you to see clearly beneath the water. Goggles are not acceptable for diving because they cannot be equalized. They can be used for snorkeling unless you feel more comfortable with your nose within the mask. Fit and comfort are the two most important features to consider. A mask should be snug but comfortable, have tempered glass and finger-wells or a nose pocket to allow access to the nose for ear clearing. The two problems I am personally confronted with are leakage and fogging. I think my mustache causes most of my leaks. Every one experiences fogging. There are liquids you can use that help prevent fogging, and you can also spit--yes, *spit*--into the inside of the lens, rub it around and rinse with water before you put it on. Consider also prescription lens masks.

Snorkel: A snorkel allows you to breathe without lifting your head out of the water while swimming on the surface. With proper buoyancy adjustment you can float or swim along on the surface and breathe through the snorkel while viewing the underwater world. Then, by holding your breath you can dive for a closer examination of any object of interest. The snorkel is also used when scuba diving to conserve tank air when on the surface. There are several types of snorkel, including contour and flexible hose. Get one that fits comfortably when attached to your mask strap. Do not get one with a ball or other so-called leak-prevention (they don't!) device on the upper end.

Swim Fins: These are for propulsion. They also free your hands for other activities. Various sizes and configurations are available in full-foot and open-heel designs. The type that best suits my purposes are the open strap type with medium length and flexibility. I always wear wet suit boots with a walking sole for a number of reasons.

With a strap I can adjust the holding tension. Boots eliminate pressure of the foot pocket on my toes. When not diving or snorkeling, I can remove the fins and not worry about stepping on glass or other sharp objects. I have learned that boots with walking soles are perfect when metal detecting in the surf. Also, boots keep my feet warm. The only problem I have encountered wearing boots is the odor that sometimes appears after several days of steady use. This doesn't hurt anything, but the boots should be thoroughly dried after use or they will rot.

Snorkeling Vest: According to Scubapro, their snorkeling vest facilitates snorkeling in several ways and adds a measure of safety. You float slightly higher, thus reducing pressure on your lungs and making it easier to breathe. Your swimming profile can be adjusted to minimize water resistance. When resting, additional air provides more buoyant resting support.

When diving, the vest offers some positive buoyancy at the surface. As you descend you are aided as buoyancy decreases. When you start up, increasing buoyancy (due to less water pressure) helps the ascent. Also, as you load your pouches with treasure, added air in the vest offsets

These buoyancy compensators (BC), described in this chapter as one of a diver's most important accessory pieces of equipment, are manufactured by Scubapro of Rancho Dominguez, CA,

357

the weight of all that you have found. Then, in emergency situations, a vest with a CO_2 cartridge will supply 15 pounds of buoyancy at the surface.

The complexities of diving multiply when you advance from snorkeling to scuba diving. You are ready for scuba when you have become thoroughly at home with your basic gear. When you are perfectly at ease with your face under water while breathing through a snorkel and when you learn to stop swimming with your arms and learn to use only your legs for propulsion, you are ready for scuba.

You should not proceed further and definitely you should not purchase scuba gear until you have taken and passed one of the recognized courses such as PADI and NAUI. Inquire at a dive shop, police or fire department or perhaps check the directories for location of an instructor. Which is the better? I took the PADI course, but I can't say that it is superior to NAUI. You'll hear pros and cons. The value you receive from a course depends ultimately upon the instructor and your efforts rather than the name of the course or its curriculum.

Select an instructor who is certified. This will enable you to apply to one of the recognized schools for your dive card upon your successful completion of the course. You must have this dive card to get air at dive shops. Select an instructor who teaches classes regularly. Also, I suggest that you select one who has a swimming pool available for course training and tests. An instructor who can supply you with all equipment except a mask, snorkel and fins earns still more pluses.

Scuba Equipment

There are several items you'll need when you begin scuba diving. The minimum scuba assembly consists of an air tank, tank valve, back pack, regulator and weight belt. Other desirable accessories are recommended. Scuba equipment allows you to remain under water for an extended period of time. It's here that you'll the most treas-

358

ure waiting! Select your equipment carefully, and you'll be rewarded with successful underwater excursions.

Air Tank: The air tank is a cylindrical metal container that safely stores fresh air under high pressure. Common sizes are 38, 50, 71.2 and 80 cubic feet. Typical air pressure is 2300 psi. Attached to the tank is the tank valve to which a two-stage regulator is attached. Covers, called "boots," are available to slip over the tank and form a shock absorbing flat bottom for handling stability.

Tank Valve: This mechanism screws into the tank and acts as a shut-off valve. The two types of valves are the K-valve which is a simple on-off device and the J-valve which has a safety alert mechanism. A spring shuts off air flow from the tank when pressure drops to 300 pounds. This is designed only to alert divers. A pressure gauge should be used to monitor the amount of air remaining.

Back Pack: A backpack secures the tank comfortably to the diver. Most back packs are designed with two shoulder straps, a waist belt and, usually, a metal strap to hold the tank to the frame. If you use a buoyancy compensator (BC), you may not need a backpack since most BCs have their own tank support assembly.

Regulator: The regulator hose routes tank air into a double stage air pressure reduction and regulation device. The regulator reduces tank air pressure and supplies air to the diver at a pressure equal to the surrounding pressure. So, regardless of water pressures, which increase as a diver descends, the regulator furnishes air at a pressure exactly equal to outside-body pressures. A very functional and desirable rig is one that offers multi-port connections to attach a regulator, a BC with an extra octopus attachment regulator and an air pressure gauge. The extra regulator permits "buddy breathing" in emergency situations. The BC with its tank supply acts as an inflatable life jacket and as a device for compensating for changing body buoyancy caused by water pressures. Some air pressure gauge attachments also feature a depth gauge. See Chap-

359

ter 29 for a suggestions on how you should take care for the various pieces of your diving gear.

Weight Belt: A weight belt is used to offset positive buoyancy, allowing the diver to achieve neutral buoyancy. The slimmer and more muscular a person is, the less weight that person requires. Lead weights are attached to a quick-release belt. No straps or gear should be worn over this belt. In an underwater emergency, a diver must be able to jettison the weight belt immediately. If it snags on an item of clothing or equipment, a diver might be in serious trouble. Some belts are available with zippered pouches that eliminate the lead weight while traveling. Just prior to diving, the belt is filled with lead shot or sand. Lead shot, however, is sometimes hard to find. Because sand is much lighter, heavier people may require a great deal of it.

Accessories and Equipment

Buoyancy Compensator: This apparatus should be considered an integral part of scuba gear. It is one of the most important accessory pieces of equipment for a diver. Other than functions explained in this chapter's Regulator Section it features a CO_2 cartridge for emergency life jacket inflation, a mouthpiece allowing the BC to be filled with lung air, overpressure and dump valves and pockets for various items. Finally, a diver who wears a BC and knows how to use it properly has a feeling of extra security. Some professionals even believe that a BC can be used in a severe deep dive emergency to permit a diver to rebreathe air for a couple or so lifesaving breaths.

Diving Watch: This is one that is watertight and has a rotating bezel with calibrated marks allowing the diver to time his dives. Luminous hands are a desirable feature.

Underwater Light: Many types are available. If dark water is expected, you'll need one.

Diving Knife: Numerous sizes, styles and models are available. It is a must for the treasure hunter. The knife is usually worn on the leg, but I caution you not to rely upon the manufacturer's supply straps. On a dive in Texas' Squaw Springs, I surfaced to find my knife missing. The sheath was still attached to my leg but the knife was gone. The handle strap had slipped over the end of the knife. Devise a method of securing your knife that will let you retrieve it quickly when needed. I suggest that you attach your own velcro strap.

Alternative Air Supply: There are several to consider. Some gold prospecting dredges have an extra air compressor that provides the underwater prospector with air. Other surface air compressors are available that float on an inflatable tube such as Brownies Third Lung, illustrated on Page 350. Air supplies other than your back-mounted tank are referred to as *hoka rigs.*

Read your instruction manual carefully whenever you use one. You must prevent engine exhaust air from entering the air compressor intake.

The *pony bottle* is a small accessory air tank with built-in

The Hydrofin, an underwater sled developed and manufactured by Hope Diving Developments, Ltd., can be towed by a boat at speeds up to five knots and is highly maneuverable.

regulator. The pony is used as a reserve system if a diver's regular scuba system fails or the main air supply is depleted.

Miscellaneous Gear

A gear bag is a must to keep a diver from dropping gear as he or she moves about. A gear bag protects equipment and provides a neat place to store it. Pack your equipment in the reverse order in which you expect that it will be needed. Your wet suit should be on top with weight belts and fins on the bottom.

Communications equipment, compasses, small gear, various bags, repair tools, dive tables and many other accessories are available. Chapters 22 and 23 describe other equipment that might be useful when you hunt for treasure beneath the water's surface.

Clothing and Gear

Comfort is essential to the enjoyment of treasure hunting. In warm weather perhaps the only clothes needed are shorts, a tee shirt and sneakers. In cold seasons protective insulation is crucial. Clothing must offer protection from from both air and water while permitting considerable freedom of movement.

Sure, you've been exposed to weather all your life! You've been hot, and you've been cold. You probably think you've learned to survive comfortably...you don't need any advice about clothing. *But, that was in air!* Survival in water is entirely different. This chapter will concern primarily these different conditions you'll encounter in the water and the type of protection they demand. Some people are hot-natured; some, cold-natured. Let these suggestions be guidelines for selecting personal gear for your greatest comfort and utility.

Beach Hunting

During warm seasons, you can wear just about what pleases you. Certainly, foot, head and skin protection are the key considerations. I wear a scarf and sometimes a neck shield that attaches to my hat. Often, I wear soft, cotton gloves. My coin and treasure pouches are water resistant and very sturdy. Sometimes I take a pancho or water-repellent beach suit along in case of rain. But, more often than not, I enjoy the rain, whether I'm treasure hunting or jogging. During my four years in the Navy aboard a ship that was continually traveling from one climate to another, I learned that weather is a friend, not an enemy. I despise TV weather forecasters who say, "Well folks we've got some pretty drab, nasty and terrible weather in store for you." Frankly, *all* types of weather are a wonder and enjoyment to me.

Dress for comfort in hot weather. Personal articles should include a canteen (I use the military type on a web belt), snacks, digging tools, sunscreen, knee pads and toilet paper.

During cold weather, out come long pants and shirts-- even thermals, if necessary. Insulated boots are good, especially if you have cold feet. A seaman's type wool cap and gloves can be life savers. During wet seasons, a pancho is good, except it often gets in the way, especially when you stoop to dig. The two-piece lightweight rain suits are better, but hotter.

Thermals, jogging suits and multilayered clothing are all good. Your primary considerations are warmth, mobility and dryness. Non-porous clothing can make you perspire. If it does not provide vents for evaporation of the moisture, you'll soon be uncomfortable. You may have to do some experimenting, but give cold weather hunting a try. You'll like it!

For digging on your knees you might try ready-made or home-built knee pads. Optimal Enterprises manufactures two styles of knee pads called Kneel-Eze. They are made of tough neoprene with a velcro elastic strap. You can write to this company at 245 Fischer Ave., D-6, Costa Mesa, CA 92626, (714) 549-5211.

Thick, tough rubber pads prevent skin abrasion and sore knees. There are two disadvantages to wearing knee pads. If the bands become too tight, they will restrict blood circulation and/or cause discomfort. The second disadvantage is that dirt and sand may work its way inside the pads, soiling your trousers. You might try making your own as Duane Caldwell wrote about in *Lost Treasure*. He described an efficient, simple method of constructing knee protectors by cutting two lengths of rubber from an automobile innertube. The sections, each a foot or more in length, are worn over the pants' legs at the knees and can be held in place by rope or strapping that comes up and attaches to the belt or clothing. Large safety pins can also be used to attach the protectors.

During warm seasons, just about anything goes in the water. I rarely wear anything more than shorts, a T-shirt (or, a light, long-sleeved shirt when sun protection is required), protective footwear, a wide-brimmed hat, neck protection and soft cotton gloves. I use lots of sunscreen, number 12 or higher. In areas where you may encounter coral, submerged logs or jellyfish, you should protect arms and legs. Sometimes I wear polarized glasses that reduce surface reflection of the sun.

One trick that works for me is wearing a soft, water-absorbent hat. Occasionally, I dip it in the water, then pull it back down over my head. The slowly evaporating water keeps my head cool and comfortable. My friend, Roy Lagal, once jokingly suggested that my brains might "cook" when the water turns to steam. Actually, the water slowly evaporates to remove heat which results in cooling of the skin. Often, I wear different styles of World War II military headgear which I purchased at Army/Navy stores.

Cold weather presents options. You can stay dry by wearing hip- or chest-high rubber boots. Under clothing, or thermals and socks will keep you warm. Arms-length neoprene gloves, with a cotton pair inside, keep your arms and hands dry and warm. This gear is available from sporting goods stores, catalogues and Army/Navy stores. Jogging suits and insulated underwear such as that worn by cross-country skiers should be considered. Select insulated articles only after some experimenting. If your inner clothing soon becomes saturated with perspiration, you've dressed too warmly. Several thin layers that let moisture escape while trapping air are the best combination. Remember, when clothing becomes wet, it loses most of its insulating properties. As noted earlier, water-protective gear must be ventilated to let moisture escape.

Should you fall in the surf or be struck by a sudden ocean wave, your boots could fill with water. You'll quickly become cold and uncomfortable. You may even find it difficult to reach shore. For such occurrences keep one or more extra sets of clothing along with you. If you have a long drive home, a pair of warm, dry socks and shoes will feel mighty good. Carry along a covering to protect your auto seats and floorboards because surfing gear will become wet and sandy--if not downright muddy.

Beautifully styled "water footwear" is now available from Nike and Reebok sportswear shoe manufacturers. Constructed of nylon or Spandex uppers with rubber soles, they provide traction and let water drain easily.

In the next section you'll read about wet and dry suits. They have their pros and cons, but they get the job done.

Diving

In warm water a bathing suit alone will be sufficient for dives of short duration. Remember, however, that water will take *25 times* more heat from your skin than air of the same temperature. Just wearing an upper sweat shirt will provide some comfort. A 1/8-inch or 3/16-inch wet suit, especially the upper section, will give you all the heat-loss protection you'll need. If you expect to encounter coral, logs and other objects on which you might snag yourself, wear the entire suit.

Gloves are a must when working around coral. I dove in the waters off Colombia without adequate hand protection and suffered the consequences. The currents were quite strong and I tried to maneuver myself around by grasping at coral growths. A few days later my fingertips

This surf hunter has carefully protected himself against waves and wind with a set of waders and a sturdy windbreaker secured at cuffs and neckline.

began to swell. My doctor, who had treated many such problems, said glass-like bits of coral had penetrated my fingers. The poisoned glass caused a swelling and burning sensation which lasted about two months. Several layers of skin peeled off.

In colder water you'll definitely need a cold weather suit. Wet suits which are the most popular, are reasonably priced and provide considerable freedom of movement. Various thicknesses from 1/8-inch to 1/4-inch are available with thicker suits needed for coldest conditions. I prefer the long-john bottoms. Trouser-like bottoms that come just to the waist are available but long-johns resemble old-fashioned farmer's overalls, complete with shoulder straps. You'll need boots for warmth. See Chapter 24 for my recommendations. During extremes, a hood should be considered, which will also mask detector headphone sound somewhat. Be certain you have sufficient neck space when you buy a hood because you don't want the hood so tight it cuts off blood supply. You'll also need gloves. When wearing a wet suit in the surf, you may need a quick-release weight belt for stability. Make certain it is the very last item you attach to your waist. You might also consider weights that you you wear around your ankles.

Some divers prefer a dry suit. Manufacturers, when touting their "better" dry suits, point out that wet suits compress as you dive. Diminishing wall thickness results in reduced insulation properties in proportion to depth. Personally, I've never noticed much loss, but most of my diving has been only to about 30 to 40 foot depths which only doubles atmospheric pressure.

On a balmy spring day this pretty girl requires only a little protection against the sun, and her feet are bare for ease in following signals right on into the water.

Dry suits are just that; they keep your body dry, whereas wet suits must trap water between your skin and the suits. The water warms up to skin temperature, and you stay comfortable. Dry suits cost more than wet suits and they don't give you the freedom of movement as thin wet suits. You can wear thin insulating pieces which give you added warmth. You can control the volume of air in some dry suits, but you should never inflate one in order to get more buoyancy so that you can bring up heavy treasure. Dry suits can also be used for dry land and beach hunting.

This *Heat Exposure Suit Chart* includes suit thickness approximations for various water temperature ranges:

TEMPERATURE ZONE (Fahrenheit)	REQUIRED WET SUIT PROTECTION	UNPROTECTED DIVER TOLERANCE TIME
WARM		
85 degrees and above	Partial	Working diver may overheat
75 degrees to 85 degrees	1/8" - 3/16"	Diver at rest chills in 1/2 hour
COOL		
65 degrees to 75 degrees	3/16"	2 1/2 hours
60 degrees to 65 degrees	3/16" to 1/4"	1 1/2 hours
COLD		
55 degrees to 60 degrees	1/4" (or dry suit)	1 hour
50 degrees to 55 degrees	1/4" (or dry suit)	1/2 hour
45 degrees to 50 degrees	3/8" (or dry suit)	Protection is critical
EXTREME COLD		
Below 45 degrees	(Special thermal suit)	Death in less than one hour

Safety

Accurate knowledge will not only help you dispel many unreasonable fears, but can materially reduce the chances of encountering problems. It is the *unknown* that we fear most. Remember the Boy Scout motto: Be Prepared.

This chapter contains three sections on safety--on the *beach,* in the *surf* and while *diving.* Study the entire chapter even though you do not intend to become involved in all three phases of treasure hunting. You may now be only a beachcomber or surf hunter. But, who knows? Someday, you may decide to take the plunge to look under the water for treasures that others are finding. And, someday you may need to instruct or help a friend in water safety.

It pays to learn and be prepared before plunging into potentially dangerous situations. Certainly, this chapter is not meant to frighten. Rather, it seeks to alert you to possible dangers. Beachcombing, surfing and diving are treasure hunting's newest frontiers, and the lost wealth is waiting to be recovered there is vast. Thousands of dedicated hobbyists regularly spend time on our beaches, in the surf and under water searching for treasure.

First of all, it'll pay you to stay in good physical condition. Diving is an especially rigorous activity, even diving in a stream in search of gold. Don't be afraid of the water! Working hard all day on the beach or in the surf can be relaxing, enjoyable and rewarding. I wouldn't say that unless I had personally experienced the rewards. Don't forget, while you are learning safety rules yourself, teach them to all family members. The best way to avoid trouble is to be ready for it at all times.

Stay Aware of Weather

Keep track of weather conditions and forecasts. Stay tuned to the NOAA weather radio station in your area. You'll need a shortwave receiver tuned to one of these mHz frequencies, 162.40, 162.475 or 162.55. Here, you can listen to continuous weather reporting that includes updates on temperature, atmospheric pressure, wind strength and direction, humidity and tides. You'll be told of expected rainfall, strong winds and severe storms of all types. You'll also hear radar reports, advisories, tornado alerts, boat warnings, regular forecasts, extended outlooks and information on storms, fronts, etc. that are moving toward you.

First Aid Kit

Regardless of your activity, you should always keep a first aid kit handy. In a container of non-crushable, waterproof construction the kit should be easy to open. If necessary, it can be taped to keep out moisture.

Many commercial kits are available. Whether you purchase one or make up your own, be sure it includes an American Red Cross First Aid textbook and other important items.

Among these are soap (antibacterial), aspirin, scissors, tweezers, safety pins, flashlight (disposable), waterproof matches, antihistamine tablets and ointments for marine life injuries and stings (also good are alcohol, vinegar and meat tenderizer), antibiotic ointments (apply after cleansing to minimize infection), lip balm, skin lotion, cleansing swabs, burn ointment, triangular bandages, adhesive compress bandages and assorted dressings, tourniquets, baking soda and a non-prescription ointment for relief of local pain. Also, two quarters taped to a card with emergency numbers and your name, address and telephone number typed or clearly printed. You will probably think of other items (some personal in nature) that you want to include.

Safety on the Beach

Probably the worst things that will befall the beachcomber are *burns* from sun and wind...even they can be easily avoided by wearing sun shades, proper clothing and using the proper sunscreen. Among other mishaps are the following:

Cutting your hands, knees and feet on broken glass.

Suffering cuts caused by fish hooks, electrical cables and other sharp wires or objects.

Getting caught in a sudden storm. Even though your chances of being struck by lightning are remote, *take cover!* Never remain on the beach during a thunderstorm. Listen to the NOAA or other weather radio stations for continuous reports.

Being physically attacked by hoodlums or drunks. If you

Author wearing the sun shield that is described several times in this book. Note that the shield will slip over most "gimme" caps to protect the neck and side of the face from excessive sun.

lack confidence in the security of an area, work in pairs--out of the water, as well as in. Some beachcombers carry a can of "mace" or similar deterrent, not stored away in a bag but where it is readily accessible to them.

Being attacked *by animals.* Often when I jog or work in unfamiliar areas, I wear a four-foot length of chain around my waist. A quick-release clip attached to one end makes a neat fastener. Only a mighty strong-willed animal will stay around after one blow from my weapon. I'm glad, though, that I've never had to use it.

Being robbed or molested. I suggest you never tell anyone, even children, the amount of treasure you are finding. The quickest way to discourage people is to show them a few pulltabs and bottlecaps. They'll suddenly lose interest and even the children won't be so anxious to help you dig. Never tell inquisitive people how much your detector is worth. Just say, "Oh, they don't cost very much; besides, this detector was a gift." In fact, it probably was a gift, either to yourself or from your spouse.

Digging up explosives. In the years since World War II some beaches have been used from time to time as bombing and artillery ranges. Now, these areas are certainly few and far between. Nevertheless, if you dig up a strange-looking device that you suspect might be a bomb or artillery shell, notify the authorities immediately. Let them take care of it. Then exercise caution when digging in that area, or just stay away entirely.

Stepping in holes. Watch where you're walking! Of course, you won't fall in the holes you dig, certainly, but joggers and others might, if you fail to cover them. *Fill your holes!*

Burns from live coals. When campfires are covered and not doused with water, coals remain very hot even till the next day and can cause severe skin burns. Watch out for coals, even when they appear cold.

Toxic waste. This presents an increasingly serious problem. Be alert you to any area (or any piece of flotsam or

374

jetsam) that looks or smells bad. or in any way. *Keep away from anything* that you suspect of being contaminated

Safety in Shallow Surf

Surf hunting is just as safe as beachcombing when safety guidelines are followed. First of all, attention must be paid to the environment in which you'll be working and playing. For example, don't take chances in water up to your neck. If you insist on working in heavy breakers, you'd better plan on being knocked flat.

Use common sense, remain alert and stay aware of potentially dangerous situations. Among possible mishaps that could befall you are:

Getting seasick. Don't laugh, especially if you are prone to seasickness when you ride in a boat or on a ship. Some ocean surfs are mighty rough. If you are unaccustomed to the rocking motion caused by breakers, you could get seasick. If that happens, just get out of the water.

Becoming fatigued. Be constantly aware of just how you're feeling...physically. When you grow even slightly tired or weary in the water, pay attention to yourself. Remember that you're in a *different* environment. Don't wait until you get in trouble. Leave the water before you become exhausted.

Sun and wind exposure. Appropriate attire and sunscreen are a must--even though some medical experts are now suggesting that sunscreen may be hazardous to our health! Apply sunscreen with a sun protection factor (SPF) of 12 or above to all exposed areas 45 minutes before exposure. Most sunscreens require time to penetrate and adhere to skin cells before their ingredients can become active. Don't wear sheer clothes but preferably dark cottons which offer greater protection than synthetics.

Suffer from hypothermia. Subnormal body temperature can occur following long exposure in water. And, it doesn't have to be wintertime for hypothermia to occur. Anytime you become drowsy, feel overly fatigued, start shivering, become dizzy or become disoriented and/or nauseous, *get out of the water* and into warm clothing. Drink hot liquids. You might need medical aid. Never underestimate the problems associated with hypothermia and long exposure in or under water. The human body is a marvelous machine and has an excellent heat regulation system in its *normal environment* of air. When the body is submerged in water, the situation changes dramatically. You can remain perfectly comfortable in air at 70 degrees. In water at this same temperature you can become chilled and dangerously uncomfortable in a surprisingly short time.

Water absorbs body heat 25 times faster than air. In cold water skin surface capillaries constrict to prevent excessive heat loss. As skin temperature drops, the body begins to shiver, resulting in muscular effort and energy outflow. Continued immersion can result in extreme discomfort and hypothermia.

The follow chart compiled by the United States Naval Institute provides guidelines to help judge *safe* times when surfing and diving. See Chapter 25 for discussions of protective clothing and dive suits.

Heat Exposure Chart

Water Temperature (Fahrenheit)	Approximate Time to Exhaustion or Unconsciousness	Approximate Time to Death
32	15 min.	15 min.-1/2 hr.
50	30 min.-1 hr.	1 to 2 hrs.
60	2 to 4 hrs.	4 to 8 hrs
70	3 to 7 hrs.	6 to 24 hrs.
80	12 hrs.	relatively safe

Making contact with dangerous sea creatures. Contact with sea urchins, jellyfish (especially the Portuguese variety), horseshoe crabs and seals or sea lions can cause misery. *Avoid them!* Jellyfish are easily seen. They look similar to small, blue or pink balloons floating on the surface. Long, stinging tentacles float underwater, sometimes to great depths. To prevent stings wear gloves and use large rubber bands or velcro to secure your trousers securely to your ankles. Do not touch dead jellyfish lying on the beach.

Water motions and currents. There are several kinds of ocean surf and river water motions and currents. Let's consider them:

Orbital currents are caused by wave and breaker motion. Water is propelled toward the shore. The resulting water that piles up on the shore rushes back into the ocean, generally in water "troughs." When you stand in these troughs, you can feel the outward pull. When the next wave breaks, it tries to propel you toward the shore. These are generally harmless water motions. Swimmers over the world regularly play in them in surf areas.

Undertows are water currents that flow back out into the ocean. When water is cast ashore it piles up before beginning its outward flow as incoming waves break. Although these currents usually present no cause for concern, on beaches that slope steeply toward the ocean, water surges can become violent. Such areas should be avoided. Generally, undertows are not considered dangerous although you can get tossed about by incoming breakers. If you get caught in an undertow, don't try to fight the force of the water. Just swim along parallel to the beach for a short distance. You'll be surprised how soon you will reach calm water.

Rip currents, sometimes called riptides, can be the most frightening...and the most dangerous. As large waves break on the beach in quick succession, water is piled up faster than it can recede back into the ocean. This larger-than-normal water volume seeks channels in which to escape. As water rushes out to sea in the "rip" channels, you may be caught and pulled into deeper water. Once again, the best advice about escaping from a rip current is *not to fight it!* Just swim parallel to the shore. After a few feet, you will reach calm water where you can move normally back to shallow water.

Some riptides cannot be seen from the shore. Watch for floating debris to indicate water movement. Ask the lifeguard to point out the locations of possible riptide areas.

Floating dangers. Watch out for boaters and surfers! Don't expect them to watch out for you. I narrowly missed being struck by a large windsurfer when a fellow came zooming into a swimming area were I was working. Be ever on the alert for motorboats, sail boats and floating logs. During times of rough surf and high winds, large logs can be propelled rapidly on or just under the surface.

River currents are often deceptive and can carry you out from shore. These currents rarely follow the contour of the riverbed even in comparatively straight stretches. Projecting land areas, islands, backwaters and windings of the river course cause currents to wander back and forth from bank to bank. In working along river banks, pay attention to these currents and when they begin to feel strong or to change direction, move to a safer area. Unusual and sometimes strong currents can be found at the junctions of rivers and at their mouths where they empty into the ocean. Opposing forces of currents and tides create these unexpected water movements.

Weeds and grasses are sometimes encountered by water hunters. In fact, some THers look for them because they often serve as a trap for coins and jewelry. These areas are not a serious menace. Quick thrashing movements of the feet and searchcoil tend to wrap the growth around the legs, searchcoil and stem. Don't panic or you might trip yourself. Slow and natural movements will let the growth untangle itself.

Hazardous bottom areas. Holes, steep slopes, vegetation, drop offs, rocks and coral can cause problems for the water hunter. Generally, when walking forward and scanning the searchcoil in a normal position, you will be able to detect most, if not all, of the above hazards. But, you should always be prepared for the unexpected.

378

Hazardous "dry" areas. In dry seasons or when, say, the level of a lake has been dropping, be on the alert for muddy sink holes. The surface may appear dry. Underneath, the soil can be very wet and soft.

Panic situations. Probably the greatest danger facing those who enter the water is panic. Sudden overwhelming fear, accompanied by loss of reasoning, contributes to almost all water accidents. Condition yourself to resist panic. Try to think calmly about each problem you face. Acting quickly and without thinking carefully can gain you nothing. Fear can be overcome. Let your reasoning take control to allow you to *think your way* out of difficult situations.

Polluted water. The best solution is to know about and stay out of unsafe water areas. Polluted water, such as a poisoned mill pond, can do worse than hurt your health; it can *kill you!* Although you carefully avoid swallowing the water, it can still sometimes cause problems...even when you don't touch it! Just *breathing its fumes* is enough. Polluted water presents the danger of infections that even modern medicine finds difficult to cure. Always be alert to the possibility of hazardous areas. Whenever in doubt, contact local public health officials or other authorities. Never rely on gossip.

Unexpected river waves. When detecting in rivers, be aware of ship movements. Large barges or ships passing by--even at a distance--can create strong and fast-moving waves powerful enough to knock a person off his feet.

Hip boot dangers. Even though hip boots may seem the ideal solution for keeping dry and warm, they can present problems. You must be on guard lest you bend over and let water spill into them. When you're working in the surf, unexpected large waves can crash over you to fill your boots. Either case can certainly spoil an otherwise pleasant afternoon of surf hunting. But, more than that, your life can be threatened. Struggling to reach shore while wearing a set of waders filled with water can be a very difficult and dangerous task. Always watch for waves, but it is well to tie a belt or rope around the upper section of chest-high boots.

Physical problems. Long exposure to water can cause leg cramps. If cramps occur, move toward shore immediately while massaging the cramping muscles. Cold water has been known to cause severe stomach cramps, especially just after eating. Apparently the water interferes with digestive processes. When hunting in the surf, develop an easy, relaxed method of scanning, digging and retrieving. With a slipped disc or a strained back you could quite suddenly find yourself in a very perilous condition, especially if you are alone.

Wear a life vest. Buy and use a good one such as the model that easily and quickly inflates whenever a CO_2 pressure cartridge is punctured. This type of vest will stay flat and not get in your way. But, it's always ready when you need it. I hope you never do!

Dangers from living creatures. Even though snake bites and attacks by sharks, alligators or crocodiles are rare occurrences, use the utmost caution when searching in or near waters where these denizens are known to live.

Safety Under Water

Always remember that *hypothermia* is more likely to be a problem when diving than when surfing. Try to remain alert to your physical condition at all times. Watch out especially for simple exhaustion. Never take chances...especially when searching under the water.

If you plan to scuba dive for treasure, it's imperative that you take one of the scuba courses such as the Professional Association of Diving Instructors (PADI) course. During the 1960s I did a fair amount of scuba diving, and even taught a scuba course at Southern Methodist University in Dallas. I later lost interest in scuba diving and was inactive for about fifteen years. When we began to develop underwater metal detectors at Garrett, I became active again to test prototypes of our new instruments. Realizing that I needed to take the PADI course to refresh my knowledge, I I was shocked at how little I knew about the latest in diving procedures or the advances made in diving equipment. It was obvious that I *needed* that course!

When you take the course and during your dive time following graduation, you'll learn a lot about safety. This is not a diving book, however, and I do not intend to expand upon the subject. I simply urge you to take an up-to-date course and learn as much about safe diving practices as possible before venturing into the deep.

Even though you use a *diver's flag*, never swim rapidly to the surface. Ascend to 10-foot depth, stop, rotate completely around while scanning the surface. Then, proceed cautiously upward. As soon as you break surface, immediately rotate and scan the entire horizon to spot any approaching boats.

Always dive with a buddy, *never alone*. Know the capabilities and limitations of your equipment and your buddy's equipment. Know the area you intend to dive, including hazards, weather conditions, local emergency numbers and weather-alert radio frequencies. Know dive limits and the location of the nearest decompression chamber. Maintain your equipment flawlessly. Never tolerate unsafe or marginal equipment.

Never "lose your cool" during the excitement of recovering treasure. Never compromise on a dive. Plan ahead and stick to your plan. Never try to get "one-more-dive" out of a low tank. Always use common sense. *Don't panic!* Know your buddy and watch out for each other.

Wreck diving can be especially dangerous. *Never go alone.* Take extra tanks and a pony tank. Always be aware of your time limits. You'll need a light for seeing and signaling and keeping close to your buddy. You'll need a dive knife and maybe a smaller backup knife. Carry a spool of line to mark your exit route and, perhaps, a kit with tools you'll need to remove a souvenir or *yourself* if you become entangled in the ship's gear.

Night Diving. It's best to dive during a full moon. If you dive from a boat, exposed lights above and below the waterline are necessary. These exposed lights will serve as beacons to guide you home. So will a shore light if you enter from land. Try to avoid swift currents, caves, wrecks and other obstacles. Carry a knife, a battery and chemical light, a compass and a whistle. A six to eight-foot buddy line with loops at each end is good but can be hazardous. Be careful not to snag yourself on anything with it!

If possible, explore the area first during daylight hours. Check your buddy's equipment and have him check yours. Plan your dive. Know your light signals. *Keep calm.* This is, at best, a very short course on the perils of night diving. I suggest that you read some of the diving books that treat this subject in depth. Then, *study the material!*

Final Cautions

Always observe "no trespassing" signs...even when you *know* you are right. Don't risk arguing with a loaded gun!

Pay attention to warnings about danger areas and underwater obstacles...even when you have dived in an area before and are *positive* there is no danger. You should test all diving areas for depth *each time* before you dive. Waterways can change their course and depth.

Never dive alone, and don't allow children in or near the water without constant supervision. Many streams, lakes and ponds--even ocean surfs--that appear peaceful and calm can be deep and cold or have swift currents.

And one sincere request: Leave each place in *better* condition than you found it.

Many natural sites represent a fragile environment that can be easily damaged or destroyed. Please leave only footprints--not pulltabs, wrappers, cans or other souvenirs of our "disposable" civilization. Remember, a fellow treasure hunter may want to work the area someday. *You may even want to come back yourself!*

Cleaning Finds

Do you remember those movie scenes where the sunken Spanish galleon lies on its side in 35 feet of water with its masts in place and fish--maybe even a shark--gliding silently over its decks? I'm sure you also remember the cannons--perhaps even shining just.a little bit--that still stood guard to protect the Spanish treasure (and, it *did* shine) that spilled from a gash in the ship's hull. All of this after 300 or more years in the salt water! Scenes like that are best forgotten.

Why should you forget it? Because, at shallow depths the action of wind and of teredo worms would have long ago reduced the ship, its rigging and its treasure to an unrecognizable heap that would now be covered by sand or encrusted with coral. It's possible you might discover by eyesight a ballast pile, a stack of coral-encrusted cannon or perhaps a badly corroded cannon or anchor resting on the bottom.

The teredos, better known as shipworms, will have devoured every trace of wood by attaching themselves to it and eating it completely in just a few years. Gold, platinum and pewter will remain unharmed, but other metals will be in various stages of chemical decomposition. Iron will either have been converted, or be in the process of conversion into crystalline magnetite. Copper and brass change chemically into chlorides that produce the familiar green color. Bronze remains in excellent condition. Non-electrical materials such as pottery and glass will remain in their original condition except for surface film or coral growth.

Common sense must certainly be considered an important factor in the successful recovery of artifacts. These items are hundreds of years old. They have been existing all that time in a relatively hostile environment. Certainly, all artifacts must be handled with utmost care if they are to survive at all, much less in a presentable condition. Objects like coins can be picked up and placed in a bag or other secure container. Fragile items should be placed in a rigid container or, better yet, hand carried to the surface. Large objects must be lifted in a basket or with lift bags.

A complete study of retrieval, cleaning and preservation should be made before attempting shipwreck salvage. The water action of wind and waves, the natural forces of marine life and the chemical action caused by sea water are the main destructive forces. Of course, some preservation will have occurred. Objects buried in soil often will be surprisingly well preserved, and coral growth can protect objects.

Retrieval of artifacts other than gold, platinum, silver, copper, bronze and pewter invites disaster unless the objects are *kept in water*. Drying of organic materials such as leather, paper, bone and rope can result in total destruction within a few minutes. Shrinkage occurs as water evaporates from wood. Rot and decay will speed up. Cracking and warpage will soon follow. Iron, when exposed to air, will deteriorate rapidly.

Although salt water is a harsher environment than fresh water, protection of objects recovered from both is essential. Buckets and plastic bags filled with water are used most often to recover objects from the bottom. Once artifacts are aboard your vessel, the task of preservation can begin immediately. Unless you have containers large enough for complete submersion of all objects, it is best to leave the larger items on the bottom until preservation can be done properly. Glassware and porcelain objects do not need water submersion but demand reasonaable care in handling.

Since this chapter presents only basic guidelines in the retrieval, storage, cleaning and preservation of artifacts, you should undertake a serious study of the conservation of objects you recover from sites beneath the water. The Bibliography contains reference sources.

Artifacts recovered from the sea are commonly encrusted with layers of calcium carbonate, magnesium hydroxide, metallic corrosion, sand, clay and various forms of marine life such as shells, coral, barnacles and plant life. Conglomerations may contain a single item or hundreds of items. Since damage to artifacts can occur when encrustation is removed, x-rays are indispensable for determining the context of an encrustation and for serving as a guide to artifact extraction. If you do not have access to a conservation laboratory, you can have conglomerates x-rayed at medical clinics and x-ray laboratories. The charge should vary between $25 and $50.

Encrustation Removal

Attempt to remove encrustation only when a substantial amount of the original metal is left. Deposits can be removed from large objects by gentle tapping with a rubber mallet or sand blasting under low pressure. Smaller objects can be cleaned chemically or in an ultrasonic bath. The chemical process consists of a bath in a solution of 10% nitric acid and 90% fresh water, followed by several washes in fresh water to remove all alkaline traces. There is a time element in this process because acid will attack silver, copper and pewter.

Chiseling along cleavage lines can release encrustation from cannon and other very large objects. Electrolysis can loosen encrustation and hasten its removal. When using mechanical means, extreme care should be used to prevent surface damage. Encrustations can also be removed from objects with pneumatic air scribes or electric scribes and vibrotools. A combination of tools can be used to free movable parts such as cannon swivels, loaded breech chambers and various components.

Encrusted breechblocks and bores of cannon can be cleaned with tube drills or by the slower process of hammer and chisel and sandblasting. Since sandblasting can cause surface pitting, care must be used.

After encrustation has been removed, the objects must be cleansed, examined and evaluated to determine correct conservation treatment. Gold needs no treatment, nor does silver; but, copper can continue to deteriorate unless treated. Ferrous metal objects present preservation difficulties as do wood and other materials. Some objects may be badly corroded but still retain their original shape. They may require a wax or other synthetic consolidant. Other specimens may be so badly oxidized and fragile that they can be saved only by replication through casting.

A Conservation Discussion

Gold and Gold Alloys: High purity gold and high gold alloys do not require any treatment. Even after thousands of years, the noble metal looks the same. Occasionally coral encrustation is present and a slight discoloration may occur if other corrosive metals were in contact with the gold. Consider carefully before you remove coral encrustation because Father Neptune's work often enhances the value of such items. Copper compounds can be removed with citric acid. Corrosion of silver in low grade gold alloys can be removed with ammonia. Ammonic hydroxide (NH_4OH) is a strong, basic solution irritating to skin, eyes and respiratory system. Use a solution below 25%.

Silver and Silver Alloys: Corrosion most commonly encountered with silver will produce silver sulfide and silver chloride. Both compounds are stable and will not corrode the remaining silver any further. In copper alloys corrosion forms cuprous chloride which can continue to corrode the copper component. Prior to conservation, marine encrustation should be removed. In some cases it can be removed by immersion in 10 to 30% formic acid solution. Concentrated formic acid ($HCoOH$) causes painful wounds when it comes in contact with skin.

There are further conservation alternatives for cleaning silver and silver alloys:

Galvanic Cleaning
Electrolytic Reduction
Chemical Processes
Stabilization and Consolidation.

Galvanic Cleaning: This treatment utilizes mossy zinc or aluminum in caustic soda followed by an intensive rinsing and dehydration in a water-miscible solvent before a covering of clear acrylic lacquer. The following treatment is preferred.

Electrolytic Reduction Cleaning: Electrolysis causes direct current to pass through an artifact, removing chloride and sulfide ions from silver chloride and silver sulfide. Silver remains in a metal state. There are two electrolytic reduction cleaning methods: normal reduction and consolidative reduction. Normal electrolytic reduction uses a fully rectified direct current power supply. Consolidative reduction employs a partially rectified asymmetrical alternating current power supply. Both techniques require that a metal core be present in the object. Use a stainless steel beaker to achieve more anode (+) surface area. Stainless steel beakers can be used for both ferrous and non-ferrous materials.

Two electrolytes, formic acid (5 to 30% HCoOH) and sodium hydroxide (2 to 15% NaOH-without aluminum crystals) are used to clean silver. Current density is .01 amp per square centimeter. Since a current with inadequate voltage can cause copper (from the crust, cathode screen or copper components) to be deposited on the artifacts, and excessive voltage (or too long an immersion electrolysis action) can cause silver to be reduced, experiments should be conducted to determine the most efficient current density and whether an alkaline or acid electrolyte is best.

Material "CC"

Suggested electrolytic reduction cleaning solutions:

For cleaning iron and steel:
- 8 oz. lye
- 2 oz. laundry soap
- 1 gal. water

For cleaning copper and brass:
- 1 oz. lye
- 5 oz. washing soda
- 2 oz. trisodium phosphate
- 1 gal. water

For cleaning tin and zinc:
- 4 oz. sodium bicarbonate
- 4 oz. washing soda
- 1 gal. water

Warnings

– When cleaning encrustation from large objects, wear gloves and safety glasses. Since removing crustations and working with various electrolytic cleaning processes is messy, old clothes should be worn. A rubberized apron and rubber gloves should be worn when working with acids.

– Caustic soda (sodium hydroxide) is strong, basic and highly active with aluminum and H_2O. That's why manufacturers add aluminum crystals to "plumber's helpers" used to unclog drains.

– Various anode materials such as platinized titanium, stainless steel and carbon are used, depending upon the desired solution. If stainless steel is used in sodium hydroxide, it will oxidize after prolonged electrolysis, resulting in the destruction of the anode and depositing iron of the anode on the silver. A mild steel anode should not be used in formic acid as it will quickly break down and invariably result in iron being deposited on the silver.

– No chemicals of any kind should be flushed into home or industrial sewage. Not only is it illegal, but your plumbing may be badly damaged. I knew someone with a copper portrait business in her home who discarded waste and diluted copper solutions into her bathtub and sink drains. drains. After about two years of using this convenient disposal method, her copper plumbing was eaten away.

The above "don'ts" reinforce the need for you to study electrolysis techniques thoroughly before attempting to use them. The Bibliography lists several excellent conservation publications.

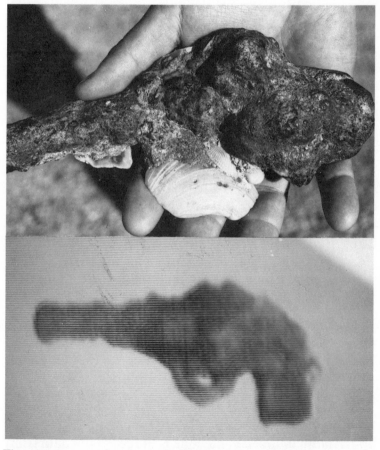

The strange, coral-encrusted object at top, which was found by Minnesotans Art and Marlette Steinke on a Texas beach, proved to be a revolver, as shown in the x-ray at bottom.

Cleaning Coins, Small Objects

Electrolysis: A simple and safe method to remove corrosion and encrustation uses a solution of citric acid and salt. This electrolyte solution contains one teaspoon of citric acid (a harmless substance primarily used as flavoring in soft drinks) and half a teaspoon of table salt dissolved in a cup of water. A stainless steel electrode plate connected to the positive wire of a low voltage (3 to 6 volts) power supply is placed in the solution on one side of a glass container. An alligator clip or other connector is attached to the coin or artifact to be cleaned and positioned on the other side of the container. A current of about 20 milliamperes flowing through the solution will cause corrosion and minor coral encrustation to loosen. The artifact can then be cleansed with a toothbrush or other soft bristle brush and a soda paste. Test various objects before attempting to clean valuable specimens.

Tumbling is a common method for cleaning coins and small objects. Tumblers are not expensive, and they are available in various sizes. Instructions and recommended cleaning agents and solutions come with each tumbler, but be sure to consider recommendations of the manufacturer. Be specific as to the type of material you have to clean. For additional information on tumblers and associated products, write to Finch Products, P. O. Box 213, Birch Run, MI 48415.

Chemical Cleaning: A great many silver objects recovered from the seabed require only limited treatment. Tarnish caused by sulfur compounds can be eliminated with commercial silver cleaning solutions.

Stabilization and Consolidation: Silver coins are sometimes found that have completely converted to silver sulfide. About all that can be done is to record the data from the impression made by the coin in the surrounding encrustation.

Ferrous Metals

Several methods are available for cleaning ferrous metals. Electrolytic cleaning is probably the best when measured by simplicity, maintenance and versatility. An electrolytic cell consists of a vat with an anode and cathode (your artifact) and a suitable conductive solution, the electrons of which are collected by the anode. Chlorides are drawn from the specimen and migrate toward the anode and walls of the vat. Positively charged ions in the artifact's surface compounds are changed to metal and remain bonded to the object's surface. Many factors must be understood and controlled in this process, such as electrolytic solution, amperage, clip construction, anode material, water purity and duration of electrolysis.

At the completion of this process, the objects should be submerged in running water for seven to ten days and brush-cleaned often, followed by another bath in distilled water for a week. Artifacts are then heated to remove all moisture. A sealant such as paraffin is used to prevent air and further moisture from making contact with the object's surface. Clear flat lacquers, epoxy or polyurethane resins or plastic sprays can also be used.

Glass/Bottle Cleaning

The weathering, corrosion and encrustation of bottles and objects made of glass depends upon the soil, nearby objects, the composition of the glass, temperature and age. Depending upon the type of body material and glaze, ceramics are affected in varying degrees. Porcelain is least damaged, although its painted exterior may be eroded away. Glazed pottery, covered with a waterproof vitreous layer, fares better than porous, unglazed pottery.

Marine growth on ceramics can be removed in a 10% solution of nitric acid. Iron and lead oxide stains can be removed in a bath of 5% solution of sulfuric acid.

If the glazed layer on pottery is imperfect, do not use acids. The pieces should be bathed in fresh water to remove salts and then dried and coated with several layers of clear plastic or lacquer spray.

Most bottles require no treatment other than soaking in a soda solution. First, remove all sediment with a high pressure hose. Tough contamination can be removed by carefully probing with a wire or small wooden dowel. Fill with a soap solution and let soak for several days. Cleaning with a bottle brush or a gentle shaking with unpopped popcorn kernels will clean most bottles. Bottles encrusted with dried algae, calcium or lime deposits can be cleaned by soaking in a water and vinegar solution. Sulfuric acid can also be used. Baby oil or lemon oil can be used to add shine and luster to badly corroded bottles.

Cleaning Coins/Jewelry

Gold is almost always recovered as bright and shiny as the day it was minted into coins or made into jewelry. It requires no preservation treatment. Soaking in a bath of 10% nitric acid should remove any tarnish caused by association with other metals.

Silver can be affected in varying degrees. Some objects will already be completely converted to silver sulfide and nothing can be done to preserve such specimens except to encase them in plastic. From the very first moment you touch these coins or items of jewelry--whether it be in surf or far beneath the ocean--special care in handling is required to prevent them from crumbling into powder.

Electrolysis can be used to clean heavily encrusted objects. Following this treatment, the objects should be further cleaned to include brushing in running water or rubbing with a paste of water and baking soda.

An important step in the initial preservation of any object is the decision you must make about just what you want to do with that specific coin, piece of jewelry or whatever the item of treasure may be. The patina that many silver coins and medallions and other pieces will have is impossible to duplicate in the laboratory. Consequently, some buyers and collectors prefer to obtain pieces with patina intact. Also, items are encrusted with coral, you should consider leaving the encrustation. This sometimes enhances the desirability of the artifact.

Copper, brass and bronze objects usually suffer little from salt water immersion. Calcareous deposits can be removed by immersion in a bath of 10% nitric acid, followed by immersion in fresh running water. The same acid bath can also be used to remove the green patina, but consideration should be given to leaving the patina. When the patina is left, corrosion continues but at a miniscule rate.

There are many commercial cleaners which are more or less satisfactory for cleaning silver and copper objects. Perhaps the most important consideration is that you must not use harsh chemicals or excessive scrubbing techniques. There is no question that scratching and marring a coin's surface will decrease its value.

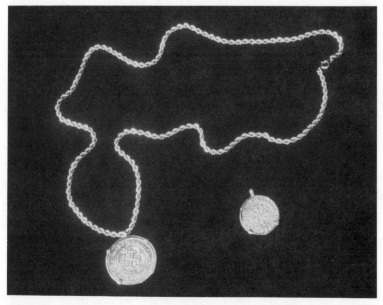

Necklaces can be a beautiful method for displaying coins of any kind, especially these handsome, gold Spanish escudos which came from a shipwreck off the Florida coast.

393

Displaying Your Treasures

Imagination plays a key role in your display of artifacts. A ship's wheel, bell or porthole looks great mounted in a paneled den. An unusual artifact such as a corroded clock or other instrument becomes a conversation piece when mounted on a wooden base. A brass porthole or door viewport can make an unusual picture frame or mirror. An unusual object such as a large, globe-shaped potato blender I once saw looked stunning when utilized as a lamp base.

Coins and other flat items can be placed in plastic-front display cases which can be purchased at most coin shops. Larger objects can be displayed in shadow-box frames, the depth of which is determined by the heights of the largest objects to be included. One enterprising individual purchased an old motorized revolving watch display case. He placed various jewelry items he had found on the "buckets." When friends wanted to see all the items he had found, they pushed a button and watched as the display rotated. Attractive displays on a neckchain can be made of unique or more valuable coins. Holders can be purchased for most coins. For shaped coins such as pieces of eight handmade holders can be made by forming flat silver strips around the coin's edge. An eyelet can then be soldered to facilitate hanging the coin on a neckchain or bracelet. If you can encase items in plastic, attractive belt buckles and other jewelry can be made.

Value from Treasures

There are always buyers for all types of found treasures. The key is to learn the value of coins, jewelry, relics and other collectibles. Learning to evaluate your finds and determining their "going rate" comes with practice and a current knowledge of gold and silver prices. Comparison shopping in jewelry stores and coin shops helps keep you abreast of values. It is important to learn coin grading so that you can correctly evaluate your coins. You'll need to learn how to determine gold content and know the meaning of various markings stamped on the silver and gold jewelry pieces.

Pure gold is 24K (karat) or 1000 fine. A gold alloy of 50% is considered 12K or 500 fine. Three-quarter gold is considered 18K or 750 fine. Most gold items are made of 10K to 18K gold. There are 20 penny-weights to the troy ounce. Each troy ounce contains 480 grains. Government regulations require that gold items be marked for purity. If you cannot locate a karat or fine stamp, then the item is not gold but made of plated-over base metal.

You can quickly and easily test jewelry with nitric acid. With a ring, make a drag mark on a piece of soapstone. With three other rings clearly marked 10K, 14K and 18K, make a mark parallel and close to the first mark. Using an applicator, spread a line of nitric acid across the four lines on the soapstone. The lowest karat line will begin to disappear more quickly than the higher karat lines. Observe which of the three ring lines disappears at the same rate as the line made by your test ring. The gold content of your ring will be the same as the content of the ring that made the comparable line.

To determine whether your ring or jewelry item is truly gold or silver and not just plated, scratch it in an inconspicuous place. The cut must penetrate the surface of the object to be tested. Drop a tiny amount of nitric acid on the cut. Most cheap alloys will fizzle and bubble under the acid. Copper and brass fizzes bubbly green. Silver turns to a creamy or slight brownish haze. Lead will haze a deep gray or black. Gold will not be affected. Thoroughly wash items in running water after testing them so that all traces of the acid will be removed.

If you plan to sell your gold jewelry, you'll need to purchase a scale that weighs several troy ounces. Knowing the gold content of your finds will help you avoid being cheated. You'll know exactly how much to ask! Dealers usually offer 50 to 75% of the actual true worth of the gold.

You may be able to develop a continuing relationship with a particular dealer who will pay you up to 90% or more. Any dealer who purchases your gold certainly has a right to make a profit. Remember that there will always be charges for smelting and refining. Consider for a moment that a smelter charge of 10% and only a 10% profit for the dealer reduces the value of your gold by 20%. Such mathematics show why it is difficult to sell gold jewelry for a price approaching the value of the gold it contains.

One way to get more for your jewelry is to sell the items directly to friends or at flea markets. People will often pay more than gold value for a nice crucifix, ring or other jewelry item. Antique jewelry can command high prices.

Knowing Prices

You will need at least a "talking knowledge" of semi-precious stones, pearls and diamonds. And, don't forget all the new, and mostly worthless, "fake" stones flooding the market. Just because that ring you found looks too old to have a synthetic stone, you could be wrong. Some synthetic stones have been around for decades.

With a scale you know how to use, it'll be easy to determine the value of your finds. Let's use the following equation to work out the *value of the gold* in an object that you found through the following example:

$$\text{Spot (\$/ounce)} \times \frac{\text{dwt (object)}}{20 \text{ (dwt/ounce)}} \times \frac{\text{object K}}{24K}$$

Spot is the value of gold for that day. Check the newspaper or call a coin shop for spot value. *Dwt (object)* is the pennyweight of the object in question. *Object K* is the karat weight of the object which will be stamped somewhere on the object.

Now, let's use the above formula to determine the exact value of the gold in a ring that you have discovered. Note that I said that we'll be considering value of just the gold metal by itself.

Your ring weighs 10 pennyweight (one-half ounce) and is made of 12K (one-half purity) gold. Spot for the day is $300 per ounce. This is how you'd calculate its value:

$$\$300 \ \times \ \frac{10 \text{ dwt}}{20} \ \times \ \frac{12K}{24} \ = \ \$75$$

The value of your ring calculates to be $75 (gold content). If your dealer offers to buy it for 60% of gold value, you'll receive $45.

The Pratical Book of Coins by Frank Sedwick is an excellent reference book. The author gives information on the history, identification, values and the buying and selling of Spanish coins.

Additional Selling Tips

You can seriously damage coins by cleaning and scrubbing them improperly. It's best you make no attempt to clean your more rare and valuable coins. Let the buyer do his own cleaning. Don't forget that silver coins are worth more than their face value. To get top value for your coins consider using the bid boards at coin shops. Chances are,

Two Spanish reales found with a detector on a Florida beach were used by Water Stark of Merrit Island, FL, to make this attractive belt buckle which he presented as a gift to the author.

397

you'll realize considerably more than the dealer will offer Heavily encrusted coins can be x-rayed to reveal the true nature of the encased item(s). Since x-ray labs generally charge $20 or more for single x-rays, examine more than one item at a time and call around for the best x-ray prices.

Take watches you find, regardless of condition, to a watch repairman. Because some parts are difficult to find, watch repairmen will often purchase old watches for parts. You can donate your finds to a charitable organization. Local museums and historical societies just love to display relics that were lost during pioneer days of the area. The Smithsonian Institution will usually accept your valuable artifacts, which may provide a short-term boost for your ego. This surge in pride, however, will subside when you realize that the Smithsonian has some 100 million (at least) items in storage. Chances are, your relic will never be viewed by the public unless it is extremely rare or valuable. Perhaps the Smithsonian Institution should auction off some of its treasure to help pay the national debt? Just a suggestion!

Antique shops will purchase your artifacts, but you might consider leaving items on consignment. You'll probably realize more from an outright sale.

Auction houses will dispose of your finds to the highest bidder. There are several to consider. One often heard about is Christies, Manson & Woods, Ltd., Rokin 91, 1012-KL, Amsterdam, The Netherlands. These auctioneers do a remarkable job of disposing of recovered sunken treasure. There are numerous auction houses in the United States. Contact your local coin shop or consult antique buyer's guides for their names.

One handler of treasure is the Joel L. Malter & Co., Inc., 16661 Ventura Blvd., Suite 518, Encino, CA 91316, (818) 784-7772. The Malter firm specializes in ancient coins, including those found with metal detectors and other treasures from the ancient worlds of Egypt,

Mesopotamia, Greece, Italy and the Orient. They publish an auction catalogue and a magazine called the *Collector's Journal of Ancient Art.*

A quarterly newsletter which reviews any and everything regarding Florida area treasure salvage, auctions, coin shows and treasure exhibits, is *Plus Ultra.* Recent issues included data regarding the history and markings of the escudos of Lima and Mexico. Book reviews and stories of famous shipwreck recoveries such as the *Atocha* are regular features. For subscription information contact *Plus Ultra,* Quarterly Newsletter of Florida Treasure Brokers, P.O. Box 1697, W. Palm Beach, FL 33402-1697.

Anchors, chains and other salvage items can be left on consignment at yards that handle used marine goods. You take a percentage when the goods are sold. Since anchors are always in good demand, you can sell them directly to your friends or other boating enthusiasts. Metal items can be sold for scrap. Keep metal items sorted by type--one barrel for brass, another for copper and still another for aluminum. Give lead sinkers to fishermen friends. Who knows, they may someday snag a valuable wreck and give you its location.

You can make your own jewelry creations and transform scrap gold and silver into handsome and salable items. Design your own rings, pendants and other jewelry items! Becoming a silversmith is not difficult and can make your leisure hours profitable.

Selling Gold Nuggets

If you have been successful in prospecting, you can sell your gold to a jeweler or gold buyer. Remember, however, that gold nuggets are almost always worth more than their gold content...when you can find the right buyer. Both women and men are ready-made buyers for nugget pendants. Learn how to mount your nuggets and you can double or triple the amount you'll get for attractive ones. Nuggets can also be designed into jewelry creations.

Selling Bottles

I am continually amazed at the quantity of bottles I locate during my underwater salvage. In one lake in East Texas where we searched for lost slot machines, we must have found five hundred bottles. I estimate there are five thousand bottles in that small lake.

Modern beer and soft drink bottles are worthless but bottles just a few years old begin having value. Flea markets are good outlets for bottles. Since they make excellent conversation pieces and decorative items, you may be able to establish markets among friends.

Buying & Selling Treasure

If you are interested in buying or selling treasure, relics and antiques, you should obtain the *Who's Buying and Selling Guide.* Its publisher, treasure hunter Charles Culbertson, developed this alphabetized guide to help sellers find those who want to buy and vice versa. If you are interested in selling or buying coins, jewelry, toys, antiques, bottles, books, knives, cookie cutters or just about anything in between, contact The Good Folks, Shiloh Publishing Company, 302 N. New St., Staunton, VA 24401.

Depending on the item involved, the process of preservation can begin as soon as the object is taken from the water as famed salvor Robert Marx is illustrating.

The Law and Taxes

Learn the applicable laws in the areas you search. With regard to a significant treasure, always try to take reasonable steps to avoid losing it through ignorance of the law. Seek counsel, if you think it may be necessary.

This must be your *first* admonition of treasure hunting!

In the realm of rules, regulations and laws, absolutes such as black and white are rare. There are, instead, many intermediate shades of complexity and interpretation. Governing citizen treasure hunters are federal and state laws and city ordinances. Many are the *local* differences.

Ignorance of the law is no excuse! This often repeated, but true, statement is one that you should keep in mind at all times. There is no excuse for not knowing laws that regulate activities you pursue. You should be familiar with every aspect of applicable regulations. For instance, if a law states that you can metal detect on a given beach, does it also say *when* you can detect? It might stipulate that metal detectors are allowed during minimal periods of swimming and recreational activity. What does *minimal* mean? It may mean that you can hunt during any season other than a stated swimming season, say from May 1 through Labor Day weekend. Or, it might mean detecting is permitted during nighttime and winter months only.

Restoration has been completed on this 16th Century Spanish icon whose discovery with a Master Hunter 7 by the author on Guadeloupe is described on Page 153-4.

If you find a coin on the beach, can you keep it? If you find a coin in the shallow water of an ocean beach surf, can you keep it? If you locate a boat in an inland lake, can you raise and keep it? Maybe you can retain those items you find, but it may be that you'll need to abide by certain laws before you become the rightful owner.

You must heed *No Trespassing* laws! In certain areas, trespassers can never be the rightful owners of any treasure they find. Without a permit or rightful claim of ownership you may not be able to keep what you find. You may not only have to give up your treasure but pay a fine for trespassing and destroying property.

It is possible for you to be jailed if you break the law. There have been those who have served jail or prison sentences when they were found guilty of either failing to pay federal and state income taxes on found treasure, or of searching historical sites. Remember that *all* land and water areas are owned by someone. Also, most property and goods are owned by someone. The law decides whether you can keep what you find. Generally, you are required by law to try to locate the owner of property you find or to turn over all found items to authorities who will attempt to locate the owner. When they cannot, within a specified time, the property usually becomes yours.

Obviously, this chapter cannot contain all you need to know concerning the laws that pertain to your treasure recovery work. There are thousands of laws concerning treasure-trove, salvage, permits, trespassing, property owner/treasure hunter search agreements, division of found treasure and a myriad of other things. This chapter, then, is intended only as a basic guide to start you in the right direction to protect yourself and to help you keep all, or as much as possible, of the treasure you find. Further study on your part is absolutely necessary.

Finders Keepers

There may be some accepted truth to that old statement, but *Finders Keepers* will not apply in all situations.

Many states have laws prohibiting the tampering with or removal of historic artifacts from on or under lands owned by the state. If *artifact* is not clearly defined, it could be anything made and lost by man, recent or otherwise. Generally, for an item to be classified as an artifact, its age, monetary value and appeal to an archaeologist or historian must be considered. We can safely believe that officials are not interested in relatively recent objects. And, too, their concern with shipwrecks and their cargo may be limited because such treasure is generally covered by Admiralty laws, although other federal laws may also apply. Also, in Texas, state laws may play a very significant role even well out into the offshore waters. A toy found on a beach, a recent coin found in a surf or an old bottle (of which there may have already been cataloged one thousand examples) found in a river, may not be of interest to anyone except you--the finder. Any object out of context (a mile from a wrecksite) will generally be of little value to an archaeologist or historian. But, when that single object is present within a wrecksite, its value can increase sharply.

Finders/Keepers may not apply to an object you find on private or posted property if the landowner decides to dispute your claim to the object. On the other hand, Finders/Keepers generally applies to any "owner-not-identified" item you find alongside a roadway, at a deserted ghost town or at a swimming hole no longer in use. We must remember that all land is owned by someone and that owner can always dispute your title to found objects (and probably *will* dispute title, if the find has significant value). It is much safer to make prior arrangements for division of the booty with the landowner and to do so in carefully drawn instruments if you anticipate recovering treasure of considerable financial worth.

In fact, *Finders/Keepers* seems to apply to just about any found object when you are not trespassing, when you are hunting legally on any public land and when the rightful owner cannot be identified. Of course, anyone can claim ownership of anything you find. It may then be left to the courts to decide who really is the rightful owner.

Treasure Trove

In the United States the term *Treasure Trove* is broadly defined as any gold or silver in coin, plate or bullion and paper currency that has been found concealed in the earth or in a house belonging to another person, even when found hidden in movable property belonging to others such as a book, bureau, safe or a piece of machinery. To be classed as *Treasure Trove,* the treasure must have been buried or otherwise concealed long enough to indicate that the original owner is dead or unknown.

Following are descriptions of the five categories of found property:

Abandoned property, as a general rule, is a tangible asset that has willfully and intentionally been disposed of, discarded or abandoned by its original owner and thus becomes the property of the first person who discovers it. An example would be a household item such as an old television set discarded into a trash receptacle. If the trash collector or anyone else decides to take the set, he can do so legally.

Concealed property is defined as being tangible property hidden by its owner to prevent its observation, inventory, acquisition or possession by other parties. In most cases, when property has been found that fits into this category, the courts order its return to the original owner. Sometimes the finder is awarded a small reward, more for his honesty in reporting the find than for his efforts in making the discovery.

Lost property is defined as property which the owner has inadvertently and unintentionally lost, yet to which he legally retains title. There is, however, a presumption of abandonment until the owner appears and claims such property, providing that the finder has taken steps to notify the owner of its discovery. Such a case might arise when someone finds a lost wallet that contains documents identifying the owner. It is the general rule that all property must be returned to its owner, who may--or may not, at his own discretion--give the finder a reward. In fact, in almost every jurisdiction, there is a criminal statute that makes it a crime to withhold "lost" property.

Misplaced (or mislaid) property is defined as property intentionally hidden or laid away by its owner who planned to retrieve it at a later date but then forgot where the item was hidden. When found, such property must be treated the same as concealed property with attempts made to find its owner. If this cannot be done, the property generally is ruled to belong to the owner or occupant on whose premises it is found, and the courts generally award the finder some amount of the object's value.

Things embedded in the soil constitute property other than that described as *Treasure Trove*, such as antique bottles or artifacts of historical value. The finder acquires no rights to the object, and possession of such objects belongs to the land owner unless declared otherwise by a court of law. Generally, the courts split the value of the find fifty-fifty between the finder and owner of the land on which the object was discovered...even if the finder did not break any laws. Remember, a person entering private property and removing objects without permission can be prosecuted for trespass and larceny, whether or not "No trespassing" signs are visible.

Some states recognize the doctrine of Treasure Trove; others do not. Some have laws that state that all found property is treated as either lost, misplaced or abandoned. In some states, each case to reach the court is treated individually at the discretion of a judge. Court cases generally occur when treasure or artifacts are found by someone on private property, or when a find is *publicized.* Then, someone claims "rightful" ownership of the find.

You may have heard the story of the Connecticut treasure hunter who found in a Fairfield County swamp a

20-pound chunk of lead which turned out to be a fragment of the statue of King George III that was toppled from its Manhattan pedestal by jubilant Patriots upon the signing of the Declaration of Independence. Research revealed that after the statue was destroyed, many of its pieces were melted down into musket balls by Patriots, while other pieces were spirited away by a Tory Loyalist who wanted to spare the king any further indignity. Thus, the court ruled that the piece of metal found by the treasure hunter was not intentionally "abandoned" but merely "mislaid" by persons who had every intention of retrieving it, meaning that it belonged to the owners of the land unless the Tories show up to reclaim it!

Miscellaneous Regulations/Laws

If you wish to search an old well or cistern, you'll need permission of the landowner. If your search leads you into a river, you'll need to contact your state's river authority. You can obtain permission to search a privately owned lake by securing permission from the landowner. But, the owner has proprietary rights to whatever is found. If a lake has a connecting navigable waterway, search rights may come under the jurisdiction of the U.S. Corps of Engineers and ownership of sunken treasure may be regulated by Admiralty antiquities laws, even though some states may still claim ownership.

To recover coins and jewelry from a swimming hole in a city park, you'll need to obtain permission from the city, generally through its park commission or board. You may be required to locate the owner or turn in found items to police who will attempt to locate rightful owners. In some states, if you find "lost" property, you must turn it in to the authorities or you risk losing it entirely. If no one claims property you turn in, it could become "finders/keepers," but the courts may decide that part of it belongs to the landowner or even the present tenant. Some states require you to obtain a permit before searching state property. Other states do not have permits, but all have rules.

If you enter the Padre Island National Seashore on the Texas Coast, a federally controlled area, you risk loss of any metal detectors in your vehicle, whether or not you are found using them in the Seashore area. In the state of Maine, there are regulations for the use of metal detectors. They do not permit metal detectors at their historic sites or memorials, and they do not allow digging in state parks, except on the beaches. Detectors are permitted on beaches only during periods of light recreational use. Upon entering a Maine State Park, you should check at the gate. They will furnish you with a permit at no cost. The reason for the permit is to know who is searching with metal detectors when someone loses a valuable piece of property such as a watch or ring.

If you will study the last sentence, you'll realize that there are laws concerning the ownership of found items. Not everything found is considered *Treasure Trove*. For instance, a detectorist found an individual's ring. Through research of the person's initials, the finder located the owner. The finder called the owner and reported the find. The finder stated that he expected the owner to pay a reward. The owner said, "No, I won't pay you anything. I own the ring, and I want it back!" The finder then stated that he wouldn't return the ring under those conditions. The owner then changed his attitude and said, "O.K., what is it worth to you? I'll pay. Where can I meet you?" When the finder met the owner at the designated place, the police arrested the finder. I haven't learned the outcome of that one yet, but I'll be willing to bet it wasn't to the finder's liking.

The moral to that story is that when you return an object, it's best not to demand a reward. If a person publishes an offer for return of a lost object, its owner must pay the stated reward. If the words *generous offer* are published, perhaps you should ask what is meant by that. What may seem generous to the owner may be peanuts to the finder.

In every jurisdiction there are laws that prohibit destroying private property. Digging a hole, even under water, is sometimes considered destroying private property. Whenever you obtain permission to search an area, make sure the person giving the permit understands you will be digging holes. But, be quick to inform him that you will also be filling your holes...and *do so!*

In some areas, federally owned lands under the jurisdiction of the Bureau of Land Management or the U.S. Forest Service permit treasure hunting. Treasure hunters are welcome, provided they do not destroy property or deface national monuments. The managers want to know you are there, however. To obtain permission, write to the park ranger in charge of the particular area you wish to search.

Beach Hunting

State laws vary considerably with regard to treasure found on beaches. In some states, beach areas between low and high water marks (usually defined as being the sand dunes above the beach area) can be searched without a permit. Neither the state or adjacent landowner can claim a share of what you find unless they can prove ownership of your found objects.

You should not enter "Posted" or "No Trespassing" beaches without obtaining permission. Even in states where all beaches are declared public, do not search fenced or posted areas without permission.

On city beaches, there may be ordinances regulating metal detecting. You may be able to hunt anytime or only during certain hours. In all likelihood, the beach you want to search will be open to you. Just the same, it is well to investigate, even if you don't see "No Metal Detecting" signs posted. It would certainly be a discomfort if you broke a law and had your vehicle and equipment confiscated and were forced to wait for some time to appear before a magistrate. It's your option whether you obtain a written permit or just accept an oral one. If you get an oral

"O.K.," at least get the name of the person and a copy of rules and regulations for metal detector users. Then, make certain you read it often to be aware of what you can and can't do.

For instance, Connecticut beach hunters should be aware of these rules stated in a Jan. l, 1984, directive issued by the Department of Environmental Protection:

"The use of metal detection devices is permitted on land under the jurisdiction of the Department of Environmental Protection under the following conditions:

"l. The activities shall be limited to surface collection except where digging is permitted in sand areas devoid of vegetation. However, no collecting or digging will be allowed in areas of sand dunes adjoining the beach area proper. Digging must be done by hand with all motorized devices prohibited. All holes dug must be refilled immediately before the collector leaves the site.

"2. Use at a swimming beach shall be limited to times of 'no swimmer' use or at staff discretion.

"3. Persons using a metal detector are required to use a trash apron to store all materials found. The collector may retain articles found, except items of a personal nature such as jewelry and watches which must be turned in to the manager in charge. Any material the collector does not wish to retain shall be placed in a waste receptacle.

"4. No specific permit is required at this time.

"5. Staff may close any area to this activity for purposes of maintaining visitor safety and preserving significant artifactual remains."

Surf Hunting

Most surf areas are open to treasure hunters but some are not. You may have to get a permit from the state or from the person to whom the state has already awarded a search permit. In areas where a person owns the beach to the water, you may be able to search in the water.

The searching of National Seashores such as Texas' Padre Island and North Carolina's Cape Hatteras is

411

prohibited. In some national park areas, you may get permission but you may be required to turn in historically valued items.

The use of motor-powered devices such as dredges is prohibited in some surf areas. And, in some surf areas where permits are required, you must fill your holes.

Unless otherwise regulated, most beach areas from the high tide mark out to beyond depths in which you can't very well hunt, are open to the public. Some beachfront landowners have been known to take it upon themselves to declare adjacent water as *their* property and force off "trespassers," sometimes at gunpoint. Territories of all navigable waterways come under the jurisdiction of the Army Corp of Engineers. They control it, they regulate it and most beach water areas are open to the public for boating, swimming and/or other activities...unless the Corp of Engineers forbids! It's best, however, never to argue with a "loaded shotgun." Leave such property owners to themselves.

Hunting Under Water

If you wish to recover a sunken yacht, you have two basic courses of action. You can offer to raise it for the owner and/or insurer and charge a fee for your services. You could also purchase the sunken vessel "as is" and raise and restore it yourself. In either case, you stand to profit. You cannot, however, simply recover the yacht and claim it as your own.

Let's take another case, the location and salvage of cargo from a 16th Century Spanish galleon. Oceanside states and states with navigable waters may require a permit or license that gives you the right to search for the vessel you are seeking. You may have to pay a fee and obtain a security bond before you can begin your search. After finding the wreck, it has to be identified, usually with old ship drawings or coins and relics found aboard.

Then, to protect your discovery against claim jumpers and to avoid legal problems, you'll first have to go into

Federal District Court to "arrest" the wreck. After you receive orders from a Federal Judge, you or a diver will act on those orders and swim to the bottom to "serve notice" on the shipwreck. The notice, encased in plastic and tethered into the wreck by a short length of rope, informs anyone who might happen along, that "a warrant shall issue for the arrest of the (name of ship), her appurtenances, her furniture, her cargo and her apparel."

The notice is part of the maze of legalities and technicalities into which modern adventurers must venture in order to hunt shipwreck treasure. The court seeks possession of the wreck until rights of possible claimants to it can be determined. In effect, you or your company are merely the custodian of whatever you bring up. The courts then determine ownership. In the case of a centuries-old Spanish shipwreck, many could step forward. These could include the modern nation of Spain itself as original owner of the vessel, a descendant of the ship's captain or even the country, perhaps Mexico or Peru, from which the treasures originally came.

If the courts decide in your favor, then the ship is yours subject to any treasure you may give to a governmental body or a charitable institution...and, of course, all applicable income tax levies. Special situations can still exist, such as on the Texas Gulf Coast. Contrary to other states, Texas lays claim to the Continental Shelf extending far out into the Gulf of Mexico. This, of course, includes *all* treasure found on its land, even under hundreds of feet of coastal water far from the shoreline.

You Should Know

When you become "custodian" of a shipwreck, you may also become responsible for all problems concerning it. If fishermen snag their nets on "your" ship or gear, you may have to pay for the loss. If your ship is ever considered a menace to navigation, you may have to have it hauled into deeper water or demolished...which could get expensive. Dismantlement costs of a big WWII cargo ship might be expensive. If someone claims injury from "your" wreck, you might be responsible.

Here are some more surprises! You may not even have 100% rights to keep others off "your" wreck. Others could recover treasure and demand and collect a fee from you under Admiralty laws. Another problem arises if, during your salvage, you discover that another ship's cargo is "mixed" with yours. You find yourself excavating two ships, including one in which you may have no legal right. What happens then? Well, I guess that's what laws and lawyers are for, to untangle problems...and ship's rigging!

Maritime Law

Called "Admiralty" because they were once administered by admirals, maritime laws regulate navigation and commerce on the world's ocean and navigable inland lakes and rivers. They regulate vessels from small boats to giant ships, and the laws pertain to insurance, property damage, contracts and personal injuries.

Maritime salvage laws are designed to reward those who rescue ships and property from the perils of the sea. These laws guarantee a monetary reward to those who salvage property and return it to its owner(s). The property in question must be lost or abandoned, its owner(s) unknown or not available and the property in unquestioned peril of the sea. If the owner is not interested in such property, it can be yours. If the owner cannot be found, you may have to make your claim in Admiralty Court where the judge can declare you rightful owner.

That is what happened when Mel Fisher's lawyers used Admiralty Salvage law to win him the right to salvage the Spanish galleon, *Atocha*, in Florida waters. Florida's own State Antiquities Law was ruled null and void as far as the State's claim on the *Atocha* was concerned. It would be well to point out here that George Sullivan in his excellent book on the *Atocha* search, *Treasure Hunt*, reported that Mel was forced to spend "almost as much in lawyers' fees as he did paying divers and equipping boats."

Income Tax Laws

All treasure hunters must pay income tax on profits derived from the sale of treasure, artifacts or any objects found. The profits received are treated as normal income. Expenses incurred in the salvage of the goods are deductible according to and regulated by income tax laws. Taxes are due during the year you sell or receive value for your found goods. If you donate artifacts and treasure to qualified recipients, you may earn a tax deduction for a charitable contribution. It will probably be necessary for such goods to be appraised by a qualified appraiser and you should have a statement from the charitable institution stating that such goods were, indeed, accepted. There are certain Internal Revenue Service rules that govern amounts that can be claimed as a deduction.

You should keep complete, accurate records of all money you spend in your activities related to treasure recovery. Expenses include equipment costs, transportation, lodging, meals, rental fees, license and legal fees. Obviously, if you don't know all your expenses (or have them properly substantiated), they cannot be charged against the profit you receive from selling treasure. Always remember that the IRS may question your expense items. These expenses are not fully deductible from other "ordinary income" if it is determined that your treasure hunting is a *hobby* rather than your principal business.

Getting Permission

You may be astonished at what you can do simply by writing a letter and requesting permission to search a given area. Don't overlook this method to obtain permission to search an otherwise "unsearchable" area. Many treasure hunters testify that it works.

Don't assume that an area such as a state park is automatically off limits. Within many park systems metal detectors can be used in non-archaeological areas such as sandy beaches. Some areas can be searched if you'll first obtain a permit from the park's chief ranger or manager. Park managers may grant you permission to search for a specific lost item, such as a ring or valuable piece of jewelry. If you get permission, you must abide by all the rules of the permit. Hunt only during stated times and in stated areas. Don't destroy buildings, vegetation or even the ground by digging a hole larger than necessary to retrieve the article. Then, *fill your holes!* Try to leave every area in as or better shape than you found it. One bad move on your part, and you and everyone else may be banned, perhaps forever, from that park and possibly even others. Park managers change jobs often. If you make an enemy of one, detector hobbyists may be banned everywhere he goes.

You may possibly secure treasure hunting rights to certain areas by agreeing to turn over to the officials all found artifacts of historical value. In return you can request to keep modern items such as coins, rings and other jewelry. Plus, you should also take out all trash you dig or find.

You and your entire club may be able to "break the ice" with reluctant public officials by offering to *adopt* the area you wish to search. You promise to remove all trash, both dug and found, cover all holes, possibly specify that only small digging tools like screwdrivers be used and agree to assume the responsibility for all clubmembers. If one doesn't abide by the rules, you can offer to repair their damage or pay some penalty. Also, you could agree to look after the park. When you find other hunters who, say, do not fill their holes, you will instruct them in proper digging and recovery procedures. Those who do not obey the rules or who attempt to damage property are to be reported to park officials.

Rules Amongst Ourselves

Clubs can invite local lawyers, archaeologists and historians to attend meetings and to serve as guest speakers. Ask them to talk on treasure trove, salvage laws, trespass-

416

ing, permits and land owner/treasure hunter search agreements, archaeology, excavation methods and archaeological and historical site information. Getting to know these professionals could lead to the "discovery" openings of numerous sites.

All metal detector hobbyists should consider joining and actively supporting local treasure hunting clubs. Participation in club activities is one of the best ways to learn about laws and regulations that treasure hunters should know about. If your club is not a member of the Federation of Metal Detector and Archaeological Clubs, Inc. (FMDAC), suggest to leadership of the club that you join. For information write FMDAC at 12 High Street, West Milford, NY 07480. The Federation actively monitors laws, restrictions and proposed legislation that affects us all. Through their efforts, our voice is being heard as never before. Restrictive laws have been abolished or modified, resulting in many new and formerly restricted areas being opened to responsible metal detector hobbyists.

It should be understood amongst ourselves that the formal Code of Ethics of the treasure hunter is in force at all times and that every team member must abide by the rules. Be quick to remind a fellow treasure hunter to discard all trash in the proper receptacle and to fill all dug holes. Police your own group. You may prevent good areas from being closed.

Code of Ethics

Learn the following rules. Keep a copy tacked in a convenient place where you can review them occasionally:

● I will respect private and public property, all historical and archaeological sites and will do no metal detecting on these lands without proper permission.

● I will keep informed on and obey all laws, regulations and rules governing federal, state and local public lands.

● I will aid law enforcement officials whenever possible.

417

- I will cause no willful damage to property of any kind, including fences, signs and buildings, and will always fill the holes I dig.
- I will not destroy property, buildings or the remains of ghost towns and other deserted structures.
- I will not leave litter or uncovered items lying around.
- I will carry all trash and dug targets with me when I leave each search area.
- I will observe the Golden Rule, using good outdoor manners and conducting myself at all times in a manner which will add to the stature and public image of all people engaged in the field of metal detection.

Dividing Finds

When you and a friend go treasure hunting, you may agree that each person keeps what he finds, or you may agree to split everything found. What happens when you make a single, valuable find? You both write down what you believe the item to be worth. The one who makes the higher bid takes the item--and pays to the other the value of his lower bid. The "winner" has the item he wanted, and his friend has been paid what he thought the article was actually worth. Both should be satisfied!

Search/Salvage Agreement

Avoid heartbreak. Insist upon an agreement between yourself and property owners. And, please notice that I used the plural term, property *owner-S.* Even though the husband/owner gives you permission, his wife may take all you find if she hasn't signed the agreement.

At the conclusion of this chapter (on a page that can be easily copied or removed from this book) is an example of a simple agreement between land owners and a treasure hunter. Depending upon the property laws applicable to the site you wish to search and the anticipated dollar value of your finds, you may want to consider a more detailed custom-drawn agreement.

This agreement is a copy of an agreement used by a treasure hunter during one particular treasure search. It should be modified to satisfy all applicable laws and requirements of all parties when and wherever it is used. Be certain the "owners" are not just *renters!*

When you are dealing with governmental agencies and the stakes are high, you should consider employing an attorney well versed in all laws pertaining to such matters.

Foreign Governments

I'm not going very far into this one...just far enough to tell you that you can fully believe that in some situations, a courtroom filled with Philadelphia lawyers, all on your side, may not be able to help you acquire what you know is *yours* based on a contract signed by you and a legal representative of a foreign government. Believe me!

It seems that the new order of the day is that many governments have decided they aren't giving *anything* away. If you find treasure in a foreign country, either within its boundaries or in its waters--either with or without a search permit--you will probably need the best legal assistance available. And, even that may not help you one bit. You may wind not only without your treasure but in danger of a prison sentence.

Another Problem

Most countries, even our U.S.A., try to attract foreign tourists with money to spend. But, when you clear customs loaded down with strange-looking equipment cases and businesslike luggage, you can expect delays and possibly confiscation of your goods, at least until you leave the country. All of your documents and letters of permission from tourist departments may be totally ignored by customs officials. I speak from experience.

I went to a South American country with the Scuba World team that had been "invited" to make a film for televising in the United States, aimed at attracting American tourist dollars to that country. When we arrived with numerous suitcases, bags and television "equipment-looking" cases, we were stopped cold at customs. Finally, we were allowed to come into the country *minus* all strange-looking equipment cases, which meant that camera equipment needed to make this "tourist-dollar" film, was held by customs until we departed a week later.

All this took place--and it is probably being repeated this very minute at a customs post somewhere in the world--because some developing countries, some that know nothing about scientific investigations and some that may have had their "antiques and relics" plundered, are suspicious of any kind of high technology investigation and explorations. They simply say *No.* Then, they are safe.

Conclusion

Don't be overly frightened by all the laws associated with treasure hunting. Still, I urge you at least to be aware that laws exist and that they may be applicable where you hunt. Remember that ignorance of the law is no excuse.

Also, *always* observe *no trespassing* signs...even when you believe they have been posted illegally. You might find yourself arguing with a loaded shotgun (which is something else you *never* want to do).

And, remember, if you think you have a legal problem, the thing to do is *seek legal counsel.* With regard to a significant treasure or a significant problem with its recovery, talk to an attorney *before* you proceed. Don't take a chance of losing a valuable prize or your freedom because you didn't understand the law.

It's always been my observation that when a treasure hunter tries to do the *right* thing and makes a sincere effort to try to do his or her best in following our Code of Ethics, particularly as it pertains to the Golden Rule, that treasure hunter seldom has any trouble.

Hunting for treasure near and under the waters of the world is often quite profitable. But, it should always be fun. Don't ruin the hobby for yourself and others by abusing laws and regulations!

Search and Salvage Agreement

This agreement dated this ___ day of _____,
19__, is between _____,
hereinafter known as the Property Owner(s), and
_____, hereinafter
known as the Salvagor.

In consideration of the Salvagor's undertaking to
devote his time and equipment in a search of the premises
described as:

(Description of property to be searched)

the Property Owner(s) hereby agree that the Salvagor
shall receive as compensation for his services:

___*(1/2 or other fraction)*___ of all money, jewelry, artifacts
and _____ discovered
by the Salvagor, subject to the laws of this community.

The Salvagor is given full authority to work in, on or about
the said premises at any reasonable time, subject only to
such notice as the Property Owners may require in advance of such work. Each party waives any possible claim
against the other for liability for any careless or negligent
act or omission of the other arising out of or in the consequence of the search herein provided for. This agreement
shall be effective for ____ months from the date thereof.

Executed at:

_____   _____
Salvagor   **Property Owner**

                                             _____
                                             Property Owner

Note: Property may be described generally as a house and lot, or a farm or
tract on a particular street or road or at a specific address, owned by the Property
Owners. Use a legal description, if available.

Equipment Maintenance

Salt water with its corrosive effects will damage practically everything. After equipment is used in the field, especially in salt water environments, cleaning and maintenance are critical factors to prolong its serviceable life.

Equipment Maintenance

Clothing: Regular and thorough washing of clothing you wear when beachcombing, surfing and diving is all the care needed. Sneakers, boots and waders should have sand rinsed out after each outing. Always dry these items in open air. Never use any sort of artificial heat source. You can use paint thinner to remove tar and oil from personal items. Baby oil works, but it does take longer.

Snorkel & Scuba Gear: All snorkel and scuba gear should be rinsed in clean fresh water as soon as possible after each use, especially when you have been working in salt water. I always hose down my gear, but whenever possible I also fill the bathtub with water and give the equipment a thorough soaking. Boots, waders, dive suits and hoods should be turned inside out. After washing away all mud and sand, the articles should be left to dry in the open air. A towel can be used to absorb excess water to hasten drying. Never use an *artificial heat source* to dry these articles. Let them dry naturally and thoroughly before storing. Whenever dive boots are worn for long periods, they may develop a disagreeable odor. Wash them in a solution of soda and water and let them dry.

Your *dive mask and snorkel* should be cleaned and all water and foreign matter blown out. Your *scuba regulator* is most critical. It should be thoroughly rinsed in clear water, using successive clean baths. Blowing through the regulator while depressing the various valves will clear out sand and other contaminants. Follow the manufacturer's recommendations concerning periodic cleaning and inspection, no matter how little the equipment may have been used. Cost is minimal. Whatever the price, it's worth it! Air tanks should be inspected according to manufacturer's recommendations. Unless dive shops find an updated inspection date, they will refuse to fill air tanks.

Tools: Iron and steel tools--and sometimes even those of stainless steel--will eventually rust. You can prevent rust to some extent by washing all items in fresh water immediately after they are used. Let them dry before storing. You'll notice I said stainless steel sometimes rusts. Therefore, you must care for these items the same as you would any other metal-fabricated tool.

Dredges/Power Equipment: Use fresh water to clean out accumulated sand and debris as soon as possible after the equipment has been used. This is especially important if the equipment has been in salt water. Always follow manufacturer's recommendations for cleaning and storing. *Caution:* never run your dredge pump dry. To do so will damage the pump. Lubricate all items as specified by the manufacturer. Always run combustion engines until the carburetor is empty of gasoline. If you don't, the next time you need the equipment, its carburetor and jets may require cleaning.

Detector Maintenance

Any detector designed and produced by Garrett or other quality manufacturer is rugged outdoor equipment....meant for everyday use. Remember, however, that it is also a scientific instrument. Treat it as such, and handle it with care. You shouldn't baby your detector, but neither should you be unnecessarily rough in using it. Give your detector reasonable care and regular maintenance. Clean it when needed. Expect your quality metal detector to give you many years of trouble-free performance.

When you use a detector or anything else on the beach, sand will somehow find its way into it. So, you're sure to get sand in your detector's stem and control housing just as it gets into everything else. Many years ago, after an extended stay on Texas' Padre Island, one member of a search group even found sand in a factory-sealed cigarette package!

The following maintenance procedures will keep your equipment in top-notch working condition. The detector stem should be completely disassembled and flushed with fresh water. A soapy solution can be used to aid removal of stubborn materials. A lubricant is *not* recommended nor desirable unless the lubricant you use is positively non-sticky and will not attract any particles of sand or grit. Wipe the detector with a damp cloth. The searchcoil can be cleaned with a garden hose. Do not let water get into the cable connector. Protect the cable from sharp blows and avoid kinking it. Open any portals and battery doors and check the interior. Clean out foreign material such as sand or leaves. Never use forced air to clean a detector. Air that is blown in a detector's control housing can force dust and debris to become lodged in the electrical controls and cause them to fail.

You can visually spot water when it gets in the housing of an underwater detector constructed with a transparent control housing. If this occurs, immediately turn the detector off and remove the access door, drain the water and let thoroughly dry for at least a day while sitting in an open area. Never place a metal detector or a searchcoil in an oven or use any other artificial heat source for drying. Normal temperature is sufficient. Dessicant packs can be dried by placing them in a 400-degree oven for one hour. The indicator card will be blue when wet, but turn pink when dry.

Properly designed underwater detectors have dual 0-ring seals that prevent water from entering the control housing. Nevertheless, detectors will eventually require maintenance. When control shafts are rotated, microscopic particles gradually work their way into the 0-ring seals to cause leaks or sticking controls. If this occurs, it is advisable to return the detector to the factory for proper repair and replacement of its seals. At the Garrett factory, after cleaning, inspection and replacement of seals, all detectors are given a six-atmosphere pressure test to insure that the equipment will locate treasure satisfactorily in water depths to 200 feet.

When using your detector, inspect all exposed connectors daily. Each time you change· batteries, carefully inspect the battery and clip connections. All contamination and corrosion should be removed. You can use a pencil eraser, but be careful not to short the terminals with the metal casing on the eraser. Any spring clips that appear to have been opened should be closed with a slight pressure of your thumb and forefinger. Visually inspect all detector components during maintenance and cleaning operations.

Field Repair

You may have already read some of the following material in one of my other books from the excellent *Garrett Guide* series entitled *You Can AVOID Detector Problems.* You *can* avoid them, too, if you'll just follow these simple instructions.

Always check the *batteries* first if your detector stops working. Some people simply overlook the need to replace batteries regularly. Now, new batteries certainly won't correct *all* your detector problems, but they are usually the source of the problem whenever a detector stops working. Always carry a fresh set of batteries on every hunt. Even though the detector's meter or other indicator may report that batteries are good, or even if it seems you *just* put a new set into the detector, always test your detector with fresh batteries any time it fails.

Make certain that you insert new batteries correctly and that they test satisfactorily. As part of your detector's regularly visual inspection check battery terminals for tightness. Carefully examine the detector by looking through any doors and portals. Observe every component for damage. Look for wires that may have been pinched when you last changed batteries. When panels are replaced, detector wires are sometimes pinched, setting up a potential problem that can result in failure in the field. If your detector is factory-sealed, *Never open it.* At best, you risk voiding your detector's warranty.

Batteries

There are four types of batteries normally used in a metal detector:

Carbon zinc batteries cost the least and deliver current for the shortest length of time. They operate most efficiently at Fahrenheit temperatures from 32 (freezing) to just over 100 degrees. They are more prone to leak corrosive acid than alkaline and NiCad batteries.

Heavy duty (zinc chloride) batteries are generally more expensive than carbon zinc but will give additional service. They are more prone to leak corrosive acid than alkaline and NiCads.

Alkaline (alkaline manganese) batteries cost more than carbon zinc and heavy duty types and give more current for a longer period of time. They last longer in storage and are less susceptible to leakage. Their performance is better in extreme temperatures. Use of this type battery is probably cheaper in the long run than carbon zinc or heavy duty types.

NiCAD (nickel cadmium) rechargeable batteries feature a manufacturer's claim that they can be recharged one thousand times. They are more expensive than other types. Longer life and best performance can be obtained if they are used often and recharged immediately at room temperature. They will take a "set" if repeatedly used for the same length of time. For example, if repeatedly used just one hour per day and then recharged, the NiCads will take a "set" and deliver maximum current for only one hour. It is therefore recommended that you let NiCad batteries run down completely before recharging at least once every three months to extend battery life. NiCads will power a given circuit 40 to 50% as long as carbon zinc. For example, if carbon zinc batteries power your detector for 20 hours, NiCads will power it for 8 to 10 hours. Since NiCad operating voltage is less than the other types, Ni-Cads will register at a lower level on meters and lights designed to check batteries on detectors.

Short Battery Life: If this occurs while you are using NiCads, study the preceding paragraph. If it occurs with regular batteries, place a fresh set into the detector and keep a record of the amount of hours the new batteries give you. You may find your batteries were actually not fresh to begin with. Use headphones instead of the speaker to extend battery life. Your detection efficiency will improve as well!

Searchcoils/Cables

Contamination: Dirt, black magnetic sand, small metal shavings or other contaminants can work into a searchcoil cover or speaker to cause erratic sounds that are annoying and appear to indicate a faulty detector. It is easy to clean a searchcoil cover. If black magnetic sand particles are sticking to the speaker cone, turn the detector upside down to let the material escape. Test the detector by activating it. Sometimes, vibration of the speaker cone will loosen particles that have magnetically attached to it. A small magnet can also be used to pull the particles out.

Cable connector: Erratic sounds can be produced when the cable is slightly twisted at the point where it enters the cable connector. Check this problem by removing the connector cable clamp screws. Remove the cable clamp and visually inspect the wiring. Rotate the wire slightly to test for broken connections. These broken connections can be repaired with a small soldering iron. Making repairs of this type, however, requires some knowledge of both electronics and soldering. As soon as possible, have a reputable technician check your emergency repairs.

Testing Searchcoils and Cables: Erratic operations and no audio can be the fault of the searchcoil and/or its cable. Pick up your detector, turn it on, grasp the searchcoil and gently twist it back and forth. Gently pull on the cable where it goes into the searchcoil to determine if the wiring is broken. If wires break in the field, you can sometimes press the searchcoil cable or tape it in such a way to permit you to finish the day's search ing. Permanent repairs will be necessary, and it is in your best interest to make them as soon as possible. Don't expect a "field expedient" to solve a problem permanently. If erratic operation persists, the searchcoil may be faulty. Replace it!

Submersion Problems: If a manufacturer states that searchcoils are submersible, you should be able to submerge them up to the end of the cable--where it connects to the detector housing. Submersible searchcoils have been known to leak, however. Some times the cable covering has been punctured either by careless handling or by thorns when the detector was brushed up against bushes, a barbed wire fence other sharp objects. Cables and even the searchcoil itself can be punctured under water by sharp coral. Water can seep into punctures and run through the cable into the searchcoil. Also, searchcoils have been known to leak when taken from the hot trunk of a car and plunged immediately into cold water. The hot, expanded air inside the searchcoil cools, causing a vacuum which pulls water in through the tiniest hole in the cable or coil.

If you suspect that water seepage is causing your searchcoil to fail, let it dry for several days in a warm place. Don't try to "hurry up" the drying by using a hot oven because this may permanently damage your searchcoil. If you can locate where the water seeped into the coil, repairs can be made with silicone material available at most hardware stores. Apply this generously to the location where you suspect the leak occurred. Let dry thoroughly before using.

Skid plates (coil covers) are recommended because they provide excellent protection for your searchcoils.

Detector Problems

Intermittent Sounds: Check the battery connections In fact, these connections should be checked regularly to make certain they are tight. Check carefully for corroded batteries. Sometimes batteries will leak a small amount of battery acid, creating corrosion on the contacts.

Non-Detection: If even a coin lying on top of the ground produces no detection, make sure your detector is correctly ground balanced. If you are using a modern detector with automatic ground balancing, this should be no problem. If you are attempting to ground balance your detector manually, make certain you adjust the detector at the correct operating height. If you adjust it while the searchcoil is high in the air and lower it to the ground, heavy mineralization can affect the detector's circuitry to such an extent that even a coin lying on the ground will not be detected. Also make certain that you have not turned your discrimination control(s) too high.

Audio Threshold Drift: If your have trouble setting an audio threshold on your detector, check the batteries. Some detectors require warmup time. Make sure you have allowed adequate warmup (5 to 10 minutes). Removing your detector from an air-conditioned car, then operating in direct hot sunlight can cause components to heat too rapidly, necessitating a few minutes of warmup.

Water Damage: After searching in the water, never elevate the searchcoil above the level of your control housing or lay down the detector with the searchcoil higher than the housing. Any water trapped in the stem could then flow into the housing. Depending on your stems, it might be necessary to remove the lower stem to drain accumulated water. Fresh water will usually ruin a detector's circuitry. Salt water will absolutely ruin it!

Audio (Sound) Problems: If the sound produced by your detector is intermittent or if the audio is unsteady, you are probably operating near high voltage power lines, television, TV transmission lines, airports or another metal detector. Citizen-band radios operating nearby have also caused this problem. Some detectors have switches that enable you to change the frequency on which your detector is operating. Of course, you can always try to move away from electromagnetic interference sources.

If the sound on your detector fails while you are using headphones, unplug them. A broken headphone wire will cause erratic operation, or you may lose audio. If this happens, you can continue searching with the speaker alone if you do not have a spare set of headphones.

No Detection Depth: If your batteries are strong, if your detector is correctly ground balanced and you achieve good threshold sound, if everything else is right...the problem is probably with *you*, my friend. A wise man once said that most detector failures can be attributed to batteries that refuse to work or operators who refuse to think.

Of course, searchcoils can fail. If you have a spare searchcoil, place it on your detector and check for depth. If the detector is still giving poor depth detection, re-read manufacturer's instructions and carefully follow operating procedures.

Owner's Manuals

It would be well to say a few words here about the important subject of owner's manuals. In short, carefully read the one pertaining to your detector. Read it again. *Study it.* Commit its instructions to memory.

The successful treasure hunter never takes any detector into the field until first carefully studying all literature supplied with it by the manufacturer. Here's a test you should apply to the owner's manual of any detector...before you buy it;

Exactly what does the owner's manual tell you about that *particular* detector?

Does it tell you how to use that detector?

Does it answer your questions?

Or, does it contain merely statistics and diagrams? (You don't buy a detector so that you can repair it. You buy it to hunt for treasure!)

Is the owner's manual pocket-sized or at least in a format suitable for taking into the field? Or, is it designed for a desk drawer? In other words, is your owner's manual designed to be *used* or to be filed and forgotten.

Problem Checklist

Many of the problems previously discussed--and even a few more--have been compiled into the following checklist. If your detector fails to operate properly, perform these checks. Of course, these are *general* instructions. Not all procedures will apply to all detector models. Be certain to check your owner's manual...and, check your batteries!

NO OPERATION (Power On)

Battery checks zero; Check battery holder and battery cable connectors.

Battery checks normal: Check for loose or disconnected search coil connectors.

NORMAL OPERATION

Battery checks zero: Check joints at battery-check switch and other wiring points.

No meter operation or battery: Look for disconnected wire to meter; check for defective meter; check joints at battery-check switch and other wiring points.

No sound: Check for disconnected speaker connector; check for loose wires at speaker; check for damaged headphone jack/plug; check to see if jack springs have opened.

Constant sound: Substitute a good coil; check pushbutton or master control switch and associated cables.

Meter operation unsatisfactory: Check for pinched wire.

Can not set audio: Substitute a good coil; check pushbutton or retune switch and associated wiring; clean connector pins with eraser.

Intermittent operation: Check for loose batteries and loose terminals on the battery holder or the batteries themselves; check for tarnish on coil connector pins.

BATTERIES (HOLDER) DIFFICULT TO INSTALL

Look for restricted wiring; use small file on battery holder or try to smooth out nicks in runners, etc.; check for bent or misaligned battery tray and mating connector pins.

MODES REVERSED

Check to see if control switch is connected backwards; check to see if wires are reversed in control switch cable connector.

ERRATIC OPERATION

Substitute a good coil; check for excessive stem movement; clean coil cable connector pins; check for loose connector and housing screws. Move away from television sets, high voltage power lines and other potential power sources; change frequencies and check your detector again.

Additional Tips

Your detector is a sensitive electronic instrument. Care in transporting and handling will extend its life. Do not subject a detector to high temperatures by storing in hot sunlight or in a heated automobile trunk.

Keep detectors clean. Wipe housing after each use. Wash the coil when necessary. Protect from dust and sand as much as possible. Disassemble stem and clean after use in sandy areas, especially after working in or near salt water.

For storage periods longer than one month, remove batteries (or battery tray/holder) from the detector.

Never use spray cleaners or lubricants on the printed circuit board or controls. Such materials leave harmful residues. Never use *any* petroleum product on, in or anywhere near your detector.

And, again, don't forget to check your headphones. They've been known to fail, especially the connecting wires where they are soldered to the earphone plug. With the detector turned on and operating, wiggle the headphone wires. Pull on them gently where they go into the headphone pieces and where the wires go into the plug. Detectors have been returned for factory repairs where the only problem was faulty headphones.

If all of the above procedures fail and your detector still won't operate, you may require repairs that must be performed at a factory or service center. If away from home for an extended period, perhaps you can locate a local dealer to examine your detector. Many dealers are factory-trained in detector repair. Some may charge a small service fee. Don't overlook this possibility as one way of getting back into the field quickly.

If the detector must be returned to the factory, pack it carefully and use lots of insulation. It is not necessary in most cases to return stems, headphones, etc. Always return a searchcoil, however. Send the one you normally use. Do not pack digging tools which only add weight and increase shipping costs. Enclose a letter with your name and address and a brief, yet complete, description of the problem; i.e., how often it occurs and the special conditions that seem to cause it.

Let's hope that your detector never fails in the field, butremember...don't baby it to protect it. *Use your detector!* Garrett and other quality detectors are built to stand up in the field during many years of hard use.

*Gold from beneath the sea...*somehow seems to bring a special THing joy, especially when earned by hours of work in the water and days spent in research.

Glossary

(Chapters 5 through 9 contain additional metal detector terminology and provide more information concerning most of the terms described in this Appendix.)

Admiralty Laws--Those rules that relate to the rights and conduct of property and persons on the high seas. So called, because in England trial of such cases is held in an Admiralty Court. These cases in the United States are in the jurisdiction of Federal District Courts.

Air Test--A method to determine the *Sensitivity* of a metal detector; i.e., how deeply it can detect. So called, because the test is performed with nothing but air between the detector's searchcoil and the object being detected. Depending primarily on soil/mineral and atmospheric conditions but also on the detector itself, depth performance in the field can vary widely from that of an air test.

All Metal Mode--The mode of operation of a metal detector in which *all* metal targets are detected. Precise *Ground Balancing* is essential in this mode to eliminate or minimize the effects of mineralization in the soil. This mode of detector operation must be used for effective *Electronic Prospecting*. It is also preferred by those operators who insist on "digging all targets." (See *Discriminate Mode*.)

A full treasure pouch...just the bonus to this beach hunter's enjoyment after a day at the ocean's edge with only the breeze, the sound of surf and sea creatures for company.

Ampere--A unit of electrical current which measures rate of flow of electrons in a conductor.

Amplifier--An electrical circuit which draws its power from a source other than the input signal and which produces an output voltage/current that is an enlarged reproduction of the essential features of the input signal.

Antenna--The component of a transmitter or receiver that actually radiates or receives the electromagnetic energy. (See *Searchcoil.*)

Audio Adjust--The control used to adjust the sound produced by a metal detector to the desired audio "threshold" or "silent" level settings. (See *Tuning.*)

Automated Detector--One of the most popular types of instruments generally used today, especially for searching beaches and hunting coins. Featuring *Automatic Ground Balance* , this type of instrument is generally referred to as a "motion detector" since it can respond to a target only while the searchcoil is being moved over that target.

Automatic (Audio) Tuning--A circuit incorporated in most modern detectors that keeps the *audio* level at a predetermined setting by automatically compensating for detector drift and changing environmental conditions that often affected audio adjustment in older model *(Non-Mortion)* instruments. Do not confuse with *Automatic Ground Balancing* (whose description follows).

Automatic Ground Balancing--A type of metal detector circuit featured on most modern instruments. With this circuit no manual adjustments are required to cancel out the detrimental effects of iron earth and salt mineralization. Some circuits on *Non-Motion Detectors* continually analyze soil beneath the detector's searchcoil and automatically adjust the detector circuitry to "ignore" minerals. This is a vitally important circuit. Do not confuse it with *automatic tuning*, above, also an integral part of most modern detectors.

BFO Detector--A type of metal detector utilizing Beat Frequency Oscillator (BFO) circuitry. Such detectors were quite popular in the 1960s and 1970s and are important in the history of metal detector development. Although some older hobbyists continue to use such models, they must be considered obsolete. Results possible with them are totally unsuitable when compared with the capabilities of modern instruments.

Black Sand--See *Magnetic Black Sand.*

Body Mount--A somewhat uncommon detector configuration in which the control housing is strapped to the front of the upper body for use by surf hunters. (See *Hip Mount.*)

Calibration--A term that generally refers to factory adjustment of a detector to specific operating performance. For instance, accurate ore-sampling requires that a detector be set at a factory-calibrated point at which the distinction between metal and mineral is clearly recognizable. Most quality models are permanently calibrated and require no adjustment.

Canceling--Obsolete and imprecise terminology that is sometimes used to refer to *Ground Balancing* or *Discrimination.*

Circuit--An electrical or electronic network providing one or more closed electrical paths. More specifically, it is a grouping of components and wiring in devices designed to perform some particular function or group of functions. Examples of circuits within a metal detector are transmitter circuit, receiver circuit, antenna circuit and audio amplifier circuit.

Circuit Board--The thin sheet of material upon which electronic components are mounted If the circuit board is completely self-contained, it is usually referred to as a "module." Circuit boards may be hand-wired or have the interconnectors printed electrochemically upon them. Such modules are designated PCB (printed circuit board).

Classification, Audio--An audible method (or methods) for classifying detected targets into conductivity classes or categories. (See *Coin Alert.*)

Classification, Visual--A visual (metered or light) method (or methods) for classifying detected targets into conductivity classes or categories.

Coil--See *Searchcoil.*

Coin Alert--An audible method of producing a special tone only when coins (or high conductivity silver and gold items) are detected. All other detected targets produce normal accept/reject signals.

Component--In a metal detector this term generally refers to an essential part of a circuit; i.e., resistor, capacitor, coil, tube, transistor, etc. The term can also refer to complete functional units of a system; i.e., transmitter, receiver, search coil, etc.

Conductance--The ability of an element, component or device to permit the passage of an electrical current; i.e, *Eddy Currents*. It is the reciprocal function of resistance.

Conductor--A wire, bar or metal mass (coin, ship's hull, cannon, etc.) capable of conducting electrical current.

Control Housing--The box or container in which is placed all or most of the electronic assembly and batteries of a metal detector. On most detectors this control housing *must* be protected from water.

Depth Detection--A term usually used to describe the ability of an instrument to detect metal objects to specific depths. (See *Sensitivity*.)

Depth Penetration--Applied to electronic metal detectors, the term is used to define the specific distance into a particular medium (soil, water, air, etc.) that the electromagnetic field of a metal detector is capable of satisfactorily penetrat. This affects the *Depth Detection* abilities of an instrument.

Detection Pattern--See *Searchcoil Detection Pattern.*

Detuning--A term that was used quite often with older model detectors to describe the "down tuning" necessary to enable precise *Pinpointing*. Modern electronic circuitry with its *Automatic Tuning* and *Electronic Pinpointing* have virtually eliminated any need for detuning.

Discriminate Mode--The mode of operation of a metal detector in which metallic targets are specifically designated by the operator are eliminated from detection. (See *Discrimination*.) Many modern detectors, particularly motion detectors, (see *Automated Detector*) can be operated only in the Discriminate mode. (See *All Metal Mode*.)

Discrimination--The ability of specific circuits within a detector to eliminate from detection certain undesirable metallic objects. Using a detector in its Discriminate mode, a detector operator chooses which targets are to be eliminated through proper manipulation of discrimination control(s). This function is also described as "elimination."

Drift--A term used to describe the inclination of an instrument's tuning to vary from its setting because of temperature, battery condition, faulty components, poor design, etc. Drift is seldom a problem with modern detectors,

Eddy Currents--Also called Foucalt currents, they are induced in a conductive mass by the variations of electromagnetic energy radiated from the detector and tend to flow in the surfacer layers of the target mass. Flow is directly proportional to frequency, the density of the electromagnetic field and the conductivity of the metal. Eddy currents flowing in a target produce the same effect as that of a shorted-turn secondary and are a primary electrical phenomenon that produces metal detection signals in all metal detectors.

Electromagnetic Field--An invisible field that surrounds the transmitter winding. Generated by the alternating radio frequency current that circulates in the transmitter antenna windings.

Electromagnetic Induction--The voltage induced in a coil (or conductive object) because of the changes in electromagnetic lines of force that pass through the coil or object.

Electronic Circuit--A circuit wherein current flows

441

through wires, resistors, inductors, capacitors, transistors and other components.

Electronic Pinpointing--A detector mode that causes a "sharpening" of detector signals when objects are detected. An electronic aid to precise target location.

Electronic Prospecting--The use of a metal detector to search for gold, silver or other precious metals in any form. Most common electronic prospecting is the search for gold nuggets with a detector that offers manual ground balancing capability.

Elimination--Terminology that is sometimes used to characterostics better described as *Ground Balancing* or *Discrimination* .

False Detection--Responses to objects or anomalies other than sought metallic targets.

Faraday Shield--The conductive covering surrounding the searchcoil antenna wires (and other components) of a metal detector. Its purpose is to provide electrostatic shielding and reduce "false detection" signals due to ground and wet grass capacitance effects.

Ferrous--Pertains to iron and iron compounds, such as nails, bottlecaps, cannons or ships hulls.

Firmware--Computer programs stored permanently as memory in a computerized microprocessor detector.

Frequency--Applied to alternating current or voltage, the term describes the number of periodic recurrences of a complete alternation or cycle zero, plus-maximum, zero, negative-maximum, zero, current or voltage levels that occur within one second.

Frequency Designations

Very Low	VLF	3-30 kHz (cycles or 1,000 Hertz)
Low	LF	30-300 kHz
Medium	MF	300-3000 kHz
High	HF	3-30 mHz (cycles/10,000 Hertz)
Very High	VHF	30-300 mHz
Ultra High	UHF	300-3,000 mHz
Super High	SHF	3,000-30,000 mHz

Gain--An increase in voltage, current power with respect to a previous quantity or a standard reference. Gain occurs in vacuum tubes, transistors, transformers, etc. as gain per component, gain per stage and gain per assembly. Such gain can be measured in terms of voltage, current, power or decibels.

Ground Balancing--The ability of a metal detector to eliminate (ignore or cancel) the detection effect of iron minerals or wetted salt. (See *Automatic* and *Manual Ground Balancing.*)

Headphones--Metal detector accessory that converts electrical energy waves into audible waves of identical form. Used by treasure hunters in place of detector loudspeakers, especially in noisy or windy locations. Because they present the audible signals more effectively than a loudspeaker headphones are recommended for use any time possible when using a metal detector. They are less susceptible to damage by rain and utilize less battery power than a speaker.

Hertz--Unit of frequency equal to one cycle per second.

Hip Mount--A common detector configuration used in many types of treasure hunting in which which the control housing is strapped to the hip. This is a popular configuration for surf hunters since a control housing on the hip can be easier to manage than one on a stem. (See *Hip Mount.*)

Hot Rock--A mineralized rock that produces a positive signal in a metal detector.

Induced Current--The current that flows in a conductor or conductive mass when a varying electromagnetic field is present. Except for eddy currents, induced or secondary currents flow only where there is a complete circuit or closed loop. Eddy currents are, in themselves, closed loops.

Magnetic Black Sand--Magnetite, a magnetic oxide of iron and, in a lesser degree, hematite. May also contain titanium and other rare-earth minerals but serves mainly as an indicator of the possible presence of placer gold.

Magnetometer--Not a metal detector even though the term is sometimes used improperly when metal detectors are discussed. Rather, this is an instrument for measuring magnetic intensity, especially the earth's magnetic field. Treasure hunters searching for a metal ship often use a magnetometer to locate the increased magnetic field density caused by the hull.

Manual Ground Balance--The type of metal detector circuit that first offered instrumentation to permit canceling (ignoring or eliminating) the detrimental effects of iron earth and salt mineralization. Not required or included on *Automated Detectors* . On some modern instruments this circuit presents an important option to *Automatic Ground Balance* when extremely precise ground balancing is required, especially in *Electronic Prospecting* . Manual Ground Balance is a feature of the so-called *Non-Motion Detector* .

Matrix--The entire area below a searchcoil that is "illuminated" by the transmitted electromagnetic field transmitted from the antenna in the coil. A matrix may wholly, partially or intermittently contain conductive and/or non-conductive targets which may be of either ferrous or nonferrous materials. The matrix may contain moisture, sulfides, metallic ores, etc. The detection pattern is only a portion of the matrix.

Metal Detector--An electronic instrument or device, usually battery-powered, capable sensing the presence of conductive objects lying underground, underneath water or otherwise out of sight; then, providing its operator with an audible and/or visual indication of that presence.

Metal/Mineral--Refers primarily to that "Zero" *Discrimination* point on a properly calibrated detector at which time any signal given by the detector will indicate that a target is metal, not mineral.

Meter--That device on a metal detector that reports information visually concerning depth and type of target, battery condition, ground conditions, etc.

Mode--The manner in which a detector operates, which can usually be controlled by the operator. Modern detectors generally offer two operating modes, *All Metal* and *Discriminate.*

Motion Detector--See *Automated Detector.*

Narrow Scan--A scan width less than full searchcoil diameter. In earlier days, TR detector searchcoils scanned an effective area equivalent to about 30-40% of the diameter of the searchcoil being used.

Non-Ferrous--Pertains to non-iron metals and compounds, such as brass, silver, gold, lead, aluminum, etc.

Non-Motion Detector--A type of instrument that permits the searchcoil to be hovered directly above a target for any length of time. Such instruments generally feature *Manual Ground Balance* and are used for *Electronic Prospecting* and cache hunting. Such detectors are not particularly applicable to beach and water hunting, except for specialized situations.

Null--A tuning or audio adjustment condition that results in "quiet" or zero audio operation.

Oscillator--The variation of an observable or otherwise detectable quantity of motion about a mean value.

Overshoot--A "false signal" characteristic once common but essentially eliminated by modern circuitry.

Penetration--The ability of a detector to penetrate earth material, air, wood, rock, water, etc. to locate metal targets. Penetration is a function of detector design and type of detector, as well as the material being penetrated.

Performance--The ability of a detector to carry out the functions of which the manufacturer has claimed this instrument is capable.

Permeability--The measure of how a material performs as a path for magnetic lines of force as measured against the permeability standard, air. Air is rated as 1 on the permeability scale, diamagnetic materials less than 1, paramagnetic materials slightly more than 1 and ferromagnetic materials much more than 1.

Phase--The angular (mathematical or time concept) relationship that exists between current and voltage in all AC circuits...regardless of type. When both voltage and current cycles rise and fall in exact unison, voltage and current are said to be in phase. When the rise of current flow lags behind the rise of voltage, the circuit is said to be inductive. Conversely, when the rise of current leads the rise of voltage, the circuit is said to be capacitive.

Phase Angle--The number of angular (mathematical concept) degrees than AC current and voltage peaks are out of phase--or out of step with each other.

Pinpointing--The ability of a detector operator to determine exactly where a detected target is located. (See *Electronic Pinpointing.*)

Placer--Pronounced like "plaster," without the "t"...the term describes an accumulation of gold, black magnetic sand and other elements of specific gravity higher than sand, rock, etc. found in the same area.

Pushbutton--A type of control used in some, generally older, types of metal detectors.

Receiver--That portion of the circuitry of a metal detector that receives information created by the presence of targets, acts upon that information and processes it according to intentions indicated by instrument design or actions of the THer; then activates the readout system in proportion to the nature of the received data.

Receiver Gain--The amplification of input signals to whatever extent required.

Response Time--Time delay in audio performance of a metal detector between detection of a target and the report of this detection by the instrument's audio and/or visual indicators. Once a critical factor, response time is virtually instantaneous on modern instruments.

Retuning--Important on older instruments, this act of restoring the audio threshold of a detector to a predetermined level, is performed automatically on new detectors. Manual retuning is offered as an option on some more expensive instruments because of its occasional importance in areas with large amounts of metallic junk or in electronic prospecting with *Manual Ground Balance.*

Scanning--The actual movement of a searchcoil over the ground or other area being searched.

Scuba--Acronym for Self-Contained Underwater Breathing Apparatus, a system of equipment used for breathing while swimming under water; usually consists of an air intake device, storage tanks, regulator and necessary hoses.

Searchcoil--The component of a metal detector that houses the transmitter and receiver antennas. The searchcoil is usually attached to the control housing by way of an adjustable connecting stem. The searchcoil is scanned over the ground, or other area being searched.

Searchcoil Detection Pattern--That portion of the electromagnetic field in which metal detection takes place. It is located out from and along the axis of the searchcoil generally, starting at full searchcoil width and tapering to a point at some distance from the searchcoil. Its actual width and depth depend upon the type and strength of signals being transmitted by the detector as well as the size and nature of any given target.

Sensitivity--The ability of a detector to sense conductivity changes in the detection pattern. Sensitivity of a detector increases in direct proportion to the level of change in conductivity required by its circuitry to produce a meaningful readout. One of the most important operational characteristics of an electronic metal detector, sensitivity determines the actual size of targets that an instrument will detect and the depth to which they can be detected. Although sensitivity is ultimately determined by design characteristics of a detector, a control on most instruments permits some regulation by the operator.

Signal--Generally describes the electromagnetic data received by the detector from a target and the audio and/or visual response generated by it.

Silent Audio--The tuning of the audio level of a detector in the "silent" (just below *Threshold*) zone. When operating in this fashion, the operator hears no sound at all until a target is detected.

Splashproof--A designation of environmental protection that indicates that minor wetting of detector's housing and/or searchcoil (light mist, dew, etc.) will not affect its operation.

Stability--Ability of metal detector circuits to remain tuned to predetermined operating points. Once a critical aspect of detector operation, now a standard operating feature of any quality detector.

Submersible--A designation of environmental protection that indicates that complete submersion of a detector's housing and/or search will not affect its operation. Always note depth to which submersibility is permitted. All Garrett searchcoils can be submerged to the connector. The Sea Hunter detector can be submerged to 200 feet, the Beach Hunter to six feet.

Super Sniper--A Garrett trademark used to describe its 4 1/2-inch searchcoil and the method for using it to enhance individual target detection in specialized situations. This type of treasure hunting is especially effective for hunting in areas with large amounts of metal "junk" or near metallic objects such as fences, posts, buildings, etc.

Surface Area--That area of a target lying parallel to the plane of the detector searchcoil; in other words, that part of the target that is "looking at" the underside of the searchcoil. This is the area through which the electromagnetic field lines pass and on which eddy currents are generated.

Sweeping--See *Scanning*.

TH--An abbreviation for Treasure Hunter, used in THer, THing, etc.

Threshold--That adjustable level of audio sound at which a metal detector is operated when searching for treasure.

Touchpad--A type of control that is quite popular on modern detectors because of its effectiveness and dependability.

TR Detector--The type of metal detector that first utilized the Transmitter-Receiver circuit, which is essentially the circuitry of all modern VLF instruments. When first developed, TR Detectors were a distinct improvement over exostomg BFO models, offering *Discrimination* and other features. As such, these instruments are important in the history of metal detector development. Although some older hobbyists continue to use TR detectors, they must be considered obsolete. Results possible with them are totally unsuitable when compared with the capabilities of modern instruments, even with the similarities in circuitry.

TR Disc--A non-motion mode of metal detector operation in which discrimination can be achieved with manual ground balance. Used almost exclusively in *Electronic Prospecting* .

Tuning--That adjustment an operator makes to bring the detector's audio level to *Threshold* . While quite important, this adjustment is no longer of particular concern to THers since it is accomplished automatically by the circuitry of modern detectors.

Universal Capabilities--Describes a metal detector that can effectively accomplish most THing tasks...beach hunting, coin hunting, surf hunting, ghost towning, electronic prospecting, cache hunting, etc. See *Versatility* below.

Versatility--A measure of the applications in which a detector can be used effectively. In other words, for how many different kinds of hunting can a particular detector be used? See *Universal Capabilities* above.

Visual Indicator--Generally means *Meter* on a THing detector, although some instruments (especially those on security devices) use other visual indicators not related to a pointer-type meter (such as lights).

VLF Detector--The initials stand for Very Low *Frequency*, a segment of the RF spectrum that includes frequencies from 3 kHz to 30 kHz. All modern instruments (except Pulse Induction-types) can be designated as VLF detectors.

Volume Control--A control, generally resistance, used to limit voltage and/or current in an audio amplifier and, thereby, control volume of sound or "loudness" when a target is encountered. Do not confuse with audio adjustments involved with *Tuning* or *Threshold.*

Waterproof--A designation of environmental protection that indicates that heavy rainfall or splashing surf on a detector's housing and/or searchcoil (light mist, dew, etc.) will not affect its operation. It does not mean that the housing and/or coil is *Submersible* .

Wetted Salt--The most prevalent mineral encountered in beach and ocean hunting. Is ignored by Pulse Induction and VLF detectors with *Ground Balancing* capabilities, either automatic or manual.

Wide Scan--Generally implies that the scanning width (detection pattern) of a detector, as the searchcoil passes over the ground, is equal to the full width (or wider) of the diameter of the searchcoil being used.

Books

Adventure Series Productions, *Diver's Almanac.* 1984.

Allen, Joan, *Glittering Prospects,* Elm Tree Books, London, 1975.

American National Red Cross, *First Aid*, Doubleday, New York, 1973.

American Red Cross, *Life Saving and Water Safety,* Doubleday, 1937.

Andrews, Evangeline Walker, *Jonathan Dickinson's Journal,* Florida Classics Library, 1981.

Australian Art Exhibitors' Corporation, Ltd., *Eldorado Colombian Gold*, Australia, 1978.

Bascom, Willard, *Deep Water, Ancient Ships*, Doubleday, New York, 1976.

Waves and Beaches, Doubleday, 1964

Boehler, Ted, *Divemaster Manual 2,* DeepStar Publishing Co., Crestline, CA, 1981.

Brady, Edward M., *Marine Salvage Operations,* Cornell, 1960.

Bridges, Lloyd, *Mask and Flippers, The Story of Skindiving*, Cornerstone Library, New York, 1960.

Brown, Tom Jr., *The Tracker,* Berkley Books, New York, 1978.

The Search, Berkley, 1980.

Tom Brown's Field Guide to Wilderness Survival, Berkley, 1982.

Tom Brown's Field Guide to Nature Observation and Tracking, Berkley, 1983.

Tom Brown's Field Guide to City and Suburban Survival, Berkley, 1984.

Tom Brown's Field Guide to Living with the Earth, Berkley, 1984.

Tom Brown's Field Guide to the Forgotten Wilderness, Berkley, 1987.

Bryfonski, Dedra, *New England Beach Book,* Walker, New York, 1975.

Burgess, Robert F., *They Found Treasure,* Dodd, Mead, New York, 1977.

Carrier, Rick & Barbara, *Dive,* Funk & Wagnalls, New York, 1973.

Coffman, F. L. *1001 Lost Buried or Sunken Treasures,* Thomas Nelson & Sons, New York, 1957.

DeLoach, Ned, *Diving Guide to Underwater Florida,* New World Publications, Jacksonville, FL, 1980.

Dixon, Sarah & Peter, *West Coast Beaches,* Sunrise Books, New York, 1978.

Erickson, Ralph D., *Search and Recovery,* PADI, Santa Ana, CA, 1983.

Fine, John Christopher, *Sunken Ships and Treasure,* Atheneum, New York, 1986.

Fletcher, E., Treasure *Hunting on the Coast,* Fletcher Publications, Redcar, Cleveland, England, 1977.

Frederick, James, *Diver's Guide to River Wrecks,* Rowe Publishing, Milwaukee, WI, 1982.

Garrett, Charles L., *Avoid Detector Problems, A Garrett Guide,* Ram Publishing, Dallas, TX, 1989.

Find Wealth in the Surf, A Garrett Guide, Ram, 1988.

Find Wealth on the Beach, A Garrett Guide, Ram, 1988.

Modern Metal Detectors, Ram, 1985.

New Successful Coin Hunting, Ram, 1989.

Gibbs, Jim, *Disaster Log of Ships,* Bonanza Books, New York, 1971.

Giguere, Jon-Paul, *Make Money in Diving,* Rowe Publications, Milwaukee, WI, 1981.

Salvage Laws for Weekend Divers, Rowe, 1981.

Golden, Hans, *Buried and Sunken Treasure,* Marshall Cavendish, London, England, 1974.

Granville, Robert, *Shallow Water Treasure Hunting Manual,* Conestoga Printing, Sacramento, CA, 1984.

Grissim, John, *Lost Treasure of the Concepcion,* William Morris, New York, 1980.

Hamilton, D.L., *Conservation of Metal Objects from Underwater Sites: A Study in Methods,* Texas Memorial Museum, Austin, TX, 1976.

Hammes, Richard B. & Zimos, Anthony G., *Safe Scuba,* NASDS, Long Beach, CA, 1979.

H.D.L. Communications, *Diver's Almanac-Guide to the West Coast from Baja to British Columbia,* Costa Mesa, CA, 1985.

Helm Associates, *Treasure Lead Generation,* Austin, TX, 1986.

Hetherington, Keith, *Beachcombing with a Metal Detector,* Gemcraft, Australia, 1980.

Hudson, L. Frank, *Lost Treasures of Florida's West Coast,* St. Petersburg, Florida, 1983.

Humphries, Lund, *Treasure of the Spanish Main,* London, England.

Jenney, James, *Advanced Wreck Diver's Manual,* Rowe Publishing, Milwaukee, WI, 1983.

Diver's Directory of Shipwreck Research, Rowe, 1982.

In Search of Shipwrecks, A.S. Barnes, New York, 1980.

Kelley, Kate & Shobe, John, *Diver's Guide to Underwater America,* Dive Sport Publishing, Branson, MO, 1982.

Lagal, Roy, *Find an Ounce of Gold a Day, A Garrett Guide,* Ram Publishing, Dallas, TX, 1987.

Gold Panning is Easy, Ram, 1988.

Weekend Prospecting, Ram, 1988.

With Garrett, Charles L. *Modern Electronic Prospecting,* Ram, 1988.

Modern Treasure Hunting, Ram, 1988.

Lyon, Eugene, *The Search for the Atocha,* Harper & Row, New York, 1979.

Martin, Robert C., *The Deep Sea Diver*, Cornell Maritime Press, Cambridge, MA, 1979.

Marx, Robert F., *Quest for Treasure*, Ram Publishing, Dallas, TX, 1982.

Buried Treasure of the United States, Ram, 1987.

The Lure of Sunken Treasure, David McKay, NY, l973.

Underwater Dig, Henry Z. Walck, New York, 1975.

Into the Deep, Van Nostrand-Rhinehold, New York, 1978.

Shipwrecks of the Western Hemisphere, David McKay, New York, 1971.

Still More Adventures, Mason/Charter, New York, 1976.

Port Royal Rediscovered, Doubleday, New York, 1973.

Sea Fever: Famous Underwater Explorers, Doubleday, 1972.

Shipwrecks in Mexican Waters,

Shipwrecks in Florida Waters,

Always Another Adventure.

They Dared the Deep: A History of Diving.

Following Columbus: The Voyage of the Nina 2.

McAllister, Evelyn Ditton, *Easy Steps to Safe Swimming*, A.S. Barnes, New York, 1973.

Merkitch, Warren, *Beachcomber's Handbook*, Examino Press, Segundo, CO.

Metzker, Edward, *Beginner's Guide to Finding Gold Nuggets by Metal Detector*, Gold Nugget Publishing, Willow, AK, 1987.

Mroczkowski, George, *Professional Treasure Hunter*, Ram Publishing, Dallas, TX, 1981.

Mueller, Karl von, *Treasure Hunter's Manual No.6*, Ram Publishing, Dallas, TX, 1977.

Treasure Hunter's Manual No. 7, Ram, 1979.

With Conatser, Estee, *Journals of Eldorado*, Ram, 1977.

Nannetti, Ettore & Diana, *New York Treasures and Metal Detecting Sites*, Metal Detector Distributors, Brooklyn, NY, 1985.

Ohrellus, Bengt, *Vasa, The King's Ship,* Chilton, Philadelphia, PA, 1959.

National Geographic Society, Washington, DC, *Exploring the Deep Frontier,* 1980.

Treasures in the Sea, 1972.

PADI, *Dive Manual.*

Divemaster Manual.

Pattee, Gerald, *Metal Detecting in Water,* Found Enterprises, 1974.

Patterson, T.W., *British Columbia Shipwrecks,* Stagecoach Publish ing, Langley, BC, Canada, 1976.

Potter, John S. Jr., *Treasure Diver's Guide,* Bonanza Books, New York, 1972.

Raisz, Erwin, General Cartography, McGraw-Hill, New York, 1948.

Rieseberg, Lieut. Harry E., *The Sea of Treasure.,* Frederick Fell, New York, 1956.

I Dive for Treasure, Frederick Fell, 1970.

Rowe, Alan R.*Relics, Water and the Kitchen Sink,* Rowe Publica tions, Milwaukee, WI, 1979.

Sedwick, Frank, *The Practical Book of Cobs,* Author, Maitland, FL, 1987.

Shiloh Publishing Company, *Who's Buying and Selling Guide,* Staun ton, VA, 1976.

Springer, Robert R., *Skin and Scuba Diver's Digest,* Follette Publishing, Chicago, IL, 1975.

Sullivan, George, *Discover Archaeology,* Doubleday, New *York, 1980.*

Treasure Hunt, Henry Holt, New York, 1987.

Throckmorton, Peter, *Diving for Treasure,* Viking Press, New York, 1977.

Time-Life Books, *Atlantic Beaches,* Alexandria, VA, 1972.

Trevillian, Bob & Carter, Frank., *Diamonds in the Surf,* Spyglass Enterprises, Glen Burnie, MD, 1982.

Diamonds in the Surf: The Second Adventure, Spyglass, 1983.

The Poor Man's Treasure Hunter, Spyglass, 1985.

Volker, Roy, *Treasure Under Your Feet,* Henry Regnery, Chicago, IL.

With Richmond, Dick, *In the Wake of the Golden Galleons,* Oro Quest Press, St. Louis, MO, 1976.

Voynick, Stephen M., *In Search of Gold*, Paladin Press, Boulder, CO, 1982.

Mid-Atlantic Treasure Coast, Middle Atlantic Press, Wallingford, PA, 1984.

Wilkes, Bill St. John., *Nautical Archaeology*, Stein & Day, New York, 1971.

Wilson, Derek, *World Atlas of Treasure,* William Collins Sons, London.

Magazines/Publishers

American West
7000 E. Tanque Verde Rd
Tucson, AZ 85715

Aqua Field Publications Inc
One East/Suite 1191
Eastern By-Pass
Montgomery, AL 36117

California Diver
P.O. Box 7260
Huntington Beach, CA 92615

California Mining Journal
P.O. Drawer 628
Santa Cruz, CA 95061

Carson Enterprises
Drawer 71
Deming, NM 88031

Diving Retailer
P.O. Box 17067
Long Beach, CA 90807

Examino Press
P.O. Box CGI
Segundo, CO 81070

Fins and Feathers
401 N. Third Street
Minneapolis, MN 55401

Gold Nuggett Publishing
P.O. 268
Willow, AK 99688

Gold Prospector
P.O. Box 507
Bonsall, CA 92003

Treasure
Jess Publishing Co.
6745 Adobe Road
Twentynine Palms,
CA 92277

Lost Treasure
P.O. Box 1589
Grove, OK 74344

Midwest Outdoors
111 Shore Drive
Hinsdale, IL 60521

PADI
1243 E. Warner Avenue
Santa Ana, CA 92705

Western and Eastern
Treasures
People's Publishing Co.
P.O. Box 1095
Arcata, CA 95521

Publisher's Weekly
205 E. 42d Street
New York, NY 10017

Research Unlimited
P.O. Box 448
Freemont, NB 68025

Scuba Pro
3105 Harcourt
Rancho Dominguez,
CA 90221

Scuba Times
147 Drew Circle
Pensacola, FL 32503

Thousand Trails, Inc.
15325 S.E. 30th Place
Bellevue, WA 98007

Searcher*
2814 National Drive
Garland, TX 75041

Skin Diver
8490 Sunset
Los Angeles, CA 90069

Treasure Hunting
Sovereign Publications
Sovereign House
Brentwood
Essex, CM14 4SE
England

TL Enterprises, Inc.
4300 Middlebury
Elkhart, IN 46516

Token Publication, Ltd.
Crossways Road
Grayshot, Hindead
Surrey GU26 6HF
England

Underwater U.S.A.
P.O. Box 705
Bloomsburg, PA 17815

Western Outdoors
3197-E Airport Loop
Costa Mesa, CA 92626

*This publication is FREE. Write to be added to mailing list.

Ram Books

Beach hunting...coin hunting...surf hunting...electronic prospecting...all of these subjects--and much more--are covered in detail in the *Treasure Hunting Texts* available from Garrett dealers. Written by professional treasure hunters, these books combine stories of adventure and discovery with practical, down-to-earth advice.

True Treasure Tales are fictionalized accounts of real treasure hunts. Share the thrill of discovery with a new metal detecting hero, Gar Starrett. In the *Garrett Guide* series a single aspect of treasure hunting is presented in each convenient, pocket-sized booklet designed to be taken into the field and used for on-the-spot help.

Treasure Hunting Texts

The New Successful Coin Hunting
The world's most authoritative guide to finding valuable coins, totally rewritten to include instructions for 21st Century detectors

$10.95

Modern Treasure Hunting
The practical guidebook to today's metal detectors; a "how-to" manual that carefully explains the "why" of modern detector performance.

$12.95

Treasure Recovery from Sand and Sea
Precise instructions for reaching the "blanket of wealth" beneath sands nearby and under the world's waters, totally rewritten for the 90's.

$14.95

Modern Electronic Prospecting
Explains how to use a modern detector to find gold nuggets and veins of precious metal.; includes illustrated instructions for panning, dredging.

$9.95

Modern Metal Detectors
Advanced handbook for field, home and classroom study to increase expertise and understanding of any kind of metal detector.

$9.95

Buried Treasure of the United States
Complete field guide for finding treasure; includes state-by-state listing of thousands of sites where treasure is believed to exist.

$10.95

Treasure Hunter's Manual #6
Quickly guides the beginner through the mysteries of full-time treasure hunting with easy explanations of equipment and technques..

$9.95

Treasure Hunter's Manual #7
The Classic book on professional methods of research, recovery and disposition of treasure; designed to supplement THer's Manual #6.

$9.95

Weekend Prospecting
Offers simple "how-to" instructions for enjoying holidays and vacations profitably by prospecting with metal detectors and gold pans.

$3.95

Gold Panning is Easy
This excellent field guide shows the beginner exactly how to find and pan gold; follow these instructions and perform like a professional.

$6.95

Treasure Hunting Pays Off
A basic introduction to all facets of treasure hunting...the equipment, the targets and the terminology; revised for 21st Century detectors.

$6.95

True Treasure Tales -- **Gar Starrett Adventures**
Each $2.95

The Secret of John Murrell's Vault
The Missing Nez Perce Gold

Garrett Guides -- **Pocket-size Field Guides**
Each $1.00

Metal Detectors Can Help You Find Wealth
Find More Treasure With the Right Metal Detectors
Metal Detectors Can Help You Find Coins
Money Caches Are Waiting to be Found
Find an Ounce of Gold a Day
Find Wealth on the Beach
Find Wealth in the Surf
Avoid Detector Problems
Use the Super Sniper

A convenient order form for these RAM books can be found following Appendix 5.
For additional information call (214) 278-6151.

Garrett Video Library

Outdoor Family Entertainment and Instructional Programs. Available in video cassette and some available in 16mm. Write for details and catalog.

Sand & Sea Treasures
   Two slide/videos that take the viewer treasure hunting in recreational areas and a castle are available on a single VHS video tape. No. 16703.
                                                    $19.95.
   Treasure Recovery from Sand & Sea--No matter what you know about treasure hunting with a metal detector on land or what you think you know about hunting in the water, this slide show video will provide valuable "how-to" tips about discovering lost wealth. A companion to this book. 25 minutes, color.
   Castle Treasures--A treasure hunter inherits a castle in Austria. This slide presentation on video is not only an interesting study of a castle, but the found treasures dramatically illustrate an exciting, eventful segment of history. 13 minutes, color.

Southwestern Treasures
   Two colorful Southwestern treasure tales are available in a single VHS video tape. No. 16701.
                                                    $19.95
   Treasures of Mexico--Host Charles Garrett invites fellow treasure hunters to accompany the Garrett field team on an outing to the fabulous Cobre Canyon, near Batopilas, Mexico. The team searches a beautiful old city, silver-laden rivers, and finally, an old mine. The video makes vividly clear how productive electronic prospeting was in these areas. 25 minutes, color.

Gold and Treasure Adventures--Charles Garrett describes a competition treasure hunt in the California desert and a treasure hunting trip to Europe. While in the desert, Charles and a field team hunt an old mining area where many good recoveries are made. Actor John Quade is featured and narrates part of the film. 25 minutes, color.

Treasure Adventures

These two treasure adventures filmed on both sides of the globe are available in one VHS video tape. No. 16702. **$19.95.**

The Silent Past--An old prospector, killed by hostile Indians after he discovers a silver mine, is transformed into a ghost whose destiny is to roam the Big Bend area of West Texas until one of his descendants comes to the area. His great-great-grandson and parents travel to the area and discover many artifacts buried during the passage of time. 25 minutes, color.

Treasures of the Indian Ocean--Robert Marx, internationally known American underwater archaeologist and treasure salvor, leads a team of professionals on a search for the 18th century wreck site of the French merchant ship, the *St. Geran*, wrecked in 1744 off Madagascar. This color/sound film of historical interest shows many different methods of recovery, as well as touching on research and archaeological procedures. 25 minutes, color.

Gold Panning is Easy

The program illustrates methods of using the *gravity trap* and other pans in both wet and dry panning for gold and other materials of high specific gravity. Tells where and how to locate gold. Techniques of Roy Lagal from the book of the same name are demonstrated in Arizona by Virgil Hutton and introduced by Charles Garrett. No. 16704, 25 minutes, color.

$19.95.

Weekend Prospecting

This production was filmed while Charles Garrett, Roy Lagal, Tommie T. Long and Virgil Hutton were actually hunting gold in the Northwestern United States. Thus, the hobby of "weekend prospecting" is accurately depicted, showing techniques for locating and recovering gold that all family members can put to productive use during vacations and weekend trips to gold country. Electronic prospecting with metal detectors and both wet and dry gold panning and recovery techniques are fully illustrated. Informative, instructional and interesting with gorgeous Northwest United States scenery. Roy Lagal's book of the same name (see Page 460) is a companion piece that covers in greater detail everything presented in this video production, which is introduced by Charles Garrett. No. 16706, 50 minutes, color.

$29.95.

Tracking Outlaw Treasure

This beautiful production in vivid color tells an exciting tale of a modern-day search for the cache hidden after a stagecoach robbery more than a century ago. The use of advanced electronic detectors and research techniques is carefully explained by Charles Garrett and his companions as they seek the treasure. No. 1670, 21 minutes, color.

$24.95

Ram Books

Please send the following books:

☐ Modern Treasure Hunting $12.95
☐ Treasure Recovery from Sand & Sea $14.95
☐ The New Successful Coin Hunting $10.95
☐ Buried Treasure of the U.S. $10.95
☐ Modern Electronic Prospecting .... $ 9.95
☐ Modern Metal Detectors .... $ 9.95
☐ Treasure Hunting Pays Off .... $ 6.95
☐ Weekend Prospecting .... $ 3.95
☐ Gold Panning Is Easy .... $ 6.95
☐ Treasure Hunter's Manual #6 .... $ 9.95
☐ Treasure Hunter's Manual #7 .... $ 9.95

True Treasure Tales

☐ Secret of John Murrell's Vault .... $ 2.95
☐ Missing Nez Perce Gold .... $ 2.95

Garrett Guides to Treasure ($1 each)
(Shipped free of charge when shipping/handling is paid for any other book)

☐ Find Wealth on the Beach
☐ Metal Detectors Can Help You Find Coins
☐ Find More Treasure With The Right Detector
☐ Find Wealth in the Surf
☐ You Can Avoid Detector Problems
☐ Use the Super Sniper
☐ Metal Detectors Can Help You Find Wealth
☐ Find An Ounce of Gold A Day
☐ Money Caches are Waiting To Be Found

Ram Publishing Company
P.O. Drawer 38649
Dallas, TX 75238

Please add $1 for
each book ordered
(maximum of $3)
for handling charges.

Total for items $_____

8% Tax (Texas residents) $_____

Handling Charge $_____

TOTAL $_____

Enclosed check or money order

I prefer to order through

☐ MasterCard
☐ Visa

Credit Card Number

Expiration Date   **Phone Number (8 a.m. to 4 p.m.)**

Signature (Credit Card orders must be signed.)

NAME

ADDRESS (For Shipping)

CITY, STATE, ZIP